TALKING TO TERRORISTS

TALKING TO TERRORISTS

WHY AMERICA MUST ENGAGE WITH ITS ENEMIES

MARK PERRY

BASIC BOOKS

A Member of the Perseus Books Group
New York

Books published by Basic Books are available at special discounts for bulk purchases in the United States by corporations, institutions, and other organizations. For more information, please contact the Special Markets Department at the Perseus Books Group, 2300 Chestnut Street, Suite 200, Philadelphia, PA 19103, or call (800) 810-4145, ext. 5000, or e-mail special.markets@perseusbooks.com.

Designed by Trish Wilkinson
Set in 12 point Goudy

Library of Congress Cataloging-in-Publication Data

Perry, Mark.
    Talking to terrorists : why America must engage with its enemies / Mark Perry.
        p. cm.
    Includes bibliographical references and index.
    ISBN 978-0-465-01117-9 (alk. paper)
    1. Terrorists—Psychology. 2. Terrorism—Prevention. 3. Muslims—Communication. 4. Qaida (Organization) 5. Harakat al-Muqawamah al-Islamiyah. 6. Hizballah (Lebanon) 7. Communication in organizations. 8. Communication in politics. 9. Communication and culture I. Title.
HV6431.P468 2009
363.325—dc22   2009032542

10 9 8 7 6 5 4 3 2 1

To the men and women of the 3rd Civil Affairs Group

1st Marine Expeditionary Force

United States Marine Corps

al-Anbar Province, Iraq

CONTENTS

To halt the momentum of an accepted idea, to reexamine assumptions, is a disturbing process and requires more courage than governments can generally summon.

—Barbara W. Tuchman
Stilwell and the American Experience in China

AUTHOR'S NOTE

THIS BOOK BEGAN as a series of articles in *Asia Times* in 2005. In 2006, Michael Dwyer of Hurst Publishing approached me with an idea: Would it be possible, he asked, to turn the *Asia Times* pieces into a book? I said that I needed to add another five parts to the five-part series. I told him that that would not be too difficult. I was wrong. The task proved more challenging than I had thought, and eventually I scrapped the idea altogether. The *Asia Times* pieces were appropriate in the aftermath of 9/11 but no longer seemed to have the immediacy they had once commanded.

By early 2006 the men and women of the 3rd Civil Affairs Group (CAG) began to talk to me about their opening to the Sunni resistance in Iraq and I began to write about it. I began to believe that the work of the 3rd CAG could be coupled with the discussions I had had with Hamas and Hezbollah. After all, the original claim of the *Asia Times* pieces was that Hamas and Hezbollah were not terrorist organizations but national resistance movements—the same claim made by the leaders of the Sunni Awakening.

The story of the 3rd CAG, then, became a foundation piece in discussing a much larger issue: whether the West, the United States and its European allies, should reconsider their view of terrorism—

and shift their policies. The result—*Talking to Terrorists*—engaged Lara Heimert at Basic Books. I had already contracted with Basic Books on another project, a biography of Douglas MacArthur. But I was intent on completing a policy book, the first one I had written in more than ten years. She told me to set aside the MacArthur book to focus on *Talking to Terrorists*, and I have spent the last two years doing so.

I have dedicated this book to the men and women of the 3rd Civil Affairs Group, 1st Marine Expeditionary Force. Without their cooperation and outspoken courage, this book could not have been completed. Their dedication has convinced a generation of policymakers that the United States has gotten the war on terror wrong—that the lazy "values" rhetoric of America and Europe masks the challenges we face. I am deeply appreciative of their willingness to tell me their story.

I was aided in my work by Jerry Jones, whose single-minded focus on this story has been of inestimable help. His deep commitment to seeing the story of the 3rd CAG published made this book possible. I hope that my editor in London, Michael Dwyer, is satisfied with the result. This was his idea, and he pushed and pushed until the final word was written. I am indebted to him and to Lara Heimert, at Basic Books, for their support and confidence. I appreciate the continued support of the editors of *Asia Times*—who have continued to publish my articles and have shown great faith in their continued importance. My appreciation also to James Clad for his continued support and friendship.

I wish to express my appreciation to Usamah Hamdan of the Islamic Resistance Movement and Nawaf Moussaoui of Hezbollah for taking the time—sometimes hours—to explain in detail their views and those of their movements. My appreciation also to those colleagues who added their own knowledge and experiences to my writing. My thanks to my colleague in this enterprise, Paul Woodward. My thanks to Boaz Karni in Israel for his friendship and to his family for their gracious hospitality. There are many others in Israel whom I wish to thank: those unnamed citizens who shout and laugh their views and have sat with me for hours, over a period of many years, talking about their dreams. My thanks to my close friend Bobby Muller, in Washington, D.C. My thanks to Solange MacArthur for her patience in allowing me to "whinge on" (as they say) about this issue.

In the West Bank, my thanks go to my lifelong friend Salah Ta'amri. My appreciation also to Omar Karmi and to Nuha Musleh, and to my hosts at Jerusalem's Golden Walls Hotel, who allowed me to wander their hallways during the darkest days of the Second Intifada.

There is a small but dedicated coterie of Americans who work—without recognition—to find a resolution of the Israeli-Palestinian conflict. They will see in *Talking to Terrorists* a reflection of their own thinking. Daniel Levy, Lara Friedman, Rob Malley, Amjad Atallah, and, especially, Jeff Aronson have allowed me to plunder their thinking—and sometimes even their words—for my own purposes. If dedication is any measure of results, this conflict would be resolved. My thanks to Paul Goldstein and Jeffrey Steinberg. In the United Kingdom, the most trenchant and focused appeals to a shift in the West's Middle East policies have come from Member of Parliament Michael Ancram and from John, Lord Alderice—both good and constant friends and supporters. My thanks also to Paul Hilder, Minal Patel, and Tom Clark.

Once again, and as always, my thanks go to my friend Gail Ross—whose support for my writing, like her friendship, has never wavered.

My thanks and my love go to my wife, Nina, and to my children, Madeleine and Cal. They have lived with the Israeli-Palestinian conflict for twenty-five years. They wish it would end. So do I.

COALITIONS

"We'll just keep going."
—Michael Ancram

In March 2006, a series of articles began to appear in *Asia Times*—an online daily news magazine—about meetings that had been held in Beirut between Americans and Europeans and the leaders of Hamas and Hezbollah. The meetings had taken place the year before. The meetings were controversial, as were the articles that described them. We were "talking to terrorists." We were "consorting with the enemy." We were "giving legitimacy to terrorists." Yet more than four years later, the meetings we inaugurated have had a significant impact on American and European policy, not simply because of what we did, but because of the help we enlisted. Most especially, the meetings we inaugurated have led to a long-overdue but substantial opening between the West and political Islam. British officials were instrumental in providing that opening.

Our meetings were attended by John Lord Alderdice, a tireless worker for reconciliation and an end to conflict. Alderdice was not alone in his travels; he was accompanied by others from the

United Kingdom—brave people who placed their reputations on the line. Additionally, over a period of years following the initial meetings, British member of Parliament Michael Ancram visited Beirut often and continued the dialogue with the leaders of Hamas and Hezbollah. He spoke openly about his meetings in the United Kingdom and then came to America to do the same. Other British officials, and many Europeans, have followed in the footsteps of Alderdice and Ancram. But we should not be surprised that it is the British who have proven to be capable of listening and talking. Britain's Prime Minister Clement Attlee normalized relations with China in 1950. It took the United States another two decades to do the same.

So too now, it is only a matter of time before many other Europeans follow the example set by the British. And it is only a matter of time before the United States does the same. "We can't be frustrated, we have to be absolutely tenacious," Ancram said in a recent visit to the United States. "We'll just keep going. We'll keep bringing people. We'll keep talking. We will just keep at it until our governments have no other choice but to talk."

Talking to Terrorists is my account of the meetings I had with political Islam in 2005. But it is also much more. One week after the first discussions in Beirut in the summer of 2005, I traveled to Amman, Jordan, to keep an appointment with a small group of Iraqi exiles. The meeting was convened in the offices of the Tabouk Group, a trading company headed by Talal al-Gaood, a former Baathist and American-educated civil engineer. The meeting had been arranged for me by Jerry Jones, a Defense Department official in the office of Secretary of Defense Donald Rumsfeld. I had gotten to know Jones by accident: I was introduced to him after briefing James Clad of the National Defense University on the Beirut dialogue. "You should meet Jerry Jones," he said. "He would be very interested in this." I followed up on Clad's recommendation by calling Jones and having lunch with him. I spoke for two hours about the meetings I had with Hamas and Hezbollah. He listened closely to what I had to say. Over the next week, he prepared a memo for Secretary Rumsfeld about what I had told him. At our next lunch together, Jones asked me more about my meetings, and at the end of our discussion he told me to go to Amman to see Sheik al-Gaood, to whom he would provide the introduction. He said that al-Gaood had "close ties to the Sunni-led Iraqi insurgency" and that he had also established an independent think tank, the Iraq Futures Foundation, that was focused on resolving the Sunni-American conflict in Iraq.

I met al-Gaood and a number of his assistants in their offices in central Amman. I told al-Gaood that I had heard rumors that senior U.S. military officers had quietly met with Iraqi insurgent leaders in Amman just the year before. I asked him if he knew anything about those meetings, which had been led by "a sheikh." Al-Gaood smiled but did not answer the question. Over the next hour he skirted my question and talked about the war on terror. He was a gracious host, but he was intent on explaining the mistakes the United States had made in Iraq. His words were tinged with anger. He spoke at length about the "endless talk you Americans engage in" about "the war of values with Islam." He scoffed at the notion and leaned across the table to stare at me. "You've got this all wrong," he said; "we don't hate your values, we hate your *policies*." He was not the first one to use this formulation, and, as I was to learn, he would not be the last.

Al-Gaood was a compelling figure: sharp-eyed and articulate, at ease with Americans and knowledgeable about American culture. He was a reader, familiar with American and European history. He was willing to share his views and experience. His offices reflected his personality: sparse, but clean and well lit. I couldn't help noticing that he dressed rather like Saddam Hussein, sporting suspenders, a plain shirt, and a walrus mustache. It was an unmistakable style. His aides, who sat nearby, allowed him to take the lead—adding only details to what he said. They nodded vigorously when he condemned the United States and claimed that the Iraqi insurgency was not an enemy of America. He made it clear that he had no great love for Saddam Hussein, but he was an Iraqi patriot. Still, I could not shake the feeling that I did not belong in that room and that I should not be talking with him. Finally, it dawned on me.

"*You're* the sheikh," I said.
"That's right."
"You're with the Iraqi insurgency," I said. "You're the political wing of the Iraqi insurgency."
"Yes, that's so."
I hesitated for only a moment. "I don't think I can be in this room," I said.
This was followed by silence, as a smile spread across his face.
"Why not?" he asked.
"Because you're killing Americans," I said.
"Yes, that's right," he said, "but don't worry. I've been meeting with American military officers in this room for the last eighteen months. They know exactly how I feel."

I returned to Washington and, again at Jones's suggestion, began to talk to those who had been involved in the exchanges with al-Gaood and the Iraqi insurgency. I met and spoke with dozens of current and former officials and military officers. Over a period of many years, I collected information on what Colonel Mike Walker of the U.S. Marine Corps called "the July Surprise"—the opening painstakingly built by the marines of the 3rd Civil Affairs Group (CAG) (and by a community of dedicated American public servants and private individuals) with al-Gaood and the insurgency in Iraq's al-Anbar Province. Slowly, but perhaps inevitably, I began to reflect on the meaning of my discussions in Amman and their relationship to the meetings we had held with Hamas and Hezbollah leaders in Beirut. The two sets of experiences, I concluded, were closely linked.

TALKING TO TERRORISTS is not a memoir, a lecture, or an essay. It is a story told by those Americans who fought the war on terror in al-Anbar and who forged the opening with Iraq's insurgency. I hope my European, and particularly my British, readers will forgive me for spending the first part of this book focusing on America's war in Iraq. I am painfully aware that it was not just the United States that was involved in that country, not just its soldiers who shed their blood. Yet England's war is left out of this account not through disdain or ignorance but as a reflection of facts. Our two nations fought together and claimed victory together as allies in World War II. The alliance was not a façade; it was essential to the defeat of Germany. We could not have been triumphant without being triumphant together. This was not true in Iraq. In World War II Americans and Brits shed our blood together; in Iraq, we shed blood separately. The Blair-Bush "coalition of the willing" was a façade.

Despite this, the story of the American fight in al-Anbar—and the meetings that a small group of U.S. marines had with representatives of the Iraqi insurgency—remains a compelling object lesson in how to begin to get things right, after getting them wrong. After all, it was Winston Churchill who supposedly said that the Americans always get it right, after trying everything else first. In Iraq, we tried everything else first. Then too, the story of the marines in al-Anbar provides a useful basis for reflections on the dialogues that I had over a period of many years with representatives of Hamas and Hezbollah. The story of the Americans in al-Anbar makes up the first half of this book. The account of my meetings in the region constitute the second half. The two stories are different in many ways, but their meaning is the same. They together tell a story of how and why we—both in the United States and in the United Kingdom—are losing the war on terror. But this account is also intended to be much more. It is the story of how U.S. (and European) policies in the Middle East—and our two societies' rhetoric about "terrorists"—have undermined our standing in the world, of how we got the war on terror wrong, and how we can begin to get it right.

CHAPTER ONE

VIGILANT RESOLVE

"It's a war, however you describe it."

—JOHN ABIZAID

ON MAY 1, 2003—the day George W. Bush announced an end to "major combat operations" in Iraq—al-Anbar's Iraqis were organizing militias to oppose the American occupation. In the weeks that followed, while the U.S. military rounded up the leaders of Iraq's Baath Party, Sunni leaders in Nasiriyah, Najaf, Kut, and Fallujah were recruiting former Saddamist soldiers to serve in militias allied with groups of radical jihadist foreign fighters. The new insurgents wanted to transform Iraq into a killing zone. Oddly, the Americans seemed not to notice. It wasn't until mid-June 2003, just forty-five days after Bush's May 1 announcement, that the U.S. military launched its first anti-insurgent operation, in Baghdad, to root out "criminal elements."

Evidence of an organized, large-scale Iraqi insurgency had emerged by the end of the year. In August 2003, a suicide bomb in Baghdad claimed the lives of U.N. envoy Sergio Vieira de Mello and twenty-four others. Ten days later, Ayatollah Mohammad Bakr al-Hakim, one of Iraq's prominent Shia leaders, was assassinated in

Najaf. By the end of 2003, American and coalition soldiers were dying in increasing numbers. The uprising spread into the new year: In February the insurgency had taken root in Irbil, and in March Shia worshippers were attacked in Karbala. Eighty-four Iraqis died in the attacks.

The strength of the insurgency took the Americans by surprise. Misled by the lack of coordination in insurgent attacks and by the seeming randomness of the killings, military leaders were unwilling to admit that there *was* an insurgency until the summer of 2003. Even then, Pentagon officials had difficulty explaining to the American public what was happening in Iraq, blaming the violence on criminal gangs, outside infiltrators, and the disaffected— as if what America faced from Basra to Kirkuk was a riot instead of a war.

The new head of U.S. Central Command (CENTCOM), General John Abizaid, purposely corrected this impression during a Pentagon briefing in July, calling the uprising "a classic guerrilla-type campaign against us," and then, lest his statement somehow be viewed as minimizing the danger, he added, "It's a war, however you describe it." Abizaid's comment was purposely blunt. He did not want anyone underestimating what was happening to Americans in Iraq. It had been less than three months since "the end of major combat operations"—an eyeblink in history, but an eternity for those carrying rifles in al-Anbar.

As the attacks in Iraq escalated, so too did public doubts about America's Iraq policy. Surprisingly, the most prominent skeptic was Secretary of Defense Donald Rumsfeld. Controversial, combative, and confrontational, Rumsfeld blustered but nevertheless harbored niggling doubts that had plagued him almost from the minute the first insurgent bomb detonated in Baghdad.

In public Rumsfeld pointedly accused the press of being overly negative about Iraq's deteriorating security situation. He counseled reporters to stop using the word "insurgency," saying the term gave leaders of the armed Sunni opposition a legitimacy they didn't deserve. "This is a group of people who don't merit the word 'insurgency,' I think," he said. Later, speaking privately, Rumsfeld said that he preferred the word "terrorist," as "these were people who loved violence for its own sake."

But in late 2003 Rumsfeld's most senior civilian aides noticed that he was increasingly uneasy with the military briefings crossing his desk. "He kept asking, 'When's this going to change, when's it going to change?'" one of these aides remembers. In the early autumn of 2003, Rumsfeld sent a high-level "personnel assessment team" to Baghdad to review the situation in the country. Led by a close personal friend, Jerry Jones, the team toured Iraq interviewing American military and civilian leaders and key Iraqis. Their report was blunt: The American effort was disorganized and uninspired, and senior officials in the American Green Zone were out of touch with the war. "For many good security reasons, we do not venture out into Baghdad," one of the assessment team members wrote. "When we do, we are massively secured and intimidating. As we have heard from State's people, once the Palace becomes the U.S. embassy this July, the isolation of Americans will only increase. This isolation will not only cause us to be even more dependent on secondary sources for what is going on in Iraq, but it will make us even more distant and undecipherable to Iraqis."

The problem started at the top, with L. Paul Bremer, the head of the Coalition Provision Authority. Bremer was isolated, imperious, and out of touch with the Iraqi people. "Get rid of Bremer," one of the members of the assessment team told Rumsfeld. "Do it now." Rumsfeld demurred: Bremer reported directly to the president. He could not be removed. "This is not my brief," he told the assessment team. "There's nothing I can do." But although Bremer was outside Rumsfeld's chain of command, the American military was not. By October, Rumsfeld was receiving regular memos suggesting the United States adopt a new strategy for Iraq—one that would relabel Iraq's "terrorists" as "insurgents" who sought a role in the new Iraqi government.

One of the most prophetic memos Rumsfeld received, dated October 2, 2003, came from the Defense Intelligence Agency (DIA). Titled "Sunni Outreach to the Governing Council and Coalition Provision Authority," the information paper was written by the director for intelligence of the Joint Staff, then Major General Ronald L. Burgess Jr., a brainy Alabaman who had spent weeks studying the insurgency. He had steeped himself in the avalanche of on-the-ground reports gleaned from combat officers serving in Sunni areas. Burgess suggested that it might be possible to dampen the insurgency by making contact with its leaders. Under the subheads "Sunni Outreach," "Sunni Perceptions of Political Manipulation," and "Responding to Sunni Outreach," Burgess detailed the in-country contacts the American military had been receiving from Iraq's tribes. Although Burgess did not say so directly, he aligned himself with those who differentiated among Sunni factions, separating "insurgents" from "terrorists"—the "dead enders" of Rumsfeld's worldview.

The more Rumsfeld studied the Burgess report, the more he was convinced it could provide a way to dampen the insurgency. The key was to separate the tribes from Iraq's radical elements, Rumsfeld told a close associate. He passed the Burgess memo on to the Pentagon's political/military cell in Baghdad, a special study group of experts tasked with shaping a response to the violence, and to Deputy Secretary of Defense Paul Wolfowitz. There was no response to the memo from Baghdad, but Rumsfeld received a reply from Wolfowitz that left little doubt about where his deputy stood. Wolfowitz returned the memo to Rumsfeld with three words scribbled in the margin: "They are Nazis!"

The outburst was not a surprise. Although Wolfowitz's critics claimed the deputy secretary was "obsessed" with protecting Israel (the reason, they argued, he had supported the Iraq invasion in the first place), others argued that Wolfowitz had been deeply affected by Saddam Hussein's slaughter of Iraq's Shias at the end of the first Gulf War. As undersecretary of defense for policy in 1991, Wolfowitz had access to classified briefings on the massacres. "He was haunted by the butchery," a colleague notes. "All of these reports were coming across his desk and it was just blood, blood, blood, and he felt responsible for it. It was mass murder. It had nothing to do with Israel. He was deeply affected by the 1991 events. That's what made him support the Shias. It kept him awake nights."

Wolfowitz was also taking cues from Ahmed Chalabi's ideas about de-Baathification. Chalabi, head of the Iraqi National Congress, had provided Douglas Feith, the undersecretary of defense for policy, with a paper on German de-Nazification at the end of World War II. The paper emphasized Chalabi's view that the successful American occupation of Germany had been due to the wholesale removal of Nazi officials in the German government, a highly suspect and controversial claim. "No one checked to see if it was true," an army colonel who reviewed the study said. "Feith and his crew just took it on faith. But even then, that's not really the point, is it? Because once you've accepted that Baathists are Nazis, you end up nodding your head and you say, 'yeah, they're all Nazis. Get rid of them.'" Feith read the paper and passed it on to Wolfowitz.

Chalabi reinforced his views on cleansing Iraq of Baathists in an opinion piece in the *Wall Street Journal* on the eve of the invasion. "Iraq needs a comprehensive program of de-Baathification even more extensive than the de-Nazification effort in Germany after World War II," Chalabi wrote. "You cannot cut off the viper's head and leave the body festering." So it was that Chalabi's logic took hold among senior civilian leaders in the Pentagon: Iraq was Germany and the Saddamists were Nazis. After the fall of Baghdad, Bremer was even more explicit in the comparison: "Just as in our occupation of Germany we had passed what were called 'de-Nazification decrees' and prosecuted senior Nazi officials," he said, "the model for the de-Baathification was to look back at that de-Nazification."

Wolfowitz's view that there was simply no choice but to smash the insurgency gained wide support among senior Pentagon policy-makers. "If you had taken a poll of the senior military at the time, you would have found very few commanders who believed we should engage in any outreach to the enemy," an officer on the Pentagon's Joint Staff said. "There might have been a few, mostly people who had been in al-Anbar, but really there were very few of them. The people around Rumsfeld were convinced the insurgency would die out once America's program for Iraq took hold." Recently retired Marine Corps Lieutenant Colonel Roy D. "Dave" Harlan, a veteran of al-Anbar, remembers the difficulties he faced in convincing Pentagon officials that "we can't paint everyone with the same brush—an insurgent is not the same as a terrorist." He said, "The bottom line back in '03 was that 'there's only one way to deal with these people.' That was the view, and those who questioned it were outside the pale. It's easy to understand. The military's job is not to stabilize societies, but to *destabilize* them. We bring down countries. If these people could be defeated, then that's what we were going to do."

But Rumsfeld continued to have doubts. So although he laid aside the Burgess memo, he queried his senior staff and American commanders on opening contacts with the insurgency. On December 19, he wrote to CENTCOM commander John Abizaid summarizing the contacts the Pentagon had received from former commanders in Saddam's military. Rumsfeld believed that one of them, General Abdul Razak Sultan al-Jibouri, could be used to dampen the insurgency. Jibouri had contacted U.S. officers in Iraq about holding discussions that would lead to the establishment of what he called "a Sunni Council" in al-Anbar, led by his own Jibouri tribe. The DIA tracked al-Jibouri at Rumsfeld's direction, producing a detailed biography of the high-profile military commander.

The DIA believed al-Jibouri was capable of independent action. He was a Sunni, an insurgent leader, a member of one of Iraq's most prominent tribes, a military man, and a commander who had refused to participate in the 1991 slaughter that haunted Wolfowitz. The DIA extolled his credentials but added a disconcerting note. "Jibouri is open-minded but self-promoting," they reported. Rumsfeld scoffed at the criticism. "This Jibouri could be the right guy," he told a senior assistant. Rumsfeld passed the report to Bremer, Abizaid, and Wolfowitz.

The response from Wolfowitz was an even more emphatic repeat of what he had said about the Burgess report. He again scrawled his answer on Rumsfeld's memo—"No!" As one of Rumsfeld's senior assistants later characterized it: "Wolfowitz was almost unbalanced about this. He thought that Sunni resistance wasn't even a resistance. You couldn't deal with them. He always described them as 'Nazis.' The word was almost a personal tic. When anyone talked about this he would get so angry he would start shaking. It was a little weird." Abizaid agreed with Wolfowitz: The insurgency could be and should be defeated. Bremer, who viewed himself as acting independently of Rumsfeld, "didn't bother to respond," a Pentagon official noted. "He just let the initiative die."

Four months later, on April 12, 2004, Rumsfeld tried again, but this time he bypassed Wolfowitz and sent a memo on insurgency contacts directly to Bremer. He also sent copies of his memo to Deputy Secretary of State Richard Armitage and to the U.S. commander in Iraq, Ricardo Sanchez. "It shows you just how desperate Rumsfeld was getting," a Pentagon official said. "Rumsfeld liked Armitage, but he hated the State Department and blamed them for everything that was going wrong in Iraq. But he was looking for allies, and he thought that Armitage might help. There was a little tension there too, because Armitage thought he should have Rumsfeld's job."

In his message to Bremer, Rumsfeld's tone was preemptory, as if he were dictating a new policy. In the memo, the defense secretary suggested that Bremer "elicit help from Sunni tribal leaders" to end the insurgency. The memo listed a series of specific recommendations that Bremer should undertake, including opening a dialogue with former senior commanders in Saddam's army. Rumsfeld included his own reflections on the issue, telling Bremer that he should "probe an opening" with the insurgency. Once again, Bremer ignored the memo. The State Department did not.

Days after receiving the memo, Armitage wrote a simple response to Rumsfeld and appended a State Department study on the insurgency titled "The Sunni Heartland: A Lost Cause." Any attempt to recruit Sunni tribal leaders to end the insurgency, the paper said, would "be a colossal miscalculation." Rumsfeld's own Iraq commander, Ricardo Sanchez, concurred with Armitage and told Rumsfeld that he supported "a more kinetic plan"— military-speak for ending the insurgency by force. "Sanchez was then rolling out what he called 'a final campaign plan' for crushing the insurgents," a retired Joint Chiefs of Staff (JCS) officer said. "He [Sanchez] kept arguing that the point of the strategy was not to talk to the insurgency, but to 'neutralize' them. That's the word he used."

By the end of 2003, the Sunni insurgency was gaining strength and Iraq was being plunged into violence. The Pentagon's response to this challenge had proven painfully slow. This inaction could have been predicted: Once senior Pentagon policymakers and military officers had determined that U.S. soldiers would be welcomed as liberators, there was no need to plan for any other contingency. Rumsfeld sensed that this belief violated the most fundamental of military principles—to prepare for the worst—and he also sensed that once policymakers had decided that Iraq's Baath Party was indistinguishable from Nazis, the United States had committed itself to a strategy that brooked no compromise. He was plagued by doubts. He wasn't alone.

By the beginning of 2004, Donald Rumsfeld's doubts about America's Iraq strategy were spreading to senior commanders in key combat positions in Iraq. Among the commanders coming to grips with the insurgency was Lieutenant General James Conway, commander of the 1st Marine Expeditionary Force (the IMEF—pronounced I-MEF) in Iraq.

In February 2004 Conway's IMEF was given the assignment of stabilizing Iraq's al-Anbar Province, which comprised one-third of the country and nearly all its Sunni population. It was a challenging assignment. Conway's marines had a stellar combat record: Under his leadership, they had destroyed nine of Saddam's divisions in the second Gulf War. The imposing Arkansan was a sound tactician and had earned a reputation for being a tough fighter. But the al-Anbar assignment was different.

When he received the assignment, Conway studied both the battle reports coming out of Iraq and the classified intelligence assessments of the insurgency. After hours of pouring through these papers, he decided that his marines faced a war different from the one they had confronted when they invaded the country in 2003. His job, he decided, was to build trust, not kill Iraqis. Then too, Conway was in no mood to expend his men in questionable operations against an elusive enemy. What al-Anbar needed, Conway decided, was economic development—and his job was to find a way to deliver it. Conway was so convinced of his views that he began to put them in place when his marines arrived in al-Anbar. He ordered his senior commanders to make certain their troops took a low profile. Their job was to help people out, get to know them, act as liberators—not occupiers. But within weeks of being deployed in al-Anbar, Conway's plan was short-circuited.

On April 3, 2004, Conway was ordered to send his men into Fallujah to punish insurgents for the deaths of four employees of Blackwater USA, a private contractor. The killings stunned the American people, particularly in the wake of television footage of Fallujah insurgents dragging the bodies through the streets of the city. Now, Conway was told, he was to launch a major operation to punish the perpetrators.

Conway was dumbfounded. "What the hell are they thinking?" he asked a subordinate. "We shouldn't be doing this. It'll only make things worse, a lot worse." According to Major Patrick Maloy—a member of Conway's staff—his commander "threw his cover [his hat] on the floor and kicked it around the room." He adds, "Have you ever met this guy? He's a gorilla. He's all of six five, about 250 pounds. I have never seen him so enraged." The order contravened everything Conway believed about what America should be doing. Sending his marines into Fallujah to look for murderers would only turn the people of the city against him. Civilians would be caught in the crossfire. The marines, in al-Anbar to help, would only be making new enemies. Conway appealed to Sanchez, hoping to reverse the order. "Conway went to the top with this," one of his subordinate commanders remembers. "He just couldn't believe it." Conway protested that going into Fallujah with guns blazing was the worst thing his marines could do. Sanchez waved him off. "I have my orders, and now you have yours," he said. "This one comes from the very top."

Continuing to question the order was not something Conway would do. Although the marine commander was proud that he was not one of the Corps's "ring knockers"—graduates of the Naval Academy—he also prided himself on his combat expertise and on his loyalty. He had commanded a marine landing team during Desert Storm and had served two combat tours during Operation Iraqi Freedom. Known for issuing blunt semi-clichés to explain his own thinking, he told his marines they should be prepared for anything. "They want us to fight, we fight," he told his staff. "They want us to build power stations, we build power stations. They want us to escort little Arab children to school, we'll do that. We'll even do windows." His pithy comments were legendary. While serving on the JCS as a deputy operations officer, Conway continually reminded his staff to "stay in your lane." But now, after questioning the order to send his men into Fallujah, Conway was not only out of his lane, he was off the highway.

Conway was so troubled by the Fallujah decision that he considered sharing his doubts with reporters. For Conway, talking to the media about anything was almost an act of mutiny. He had never done it before. "He came close to just saying 'No,'" a subordinate said. Conway relented, vowing that in due time he would tell someone how he felt. Months later, he shared his hesitation over the Fallujah operation with the *Washington Post*'s Rajiv Chandrasekaran: "When we were told to attack Fallujah, I think we certainly increased the level of animosity that existed," Conway said. He added that he preferred an engagement with Fallujah's political leaders to an armed confrontation with the city insurgents. Conway believed that the White House was micromanaging the war and told one of his staff assistants that the Fallujah operation would "set the country on fire." This same subordinate discovered Conway pacing his office floor on the eve of the Fallujah offensive, muttering angrily to himself, "This is just stupid, stupid, stupid. It'll just make things worse." But there was more to the issue than Conway had bothered to tell his senior commanders.

In mid-March, Conway had sent a group of officers from IMEF's 3rd Civil Affairs Group to Amman for a meeting with al-Anbar business leaders. Their goal was to determine how to jump-start economic development in the province. The 3rd CAG was a comparatively new outfit, established in 1985 as a reserve unit to support the IMEF's combat activities. The unit was an eclectic group: schoolteachers, city administrators, police officers, drug enforcement agents, university professors, attorneys, and construction contractors—a tightly knit cohort of about 150 officers who were deployed in postcombat operations to distribute humanitarian relief supplies, oversee rebuilding projects, resettle refugees, and promote stability. It was, Conway thought, a nearly impossible job, and one that could not be done at all unless key CAG officers decided to make contact with al-Anbar's most important political leaders.

In the months and years ahead, the officers of Conway's 3rd Civil Affairs Group attended innumerable conferences, seminars, and private meetings, mixing easily with al-Anbar's tribal leaders and disbursing emergency funds to keep the province's infrastructure from collapse. The 3rd CAG's officers had little doubt who they were helping: According to CAG officer Pat Maloy, many of the recipients of their aid were "a part of the insurgency." For Conway, the order to go into Fallujah was an added headache; having made initial contact with the insurgency, his marines were now being ordered to fight them. Orders or no orders, he thought it was a bad idea.

By the morning of April 5, Conway's marines had surrounded Fallujah and had begun the painstaking process of reducing insurgent strongholds. They were supported by bombing runs from Cobra helicopters. But after days of fighting (a journalist who had covered the Vietnam conflict called Fallujah "a second Hue"), the marines had barely penetrated the insurgency's defenses. One exhausted commander reported that after ninety hours of constant combat, his team had "pacified" just 25 percent of the city. Finally, on April 9—and under pressure from the Iraqi government— Conway was ordered to end the offensive. At that point, upwards of six hundred Iraqis had been killed, many of them civilians. On April 19, the marines and the city militia reached an uneasy truce.

But Conway's prophecy that Operation Vigilant Resolve would "set the country on fire" proved prescient.

In the ensuing weeks, the fighting in Fallujah spread into the lower Euphrates Valley and militiamen in al-Anbar all but took over the province. Months later, Conway was still seething: "We felt like we had a method that we wanted to apply to Fallujah: that we ought to probably let the situation settle before we appeared to be attacking out of revenge. Would our system have been better? Would we have been able to bring over the people of Fallujah with our methods? You'll never know that for sure, but at the time we certainly thought so."

Even before the Fallujah operation had ended, Conway told Colonel Mike Walker, the 3rd CAG commander, to accelerate his search for ways to "do things a little differently in Anbar." Walker, a plainspoken and contemplative Californian, needed little encouragement. After the fight in Fallujah ("the worst fiasco I have ever seen in my life," as he later described it), Walker worked tirelessly to shift the IMEF's focus from "shooting at the bad guys" into building programs that would "reintegrate the province with the rest of the country." Walker wanted to find a quick way to dampen the insurgency by focusing on meeting the day-to-day needs of al-Anbar's Sunnis. "This wasn't just about business; it was governance and security too," he later said. "We needed to find a way to give people hope, and the only way to do that was to focus on development."

One month after the Fallujah fiasco, Walker showed up in Amman at the suggestion of Colonel Dave Harlan, the 3rd CAG's liaison officer in Jordan. The two had met back at Camp Pendleton and trusted each other. Harlan told Walker that he thought he should meet with Talal al-Gaood. The outgoing Sunni businessman knew how to cultivate friendships and was well-known in Iraqi business circles. Walker met with him in his office in Amman, and the two hit it off. "He gave the best briefing I think I've ever heard," Walker said, "and he had a dynamite group of people around him. He understood al-Anbar. He knew everyone." Al-Gaood told Walker that he could provide a network of business contacts interested in developing al-Anbar, people who were willing to work with the Americans, and he pleaded with Walker to help him in al-Anbar. "The Sunnis are suffering," al-Gaood said. "You've got to help us."

Walker briefed Conway on al-Gaood and received permission to attend a business conference in Bahrain. The conference, Walker said, would include businessmen with ties to the al-Anbar insurgency. Conway had no objections. In March 2004, Walker spent three days in Bahrain, meeting people and listening to what they had to say. "It was a good conference," he said, "but the thing that I noticed is that even then, people at the conference were on the phone with people in al-Anbar. So things were starting to move."

While in Bahrain, Walker received word from Harlan that al-Gaood wanted to hold a larger meeting in early summer on how to spark business development in al-Anbar Province. "You know, you can hold all kinds of conferences and sit and talk," Walker remembers, "but I knew this one would be different. Talal was a serious guy." Then too, as Walker learned from Harlan, al-Gaood's June conference would be different both from the small meeting Walker had attended in Amman and from the larger conference in Bahrain. Talal, Harlan said, would put together a room of businessmen from the province's most important tribes. This was exactly what Walker—and Conway—wanted. Inevitably, they concluded, the marines would "begin to penetrate just how the province worked, moving from the outer circles to the inner."

Conway and Walker were convinced that the insurgency was much less united than the American government believed and that, with a little pressure, parts of it could be persuaded to side with the Americans. Viewed by many of the marines of his division as "a tough guy" and a "trigger puller," Conway had studied the problem in the months prior to the IMEF deployment. "He wanted to find a way to unlock the province," Major Pat Maloy said. "He knew that just going in and fighting was not going to get it done."

After learning everything he could about al-Anbar and its tribes, Conway focused on economic development—on "building schools and creating jobs"—for al-Anbar's Sunni population. Walker remembers that, prior to the IMEF's deployment to al-Anbar, Conway had written personal letters to a group of California-based sporting goods companies, asking them to donate soccer balls for Sunni children. Conway sat at his desk at Camp Pendleton, every morning, writing the letters in longhand. He always added a postscript: "In addition, we would like to have school supplies for the Iraqi children," he wrote. He received no replies.

JAMES CONWAY DID not know it at the time, but he was about to receive help from an unlikely source—a Texas businessman named Kenneth Wischkaemper. Wischkaemper is a quintessential Texan: He can switch on a romantic Lone Star drawl and has little problem acting the part of an oil mogul. The fifty-eight-year-old businessman, the owner of "a sleek BMW sportster and 10,000 acres of prime north Texas real estate," might be easily mistaken for a "fast cars and easy money" Republican (he bears an uncanny resemblance to Dwight Eisenhower), but he is outspoken and ambitious—and one of the world's experts in agricultural seed exports.

Wischkaemper is the guiding mind behind Agricultural Development International (ADI), the most important industry in Shamrock, Texas. "You can't believe how complicated this business is," he said. "If you're going to export seeds, you have to keep them at a certain temperature for a certain period of time and you have to ship them that way. There are thousands of regulations about shipping seeds and thousands of forms that have to be filled out, but there's good reason for it. Seeds grow food, but they also spread disease. You can't make a mistake." In 2003 Wischkaemper was well into his third decade as an agricultural expert and was a cosmopolitan presence at international agricultural conferences, where his easygoing manner and "pay me when you can" attitude made him lifelong friends from the Middle East to Africa. Wischkaemper is nearly evangelical in his faith in his company and its ability to feed the world—and he has set out to do it. Over the years Wischkaemper had met prime ministers and presidents, and ADI had built a solid reputation for helping developing countries increase their agricultural output.

"I was in Russia in late 2003 and I heard that the Massey Ferguson franchise for Iraq was available," Wischkaemper remembers, "so I obtained the name of a contact and I headed to Amman." In Amman, Wischkaemper and his partner, Bob Teweles, met with the Middle East representative of one of the largest farm equipment manufacturers in the world, who told them to contact Talal al-Gaood, a solid businessman with a wide network of friends in Baghdad, Amman, and Damascus. Wischkaemper's business contact told him that al-Gaood owned a highly successful Amman-based trading corporation, the Tabouk Group, and was an ex-Baathist whose tribe had close contact with officials in Iraq's new government. The official added that al-Gaood spoke perfect English, was highly educated, and had a civil engineering degree from the University of Southern California.

Wischkaemper and Teweles called al-Gaood, and the three arranged a meeting at the bar of the Four Seasons Hotel in Amman. "Talal was a very serious man, a good businessman, and we got along very well," Wischkaemper remembers. "At one point we stopped talking about agricultural products and started talking about Iraq. And he turned to me and he said, 'You know, I need your help. The Sunnis need your help. Anbar needs your help.

We are suffering. Will you help us?'" It was the same message that al-Gaood had given to Mike Walker just weeks before. Wischkaemper hesitated only a moment. "What is it you want me to do?" he asked. Al-Gaood told Wischkaemper that he believed the U.S. military program of defeating the Iraqi insurgency through military means wouldn't work. What was needed, he said, was an economics-based program that focused on business development. Wischkaemper was intrigued by al-Gaood's proposal; it was almost as if al-Gaood was reading his mind.

In March 2004, Wischkaemper returned to Amman to talk with al-Gaood. The two were thinking along the same lines: Now would be a good time for the United States to start an economic development program for al-Anbar. "We went up to his home in Amman and I met his wife, and we sat down to dinner and he treated me like an old friend," Wischkaemper remembers. "He was very sincere, a family man, an Iraqi patriot. I felt comfortable with him." Al-Gaood told Wischkaemper that the one way to dampen the Iraqi resistance was for the United States to establish a comprehensive and well-funded program for al-Anbar's economic development. Al-Gaood asked Wischkaemper whether he would be willing to put together a team of U.S. government officials and business executives to meet with Sunni businessmen to discuss al-Anbar's economic development. The business conference could be held in Beirut, in Amman, or even in Baghdad, al-Gaood said.

Al-Gaood also handed Wischkaemper a proposal for an Iraqi constitutional convention that would empower Iraqi Sunnis. Al-Gaood's proposal called for broad reconciliation of Iraq's Sunnis and Shias, shaping a government that would protect the Sunni minority and give them a greater voice in the running of the country.

Wischkaemper told al-Gaood that he would think about his ideas on a business conference and talk to people in Washington about them. "I sat down and I thought about it for about three days and nights and I decided if there was ever a guy who needed help it was Talal al-Gaood," he remembers. When he returned to Shamrock, he put in a call to Larry Meyers, a Washington insider and an old friend who served as ADI's executive vice president. Wischkaemper told Meyers about al-Gaood and asked him to arrange a series of meetings at the Pentagon with officials who Meyers thought might be interested in helping.

Meyers's first call was to Lawrence Di Rita, Rumsfeld's outspoken and combative public affairs spokesman. But Di Rita refused to help: "Larry just dismissed Meyers," one of Rumsfeld's assistants said. "He wasn't interested. I got the impression that he thought any outreach to the Sunnis was just silly—that it was vaguely anti-American." Both Wischkaemper and Meyers came to believe that Di Rita "was purposely putting obstacles in our way."

When contact with Di Rita went nowhere, Meyers contacted Mark Zell, an attorney and former law partner of Douglas Feith, the Pentagon's undersecretary for policy. Zell dragged his feet. "The contact went absolutely nowhere," Wischkaemper remembers. "Zell wasn't interested in having anything to do with the Sunnis in Iraq, and his law partner [Feith] wouldn't even pick up the phone."

Increasingly aware that doing business with Sunnis in Iraq was controversial, Meyers next turned to Marty Hoffman—an old friend, influential Washington lawyer, and former secretary of the army who had an office at the Pentagon. In the aftermath of the 9/11 attacks, but prior to the Iraq invasion, Hoffman and Meyers had worked together on a team assessing Afghan business development—what a friend of Meyers describes as the Afghan reach-back effort—so Meyers thought Hoffman might be open to Wischkaemper's ideas. Hoffman agreed to meet with Meyers and Wischkaemper and to do what he could to help them. The meeting took place in mid-April in Hoffman's Pentagon office. "We briefed Marty on Ken's trip to Amman and he was intrigued by a potential opening to the Sunnis," Meyers remembers, "and at the end of our conversation he picked up the phone and called Jerry Jones."

Jones and Hoffman, both Texans, had worked together in past Republican administrations, knew how to access the labyrinthine Pentagon system, and were confident in their abilities to help Wischkaemper. "In West Texas you do business with a handshake," Jones remembers, "and that's the way Wischkaemper was. And he told me that that was the way that al-Gaood was. So I was intrigued by the idea of setting up something in al-Anbar that would spark economic development. Helping the Sunnis made a lot of sense."

Jones supported the opening to al-Gaood, believing that his ideas on business development could yield tangible benefits for the American program in Iraq. But Jones was uncomfortable with a wider and more political effort. He considered al-Gaood's proposal to hold a constitutional convention out of the question—it was too controversial and would raise questions about Pentagon contacts with disaffected Sunnis, sparking the kind of response that Rumsfeld had gotten at the end of 2003. But, Jones thought, an al-Anbar business conference hosted by Iraqis seemed the perfect solution to the problems he had come across when he had headed Rumsfeld's "personnel assessment team" in late 2003. Then too, such a conference would be "under the radar": American attendance would not have to be signed off on by Rumsfeld—or by Wolfowitz.

By the end of their mid-April meeting, Hoffman had agreed to access the Pentagon's higher reaches to help Wischkaemper determine what kind of economic help might be available to al-Anbar's Sunnis. Jones e-mailed al-Gaood to find out how serious he was about bringing Sunni Arabs to meet with American businessmen. Al-Gaood responded by repeating his offer and added

that he would also be willing to use his contacts in al-Anbar to end
the fighting in the province. Jones was intrigued by al-Gaood's proposal, believing that al-Gaood's midsummer business conference
provided a credible follow-up to the outreach efforts he had detailed in his 2003 assessment to Rumsfeld.

Years later, Larry Meyers and Ken Wischkaemper identified a
core group of anti-Sunni officials around Paul Wolfowitz who had
failed to recognize how an opening with al-Anbar's tribes could
help save American lives. But Jerry Jones insists that despite the
obvious caution of Wolfowitz and Feith—and their allies inside
the defense department—he had no sense that they had worked
against the al-Gaood initiative. "Feith just wasn't a player at this
time," he notes. "There's no question that this was really under
the radar, but not because I thought that anyone would try to derail it. This was a simple business conference proposal and it was
going to be hosted by the Iraqis. A few of us would be going out
as their guests, so it's not as if this was a U.S. initiative. And I
thought the conference provided a way of sparking economic development in Anbar. It just wasn't that controversial."

Even so, Wolfowitz was known for his hard-line views on Iraq's
Sunnis, and rumors of his determined opposition to an opening
had spread through the Pentagon's upper echelons. "If anyone had
found out Jerry was dealing with al-Anbar Sunnis, it would have
been all over for him, and people were watching. He had to tread
lightly," Larry Meyers said. "Jerry was upset about what was happening in Iraq. He didn't want to see a repeat of what we [the
United States] had done so many times before, you know—'We're
in, we're out, and to hell with you, you're on your own.'"

As uncontroversial as a conference on economic development
in al-Anbar seemed at the time, Wischkaemper warned al-Gaood
about the obstacles they faced. "Please know that there is a deep,
deep divide at the Pentagon," he wrote in a May 8 memo. "It is
the Z group [the Zell group—Wolfowitz, Feith, and their allies]

versus the Rum [R] group. Please know that the R group favors our methodology at the expense of the methodology of the Z group. . . . It appears that the R group may be finally gaining the upper hand. Please know that your and your guys' support is of extreme importance."

In the same memo, Wischkaemper reassured al-Gaood that his information went directly to Rumsfeld; it did not pass through the Z group:

> It is of extreme importance that you be aware that Z and group were not, repeat—not—the conduit through which the information reached the top. Due to developments occurring after I left Amman and before I left Washington . . . it became evident that Z and group could very possibly have an agenda that did not work in our best interests. Z and group are totally unaware that our/your names and proposals have reached the top, thus should any approach be made to you from this Z group, please bear this in mind.

Jerry Jones is wiry, self-effacing, and mentally tough. He was never afraid of taking chances. This quality had brought him into the Nixon White House and had seen him through thirty years of service to a host of Republican presidents, including Richard M. Nixon, Gerald R. Ford, and George H. W. Bush. "There were about ten of us who kept the country together for eighteen months or so during the Watergate crisis," said former Pentagon official Noel Koch, who had worked with Jones in the Nixon White House. "It was Al Haig and Don Rumsfeld and a lot of unnamed heroes, and Jerry was one of them. He was tireless, dedicated."

One day in 1974, while working at his desk in the Old Executive Office Building, Jones looked up and saw Alexander Haig, the White House chief of staff, standing in front of his desk. Haig gave him a new assignment: In addition to his duties as staff secretary, he was to be the keeper of the Oval Office tapes. For at least a part of each day, Jones was to sit in a vaulted room and sign out the Oval Office tapes and make certain they were returned. The thankless task kept Jones sequestered in a silent room into the night, as the president's lawyers reviewed Nixon's Oval Office discussions. One night, as Jones remembers, he was sitting at his desk when Nixon lawyer Fred Buzhardt came into the room and "laid the tape for June 23, 1971, on the table in front of me. And he looked up at me and he said, 'that's it Jerry, it's all over.'" The June 23 tape was the smoking gun: proof that Nixon had covered up the Watergate break-in and would be forced to resign.

Jones's willingness to take on tough tasks and his close relationship with Republican insiders made him a valuable addition to Rumsfeld's staff. He was Rumsfeld's eyes and ears at the Pentagon and was available for special tasks. Over the years he had proven a trusted resource as Rumsfeld's personal intelligence-provider, ferreting out hard-to-find information and taking on sensitive issues, from charting the influence of the Middle East's most important Shia families (at one point he provided Rumsfeld with the Sadr family tree, to show the relationship between Iraqi Shias and Lebanon's Party of God), to organizing Paul Wolfowitz's chaotic office (the deputy secretary's office was not running well until Jones hired Dave Patterson, one of the building's best managers, as Wolfowitz's chief of staff).

Jones was masterful in reading Rumsfeld's moods. By the end of 2003 he knew that the defense secretary was worried about Bremer and about the growing insurgency, despite his gruff talk to the press. Then too, Jones had skin in the game: Three of his children were in the military, and all were on their way to, in, or coming back from Iraq. Perhaps as a result, Jones was outspoken about America's mistakes in the country. Usually cool and self-effacing, and rarely given to anger, Jones turned on one of his colleagues in the spring of 2004 with an unusually harsh verdict: "We're not only losing," he said, "we're on the wrong side."

By the end of June, Jones and al-Gaood had sketched out the details of a business conference to be held at the Amman Sheraton Hotel in July. "Talal wanted to make the conference in Baghdad," Larry Meyers remembers, "but he just couldn't do it. Security was a huge issue for him. He didn't think we'd be safe." By early July, Jones and al-Gaood had produced an extensive briefing paper containing an agenda and fact sheets on Iraq's Sunni population.

Al-Gaood also began recruiting Iraqi participants, reassuring Jones that the group that would meet would be "very selective and very small." But al-Gaood was also thinking beyond the conference, shuttling political papers to Wischkaemper that he knew would be passed on to the Pentagon. The papers were deeply critical of Baghdad's interim government. In one message, al-Gaood outlined why the Americans were failing in Iraq: "The governing council and its appointed Ministers have failed to meet the needs and hopes of [the] Iraqi people in establishing proper services, maintaining security and commencing the reconstruction efforts," al-Gaood said.

By early July 2004, Jerry Jones had finished putting together the U.S. conference delegation. In addition to Wischkaemper and Meyers, Jones invited officials representing a broad section of the American government and international business community: Evan Galbraith, Rumsfeld's representative in Europe, Dulce Zahniser and James Clad of the Overseas Private Investment Corporation, James Flowers from the economic section of the U.S. embassy in Amman, two Japanese officials from the Japan Bank for International Cooperation—including Tadashi Maeda, the director general for energy at the bank—and U.S. Marine Colonel Mike Walker.

On July 12, just six days before the opening of the Amman meeting, Jones penned a note to Ambassador James Jeffrey, Condoleezza

Rice's senior adviser on Iraq and the U.S. deputy chief of mission in Baghdad. Jones reassured him that he would be attending a "really non-controversial" and "rather straightforward business conference" in Amman in July. "We DoD types would like to attend, but those of you in Baghdad are the key players," Jones wrote. "I hope you will attend and if you cannot, that you will send appropriate people to hear this group out. Please let me know how you think this outreach effort can best go forward. You should take the lead; outreach and economic development leading to improved security will only work if you in Baghdad make it happen."

After sending off his memo, Jones spent the next days in intense preparation for the Amman conference. Months later, he reflected on his expectations. "I had never met Talal," he said,

> and was simply going on the faith of Ken Wischkaemper's recommendations. I knew that I could absolutely trust Ken and I trusted his handshake. We just connected. And we had Dave Harlan on the ground assessing Talal and he liked him. So that was good enough for me. Expectations? They were very modest, but important: I had hopes that we could find a group that could step forward and lead Iraq toward a secular, pro-Western, technocratically oriented modern state. We would encourage them, support them, and help them make their views known. At the very least, we were reaching out to political people in Anbar and I thought that was badly needed. You know, I wanted to see what would happen.

Jones then turned reflective:

> This really wasn't all that earth-shattering, you know. It was going to be a very simple discussion that we hoped would lead to a very simple program. We would introduce Iraqi Sunnis to a group of business people and agricultural specialists and they

would take it from there. This was soft power at its finest. At the very least, Ken Wischkaemper and other agriculturalists could provide the expertise that Anbar needed. You know, his idea was that this would be pretty simple. We give them seeds, they plant them and they feed their people.

Jones smiled innocently. "It's like that program in the Middle East. What is it called? Oh yes, seeds for peace. That's what it is. Seeds for peace. They turn in their guns and we give them seeds. And when the crops come in and they become prosperous, they won't be shooting at us anymore." Jones shrugged and laughed self-consciously; his explanation sounded just the right note. For anyone who heard it, it sounded almost naive.

CHAPTER TWO

THE JULY SURPRISE

"He was the real deal."
—MIKE WALKER

IT IS DIFFICULT to exaggerate the abilities of Talal al-Gaood. The Iraqi businessman had an uncanny talent for putting together and penetrating complex political, economic, military, and social networks. Al-Gaood met Wischkaemper in December 2003, was introduced to Marine Corps Lieutenant Colonel Dave Harlan in February 2004, hosted Ken Wischkaemper at his home in Amman in March, opened a correspondence with Jerry Jones in April, and met 3rd CAG commander Mike Walker in Amman in May. Al-Gaood cultivated contacts inside the U.S. military that went all the way up the American chain of command: By June 2004—largely as a result of Wischkaemper's and Walker's Pentagon contacts—he was sending e-mails to retired Lieutenant General Claude M. "Mick" Kicklighter, the head of the Pentagon's Iraq/Afghanistan transition team.

Al-Gaood also built strong contacts with the al-Anbar's most important political figures. He kept on good terms with the Jordanian government, which was monitoring his discussions with the Americans, and made a point of meeting with Jordan's King Abdullah. Al-Gaood's Iraqi network was even more impressive. Al-Gaood was a patriot, to be sure (he was proud of his Iraqi heritage and history), but he was also, like Wischkaemper, a talented businessman. It was no surprise, then, given his family background and his sense of the importance of personal relations in making a profit, that he knew every sheik in al-Anbar, maintained strong relations with the province's more powerful tribes, and built political alliances with exiled Baath officials and Iraqi military commanders in Amman and Damascus.

To coordinate these political networks, al-Gaood established a command center in the offices of the Tabouk Group in Amman that was made up of exiles who were familiar with al-Anbar and who had been influential either in Saddam Hussein's government or in the Coalition Provisional Authority (CPA). In 2003 al-Gaood's center became first the Iraq House for Future Studies and then the Iraq Futures Foundation, a small think tank for Iraqi Sunnis. Nearly anyone of any importance who came to Amman from Iraq or Syria made a point of stopping by his offices.

One of the most important men to get in touch with in al-Gaood's foundation was Lieutenant General Ra'ad al-Hamdani, a former senior commander in Saddam's Republican Guard. When the Americans invaded Iraq in March 2003, Saddam gave al-Hamdani command of six divisions "with orders to hold a 130-mile swath of territory south of Baghdad." Al-Hamdani's forces put up a good fight, slowing the American military advance through Nasiriyah, but his divisions were eventually cut to pieces. In June al-Hamdani was arrested by the Americans. They came to his home and forced him onto the floor, where a U.S. soldier held him with a boot on his neck, in front of his wife and four children. In the autumn of 2003, al-Hamdani survived two separate assassination attempts by Shia-led death squads. By the end of that year, al-Hamdani came to Amman and contacted al-Gaood. He was named head of the military department of the Iraq Futures Foundation (IFF), and in May he began work on a presentation titled "Iraqi Perspective of U.S. Military Strategy in Iraq" to be given to the Americans during al-Gaood's July business conference.

Among the small group of exiled Iraqis who joined al-Gaood and al-Hamdani was Jaber Awad, a soft-spoken, brainy political operator who came from a distinguished family. In 1998 Awad had become a sheikh of the Jibouri tribe (the same tribe that piqued Donald Rumsfeld's interest in December 2003). After graduating from Baghdad University, Awad left Iraq, settled in Paris, received a degree in internal medicine, and established his own medical practice; he soon became an important figure in the Iraqi opposition abroad.

Because of his background and Middle East expertise, in the late 1990s Awad was hired as a consultant for Science Applications International Corporation—a Washington, D.C.–based Pentagon contractor. In early March 2003 he received a letter from the Pentagon asking him to be a member of General Jay Garner's team working on Iraqi reconstruction. "I was surprised and pleased," Awad said. "I hated Saddam and what he had done to my country. I looked at the Americans as liberators, and I thought it the duty of all Iraqis to help them." Awad reported to Garner in Kuwait on the eve of the American invasion and was told he would be among the first group of Iraqis to enter the country after Saddam's defeat.

Garner's staff had three objectives: to get the Iraqi government running, to provide shelter for the large numbers of refugees left homeless by the war, and to provide fresh water, sanitation, and electricity to the population. Although Garner knew that his team would not be welcomed by Iraq's Sunni political leadership, he hoped that with a little time and effort he could win their trust. Awad's job would be to provide Garner with introductions to the nation's most important Sunni leaders.

Garner's plan was simple: Wherever possible, he would leave the Sunni leadership in place to ensure the continuation of government programs. Awad agreed with Garner's strategy; the government could not run without Saddam's bureaucrats. As Garner later explained, "We knew we had to pay the civil servants to get them back to work, to run the ministries. We had to pay the army, had to pay the police force. We wanted to bring them back. Then you have pensioners, an awful lot of pensioners; we had to pay those. We had plans to rapidly begin the back pay and then get everybody back to work."

Garner and his team arrived in Baghdad on April 20, 2003. Their immediate task was to restore the nation's electrical grid and inspect its medical facilities. Within his first twenty-four hours in Iraq, Garner had put his people in place to begin that process, but his own work was more political: to make sure they had the support they needed to get the job done. So the day after arriving in Baghdad, Garner traveled north to meet with Kurdish leaders Jalal Talabani and Massoud Barzani. Garner had worked with both men when he was commander of Operation Provide Comfort, the U.S.-led humanitarian effort in the Kurdish areas of northern Iraq in 1991. After his meetings with Talabani and Barzani, Garner returned to Baghdad, where 150 members of his reconstruction team, including Awad, were waiting. He had started to build the political bridges needed for them to get the job done; now he passed on to them the message he had received from the Kurdish leaders he had met. "We have to do this fast and do this well," he said. "The Iraqi people are watching us." Awad immediately set to work opening communications with Iraq's most important tribal leaders.

But on April 24, four days after arriving in Baghdad, Garner received a telephone call from Donald Rumsfeld. "Hey, I'm calling just to tell you what a great job you're doing," Rumsfeld said. "It looks like things are really moving. Watched everything going on, and just keep up the good work and all that. And by the way,

I wanted to let you know that today the president chose [L. Paul] Jerry Bremer to be his presidential envoy, and he'll be coming over there." Garner was stunned. His job was ending. He was being pushed aside.

Bremer arrived in Baghdad on May 13. "Bremer changed everything," Awad remembers. "One day Garner was there and the next day he was gone. We had our first meeting with Bremer, and he made it clear to us that the Sunnis were not going to be listened to. There would be no pay to civil servants, no pay to the army, no pay to the police, and all the government departments would be cleaned out. He reversed all of Garner's plans."

Horrified, Awad asked for a private meeting with Bremer. "I told him that his plan for the Sunnis was a mistake. 'This is not the plan, it won't work. It's going to be a disaster.'" Bremer dismissed Awad's worries. "Every Sunni is a Baathist, every Baathist is a Saddamist, and every Saddamist is a Nazi," Bremer told him.

Within weeks Awad had resigned from the CPA and was trying to "organize with the good people on the American side." His main focus was to "bring people together with the Americans and just let them talk. And make the Americans listen—military people, professionals, people like that. The Sunni elite." Prior to his departure from Baghdad, Awad had one final meeting with Bremer. "I wanted to make sure that I got what I thought off of my chest," he later remembered. "So I told him what I thought: 'You're being used, you're being manipulated by the Iranians—you're making common cause with Iraq's enemies.' He just waved me away; he wouldn't listen."

A member of Garner's staff who had stood on the roof of one of Saddam's palaces on the day American forces entered Baghdad, peering into the distance, saw red flares arcing into the sky—a sign that commanders of Iraq's Republican Guard units were "coming in" to surrender. "It was really quite a poignant scene," he remembers. "We saw the flares go up and we thought that not only were we going to win the war, we were going to win the peace."

In the weeks that followed, Colonel Paul Hughes, a gangly and outspoken army veteran who served on Garner's staff, began negotiations with senior Iraqi commanders on demobilization and disarmament and on whether senior officers and soldiers would be granted pensions. "The idea was to keep them on our side," Hughes said. "So we would meet with the commanders and talk with them about what they needed." By the end of April, Hughes and senior Iraqi military officers were close to an agreement. "We had decided on most of the details," Hughes said. "The units would come in in good form and under their officers, they would stack arms, and they would be sent home. It was important to get a formal surrender."

But the surrender never took place. As Hughes and the American team were concluding their talks, a handful of Pentagon officials were discussing the subject at the Pentagon. The meeting that decided the fate of the Iraqi army took place on May 10 and included Bremer, Paul Wolfowitz, and former undersecretary of defense for policy Walter Slocombe. All three agreed: Iraq must be cleansed of all Baathist influence.

A formal surrender would be tantamount to admitting that the Iraqi army still had standing inside the country—a proposition that none of them wanted to accept. "I heard about the decision on television," Hughes remembers, "and I was just enraged. I couldn't believe it. But I didn't have any choice. So I told the Iraqi officers I knew, that they should go home." Hughes recounts their response: "I can remember one of the senior officers just looked at me for a few seconds, and then he said, 'Do you know what this means? Do you know what you've just done? There are 340,000 soldiers out there who need to feed their families. How do you think they're going to do it?'"

In the years that followed, numerous commentators would attempt to place an exact date on the beginning of the insurgency.

For Hughes, the insurgency began on May 10, "and Wolfowitz, Slocombe and Bremer started it."

ON THE MORNING of July 19, 2004, Marine Colonel Mike Walker strolled into the Amman Sheraton Hotel, where he was greeted by Talal al-Gaood. Walker remembers, "This was a small economic thing, so I thought it wasn't that big of a deal and I looked around and there was a guy in the lobby from the embassy, a very low-level guy, and really he was as green as grass. He looked around, and I guess he decided there wasn't much happening and he left." There were other Americans already standing in the lobby—Ken Wischkaemper, Jerry Jones, Evan Galbraith, and James Clad—and other marines, including Major Pat Maloy (whom Walker knew), Lieutenant Colonel Christian Shomber (from Marine headquarters, Baghdad), and Lieutenant Colonel Dave Harlan, who had come over from the American embassy in Amman. They were all friends.

Walker was introduced to two officials from the Japan Bank for International Cooperation, the Japanese government's international aid arm. The Americans and the Japanese had coffee with al-Gaood and his colleagues in the hotel's VIP lounge and then, "you know, just milled about," as Clad remembers. Al-Gaood then motioned the group down a hall and into a conference room. "When we walked in, I remember there was a lot of tension in the room, and people who were there stopped talking and just looked at us. I mean, there was total silence," Clad said.

The Americans were shocked by the number of people in the room. A large group of Iraqis were seated in rows of conference chairs facing a long table, and other tables were set out along the walls. It occurred to Jones that this was more than a small business conference. "I was really taken aback," he remembers. Walker could hardly contain his shock. "I remember thinking, 'Well, this is not exactly what I had in mind.'"

To their surprise, the Americans would be the focus of the meeting. Al-Gaood gestured to them to accompany him to the front of the room. Following al-Gaood's instruction, Jones, Clad, Harlan, Walker, Larry Meyers, Galbraith, Bob Teweles, Wischkaemper, and Japanese banking official Tadashi Maeda took their seats facing the delegates. "It was a pretty uncomfortable scene," Clad remembers.

Al-Gaood strode to the front lectern and broke the silence. "Dear friends and guests," he began, "it is my pleasure to welcome you to Amman and I would like to thank his majesty King Abdullah, may God bless him, for his effort to help the Iraqi people." Al-Gaood described the "suffering of the Iraqi people" and then announced that the agenda for the conference was to focus on economic development. But al-Gaood's comments soon turned political. The violence in Iraq, he said, "is being created by two kinds of people"—those who did not accept the occupation and those who "came from outside the country, the thieves and criminals who don't want to see a peaceful and strong Iraq."

When al-Gaood finished, Iraqis in the audience rose from their seats to talk about their own experiences under the American occupation. Their words were blunt and tinged with anger. As James Clad later remembered, "I have never heard such denunciations. We sat there and took it, allowed them to have their say. We were like department store mannequins. We just kind of looked at our shoes."

The accusations continued through the morning. "Talal was masterful," Jerry Jones remembers. "He wasn't going to defend Saddam Hussein and he wasn't going to flat-out condemn the Americans. He kept reminding people that we were his guests, but he let people have their say." The Americans kept looking for an opening to respond. "People were just ranting," James Clad remembers, "but we weren't about to leave. We had come thousands of miles to talk." But there was also anger among the Americans. "You could never say that Saddam was good for Iraq," Mike

Walker said. "For all the things that we got wrong, the one thing we didn't get wrong was getting rid of him."

At the end of the morning, after shifting uncomfortably in his chair, Tadashi Maeda indicated to al-Gaood that he would like to speak. "Tadashi was a very courtly man, very courteous and very straightforward," Clad remembers, "so when he got up to talk it was clear that he would wait until the room was silent before he started to speak." Tadashi began by thanking people for speaking their minds. "I have heard and we have all heard what you have said," he began, "and so now I think that I should like to say something." Tadashi was silent for a moment, gathering his thoughts. "My mother was in Hiroshima," he said.

> And I can remember when it happened and I lost her. And I thought that when the bomb was dropped that Japan was absolutely finished. I never thought that we would rise from the ashes. But my country decided to turn to the future. The Americans are not perfect people. But they wanted to help us. We accepted that because we had to put the past behind us. So now your country is also in ruins. But you must put the past behind you. You must rise from the ashes. You have to build your new country, as my people built mine.

"You could have heard a pin drop," Clad said. "It was a profound moment. I thought right then that we could make progress." Walker and the other marines agreed, but they were uncomfortable with the continuing criticism.

After the morning session, Walker ambled over to a group of Iraqis who were drinking coffee in the hallway. He wanted to break the ice. "I told them that I understood a lot of their complaints," he remembers. "But I told them that they could stop their cheerleading about Saddam. I was pretty blunt: 'He was corrupt, a complete dictator, he stole money and food from his own people.' I didn't raise my voice, I didn't get angry, but I told them, 'The Baath Party is as dead as the Nazi Party.' And I told them to stop defending Saddam because he was a monster and they knew it. They got the point."

At the end of the morning session, al-Gaood brought the Americans together with a smaller group of Iraqis to cool tempers. The group stood outside the conference room, well away from the other delegates, talking. Among the group was former general Ra'ad al-Hamdani. Al-Hamdani told the group about his experiences after the war. "He was angry, very angry," Jones remembers. Al-Hamdani told the marines about his arrest. "They threw me on the floor," he said; "they humiliated me in front of my family." He was enraged that a young American soldier had put a boot on his neck. The Americans were silent.

The general nodded a bit and looked at the marines and then smiled uncomfortably, before continuing. He said that he did not want the talks to end. "I have been a commander, a soldier, so I know these things," he said. "These were boys, you know. Nineteen or so. And I suppose that if I was a young soldier maybe I would have done the same thing." James Clad remembers there were tears in al-Hamdani's eyes. "I am an old person now," General al-Hamdani said. "So I can forgive them."

Clad looked at al-Hamdani. "What we did was shameful, it should have never happened, and we apologize unreservedly," he said. "There was no intention to bring dishonor on your family." As Jones remembered, "Word got around about what Clad had done. It made a difference; it made a big difference."

DURING THE AFTERNOON session, al-Gaood distributed a paper dividing the conference into working groups—a steering committee, a political committee, an economic committee, a military and security committee, and a committee of sheikhs. Among the attendees were some of the most trusted officials in Saddam's former government: Nouri Ali Taih (the head of the Legal Directorate of the Ministry of Military Industrialization), Sami Ahmed Kareem (a twenty-four-year veteran of the Iraq Ministry of Foreign Affairs), Humam al-Shamaa (a senior economist at Baghdad University), Sheikh Ismail Sajir Jasim (the head of the al-Malahma tribe in al-Anbar), General Shaker Turki Asal (the head of a division in Saddam's Iraqi Republican Guard), and Sheikh Abdul Razzak Farhan (the head of a major al-Anbar tribe).

There were seventy-eight Iraqis attending the conference in Amman, and they were the core of the political wing of the insurgency. In a memorandum written after the meeting, Mike Walker noted that among the seventy-eight was a core "opposition group" with strong insurgent ties. "This group, numbering twenty-three, did not come simply to discuss private sector development; they came to present the position of the parties that oppose the U.S. role in Iraq. . . . The group represented those who had felt they had been systematically excluded from any legitimate role in determining the future of Iraq. They have enough resources, people and money in Iraq to ensure they will continue to have a position of power. As such, they have to be dealt with. They were very well organized and prepared."

At the end of the first day, al-Gaood told the Americans that he wanted to introduce them to "a messenger from the insurgents; a man who represented the insurgent groups." Walker was intrigued. "Jerry [Jones] came to meet at the end of the day and said we had a chance to meet an emissary with the insurgency," Walker remembers. "He said we were going to meet with a guy called 'the doctor.'" Less than one hour later, Walker, Harlan, Jones, al-Gaood, an Iraqi translator, and "the doctor" crowded into Jones's suite and arrayed themselves around a coffee table. Walker and Jones were on one side of the table and "the doctor" was on the other.

"There was a guy on the couch and I swear he was almost in a fetal position," Jones said. "He was very wary. A middle-aged man, a professional. It took some time, but he opened up. He intro-duced himself as Dr. Ismail." Over the next months, it would be-come clear that "Dr. Ismail" was not only a ranking official in the insurgency in Fallujah, but also a representative of sixteen insur-gent groups that spread from al-Anbar Province into central Iraq. The sixteen groups were the heart of the insurgency.

Mike Walker remembers the meeting: "It was clear the man was very uncomfortable. We later learned he thought it was possible that some of us would kill him. He was very insecure; he wouldn't make eye contact. He was outnumbered, knew it, and was probably wondering what he had gotten himself into." After a short intro-duction, Dr. Ismail began to talk.

"It started as a rehash of what we had heard all day," Walker re-calls. "He was very critical, so there were some tense moments. He told us bluntly that we were on the wrong side and that we would lose, that we had given power to the Iranians. He was very angry when he said this. He asked us, 'How could you have done Abu Ghraib? What is wrong with you people?' I told him we were em-barrassed by Abu Ghraib and we wanted to make things right. He came right back at me: If you want to make things right, then get out of our cities. Leave security to us. Leave the Iranians to us; we know how to take care of them.'"

After hearing this, Jerry Jones suggested that "it might be good to start an exchange." Dr. Ismail was blunt: "We can start when you get your troops out of our cities," he said, and he added, "You have gotten your intelligence wrong from top to bottom. We know this because our people are everywhere, in every ministry in Baghdad, in every city and village. We know what you're going to do and when you're going to do it. We even have a source inside the prime minister's office. You give us what we want, and we will give you security."

Dr. Ismail talked about al-Anbar. "We are not your enemy," he said. "Al Qaeda is your enemy. If you let us, we will get rid of them. But you can't fight us at the same time. We're different. We will stop shooting and take care of the real terrorists. We're not terrorists, we're the insurgents. There's a difference."

Despite the harsh words, Dr. Ismail never raised his voice. "I thought the meeting was actually quite substantive, and very useful," Jones remembers. "This was significant. The doctor had requested the meeting, and he was willing to trust the Americans. That's why he was there. I think we all knew that what was happening in that room was momentous. We were on the verge of a real breakthrough."

Jones turned to Walker. "Maybe you should talk to General Conway about this," he said. "We have an offer here of something." Dr. Ismail looked at Walker. "Conway should pull out of al-Anbar," he said to him, "and activate the old army. They're professionals, not Saddamists, but military men." Walker looked from Jones to Dr. Ismail. "Okay," he said, "I'll go to Conway."

At the end of the meeting, Walker asked Dr. Ismail for proof that he could deliver what he had promised. "This was all about testing their command and control," Jerry Jones later reflected. "We needed to determine whether they could deliver what they promised." Walker asked Dr. Ismail how he could be contacted. "Just go to the mayor of Fallujah," he said, "and tell him you want to meet with me." Walker masked his surprise. The mayor of Fallujah had helped Conway and the marines—and was viewed as pro-American. Dr. Ismail smiled: "He's one of us," he said.

Although Mike Walker later admitted that he "simply did not believe that we accomplished that much that first day in Amman," he confirmed that the meeting with Dr. Ismail was crucial. As he remembers, "I was very surprised that this man was there and was talking with us. It wasn't something we thought would happen, not in our wildest dreams. And yet, there he was. It was our first inkling that the insurgents wanted to turn their guns on al Qaeda. That they wanted to switch sides. I was stunned." The doctor's real name remains unknown, but there is little doubt that he was an important conduit of information not only to al-Anbar's insurgent militias but also to the most important disaffected nationalist groups in Iraq. "He was the real deal," Walker said.

THE NEXT MORNING, a delegation of Americans from the conference arrived at the U.S. embassy in Amman to brief the chargé d'affaires on their meetings. Walker emphasized the economic focus of the conference, then sent an e-mail message to Colonel John Coleman, Conway's chief of staff. The e-mail contained a lengthy narrative of the previous day's events and an attachment listing the meeting's attendees. Another attachment listed seven conclusions that Walker had reached as a result of his discussion with Dr. Ismail.

Walker now believed the insurgents in al-Anbar would work to separate themselves from the province's foreign elements. The key test was whether the insurgent groups the doctor represented would be able to impose command discipline over their militias. In a covering note, Walker requested that Coleman share the e-mail with the "inner circle" at IMEF: Lieutenant General James Conway, Brigadier General Dennis Hajlik (the deputy commander), and the division's senior intelligence officers. But Walker was plagued by doubts.

Schooled in the harsh reality of actually fighting the insurgents and having been a part of the Fallujah "fiasco," Walker was skeptical that the insurgency was either united enough or competent enough to act in unison. Then too, he believed, it would be difficult to convince either marines or insurgents to agree to stop fighting, given the bitter experiences of the past. The talks with the doctor had been promising, but he feared that too much blood had already been spilled for either side to engage in the kind of cooperation necessary to bring the al-Anbar fighting to an end. "My perspective about the skeptical treatment of the meeting is that it was a direct result of the muddled negotiation affairs in the immediate aftermath of Operation Vigilant Resolve [the Fallujah fight of April 2004]," he later wrote.

In the wake of the Fallujah fight, Walker had watched the negotiators representing the insurgents in the city come and go. The marines were never certain whom to believe. And the Americans were in a weak position. "Our negotiating position was hopeless," Walker said. "The only real card we could play was the resumption of ground combat operations. Of course that card had been removed [by Washington and the Iraqi interim government], and the enemy in Fallujah knew it." He went on to note, "As my professor of negotiations from the Harvard Business School used to point out, make sure you are negotiating with people who matter. Easier said than done in Iraq in 2004."

Eventually, the marines had turned Fallujah over to the Fallujah Brigade—a collection of former Saddamists led by General Jassim Mohammed Saleh. Saleh had responded to Saddam's order to put down the Shia uprising in the wake of the first Gulf War by slaughtering Shias in city after city in the south. The marines knew he was a thug. "We had no illusions about how terrible the Saddam regime was," Mike Walker said. "They were horrific. We had videos of what they did. You became a made man in that regime by torturing people. By showing you could do it. But the people who sat around saying 'A Baathist is a Baathist is a Baathist' didn't know what they were talking about. This was not like the Nazi or the Communist Party. Being a Baathist wasn't some great honor. Everyone was a Baathist. At least with them there was a way forward. You could talk with them. You couldn't ever talk with al Qaeda, ever."

When Saleh marched into Fallujah in early May 2004, he wore his Republican Guard uniform. It was an openly defiant message to the Shia-dominated government in Baghdad and to their American supporters in the Green Zone. As the Fallujah Brigade marched into the city, loudspeakers in the mosques announced, "God has given this town victory over the Americans." James Conway ignored the announcement, explaining that the brigade "marked the formation of a military partnership that has the potential to bring a lasting, durable climate of peace and stability to Fallujah and Al Anbar Province as a whole."

American diplomats in Baghdad were not so sanguine. They scrambled to explain Saleh's place at the head of an army that looked a lot like Saddam Hussein's old Republican Guard. None of their explanations sounded credible. The press picked up the story: *San Francisco Chronicle* reporter Colin Freeman noted that the turnover of Fallujah showed that "political niceties have been sacrificed to battlefield pragmatism," and *New York Times* reporter John Kifner noted that the American command seemed "somewhat confused over the sudden turnabout here in which old enemies have become new allies." Other reporters cynically noted that if Saleh used the same tactics against the foreign fighters of Fallujah as he had against the Shias in 1991, the marines would be more than happy. "The Iraqi armies do not fuck about," one colonel was quoted as saying. "They will just shoot any Iraqi who does not tell them where the insurgents are. It is the kind of methods the Americans would love to use, but cannot be seen to."

After four days, the marines in Fallujah gave in to the mounting criticisms and replaced Saleh with General Muhammed Latif, a former Baathist who had been jailed by Saddam. The change fooled no one: Saleh was still in charge in Fallujah. Then too, as Mike Walker knew, al-Gaood and Saleh were friends. On the first day of the conference, Walker had seen Saleh in the lobby outside the meeting, and he later learned that al-Gaood had pleaded with Wischkaemper to support Selah in creating a "good, clean, strong administration" in al-Anbar.

That Saleh was the head of the Fallujah Brigade didn't bother James Conway even a little. The IMEF commander was still seething about the April order sending his marines into Fallujah in the first place. He remained enraged by those in the CPA headquarters in Baghdad who seemed insensitive to the fact that his marines were "leaking blood" in al-Anbar. To Conway, the political leadership in Baghdad was out of touch with reality and incapable of making the tough political decisions that would broaden the appeal of the Iraqi government.

Conway suspected that his recommendations didn't carry the same weight as did those of the Iraqi Governing Council. When he recommended staying out of Fallujah, his arguments were dismissed, but when the Iraqi Governing Council recommended ending the operation, the White House readily agreed. "This is a simple dimple story," a marine on Conway's staff recounts. "We were told to go into Fallujah and Conway said, 'That's stupid,' but we went anyway. And we were like a knife through butter and we could have and should have kept going. But then the IGC [the Iraqi Governing Council] didn't like what they were seeing on al-Jazeera and they howled. There was too much blood for them. And the IGC told Bremer to pull back and Bremer told Abizaid to pull back and Abizaid told Conway."

Abizaid knew that Conway was enraged by the contradictory orders coming from the Green Zone, so he decided to talk with Conway personally to explain why, after all the bloodletting, the marines were now being told to stand down—to "pull back." When his helicopter set down at Camp Fallujah, Abizaid vaulted from it to shake Conway's hand. "Conway just looked at him. He couldn't believe it," the same staff member said. "I remember them standing there, and Abizaid kind of shuffling his feet. It was a pretty bad scene." Since when did a foreign government dictate U.S. military operations? "That's when we began to take casualties in Fallujah," Mike Walker now says. "When we backed off. The insurgents came in and took our former positions and just poured it on us."

Although the deal struck by Conway with the Fallujah Brigade was approved through the chain of command, no one co-ordinated the decision with the Coalition Provisional Authority. Bremer was blindsided; the Iraqi interim government was circum-vented. This was a military decision, Conway told Abizaid. In Baghdad, Bremer was furious. "Bremer disbanded the Iraqi army, disbanded the Baath Party, and wasn't doing anything to support us in Anbar," a marine officer on Conway's staff said. "It's not like Conway took matters into his own hands. He went up the chain of command with his request. He received approval and saved lives. Which is more than you could ever say for Bremer."

The IMEF's disdain for Bremer and the CPA was palpable. Key senior IMEF officers were convinced that Bremer was out of touch with the situation in al-Anbar and viewed the marines as an expendable commodity. "The people in the Green Zone were living in an aquarium," one of Conway's staff now says;

> they were faking it. We were fighting a squad leader war out there in Anbar and we just weren't going to win a squad leader war. And the people in the aquarium were looking at their OB [order of battle] charts and saying, "We have the strongest mili-tary in the world" so "let's just crush 'em." You know, these people were just idiots. We weren't going to crush anyone. Hell, Anbar is as big as Texas. That just wasn't going to happen. I went into Baghdad and saw them. Saw what they were doing. It was cocktail hour in the aquarium; it was China Beach [in Vietnam]. Bremer and his crew were playing fraternity games. For Christ's sake, they didn't even know why they were there.

The biggest problem with the American war effort in Iraq, as a large number of Conway's senior officers viewed it, was the lack of information—the absence of sound human intelligence that would give an accurate picture of what was going on in the country. "The people in the aquarium were giving us reports of what was going on on the ground, and it was just wrong. So it came down to 'Who was who in the zoo.' They had nobody, and we had General Saleh. We could have relied on their nobody or we could rely on Saleh. In the end we made the only choice we had. Either that, or we could have sat around the pool in Baghdad, sipped our cocktails, and talked about the unfairness of it all."

But the creation of the Fallujah Brigade had not helped bring peace to either Fallujah or al-Anbar. Attacks on the marines continued. Mortar attacks were regularly launched from neighborhoods inside the city. Walker read the reports, noting the sameness of the descriptions: "Died in action from mortar attacks . . . died in action from mortar attacks."

At the end of May, an improvised explosive device (IED) killed two marines outside Fallujah. Intelligence officers of the IMEF were convinced the device had been planted by foreign fighters entrenched inside the city. The attacks continued through June. Even though the marines had worked hard to train Fallujah's new police force as an adjunct to Saleh's brigade, there were difficulties in separating Iraqi nationals from foreign fighters. The Marines found it hard to distinguish Arab insurgents not from Iraq from those who *were* from Iraq—a problem Saleh and his colleagues said they would address. A vicious suicide bombing took place during the third week of June. The marines responded, sending Thunderbolt fighter planes against foreign-insurgent positions inside the city, taking down entire buildings identified as foreign strongholds. By mid-June the cease-fire was a thin fiction. It is no wonder that, seated across from Dr. Ismail in Jerry Jones's suite in Amman, Mike Walker harbored deep doubts that a cease-fire and a new understanding with al-Anbar's insurgents would yield any results. He eyed the doctor skeptically, but when Jones suggested Walker go to Conway, Walker assented. Despite the past, he believed, the marines had to give Dr. Ismail's plea for a cease-fire another chance.

Dr. Ismail sensed Walker's skepticism and admitted that the preceding two months in al-Anbar had been difficult—for both the marines and the insurgents. But he was adamant: If the marines were willing to try once more to stop the fighting, he would use his influence with the insurgents to make certain a cease-fire was implemented. Seated in Jones's suite at the Sheraton Hotel, he promised he would visit the higher council of the resistance to determine whether a series of cease-fires could be arranged in the province. But what exactly, he asked, did the marines want? Walker thought for a moment and then began to lay out a broad understanding on what the insurgents and the Americans could do—together—to dampen the violence in the province. The understanding included a series of detailed confidence-building measures that would start in al-Anbar's biggest cities and spread throughout the province.

On the morning of July 20, Walker sent a summary of these understandings to John Coleman. He was careful to note that the agreement was not yet final but was dependent on the final approval of the insurgency's higher council:

> The main highlights of the agreement to be finalized: 1. Stopping the military operations for three days. . . . 2. Fallujah people will ask the foreign fighters to leave. 3. The Iraqi national guard will take positions in the city. 4. They will call through mosques to the people of Fallujah to deliver all weapons considered non personal weapons. . . . 5. IIG [Iraqi Interim Government] will commit itself not to [arrest] people who do not commit criminal acts. 6. Free all prisoners except criminals. 7. Reconstruction of the city and reparation payments for all people.

For Walker, the key to these understandings was whether Iraq's insurgent commanders were powerful enough to take on al Qaeda and the foreign fighters in al-Anbar.

After he sent the e-mail, Walker returned to the conference. "When Coleman received the e-mail, he was really enthusiastic," Walker recalls. "He was all for it. But I have to admit, I was still pretty pessimistic." Later, at the end of the conference, Walker documented the American agreement with the insurgency. The key military test would come not in Fallujah but in Samarra, where a twenty-four-hour stand-down would test the insurgency's command-and-control discipline. If successful, the Samarra stand-down would be extended through the rest of the country.

KEN WISCHKAEMPER ADMIRED Talal al-Gaood and had praised him to Jerry Jones. Jones understood Wischkaemper's empathy for the Iraqi; the two were much alike. Personable, articulate, and intelligent, al-Gaood seemed to have accomplished the impossible: He had brought together Americans and Iraqis to find a way to end their conflict. But al-Gaood, as many Americans would later admit, was also a survivor of Saddam Hussein's Iraq, where failure could bring death. The result was not simply that al-Gaood was an accomplished businessman; he had in addition become a tough and often uncompromising political infighter. Slowly, inevitably, the Americans in Amman began to understand that al-Gaood was more than simply a bridge to the insurgency; he was a man of influence and power. And he knew how to use it.

The second day of the conference was marked by a disturbing meeting in Talal al-Gaood's suite with the mayor of Ramadi and al-Anbar governor Abd al-Karim Barjas—known to the marines as "Mamood." It was a stormy session. During the meeting, al-Gaood reconciled with Ramadi's mayor, but, as Walker later reported, he attacked Barjas as "greedy" and "undesirable."

Al-Gaood screamed at Barjas as Walker looked on. "It was unsettling to listen to the degree of outrage that Talal had for him," Walker later noted. It seemed like a family quarrel. "He called him all kinds of names," Walker said. "A thief and a corrupt and contemptible official." Barjas remained defiant, but his defenses were down, and Walker could see that he was attempting to mask his fear. "You filthy thief," al-Gaood said, and he shook his finger at him. "You are stealing from the Iraqi people."

There was no doubt that al-Gaood could command respect and could tyrannize his opponents; Walker could see the fear in Barjas's eyes. "It was an amazing scene," Walker remembers. "It was honestly and deeply felt, but in retrospect it was also a drama played out for us. Talal wanted to show us that he had the power to do things in Anbar. That he could get the things done that he needed to get done." Barjas left the hotel the same day.

One week later, Barjas's three sons were kidnapped from his home by masked terrorists. The governor was told that unless he resigned his position, they would be killed. Three days later Barjas appeared in public, his faced streaked with tears, to issue a statement: "I am Abd al-Karim Barjas, governor of Al-Anbar. I declare before God and you my repentance of any action I did against the mujahedin, or any act in cooperation with the infidel, the Americans, and I announce my resignation of my post."

Walker took the measure of al-Gaood. "The Iraqis were always talking about how we would break down their doors and terrorize them and humiliate them," he reflected, "and they went to great lengths to tell us how this was not a part of their culture. But they really never had any problem doing it to us—or to each other." After the Barjas incident, al-Gaood chatted with Ramadi's mayor, talked of his family, and told him, "*Inshallah* [God willing], the troubles soon will be over in your city, with the help of our friends here." He motioned to the marines. This seemed to Walker and the marines "like a blessing of him. As if he was choosing him to be the next governor of Anbar. After Barjas was gone."

THE AFTERNOON OF the conference's second day was taken up by the reports of its five standing committees. This was a difficult process and included debate on a wide range of Iraq's political, economic, and social problems. But the anger of the first day was gone—and with it the harsh and accusatory language between Iraqis and Americans—replaced by a growing atmosphere of trust. "The papers were presented by each committee leader to the entire session," Jerry Jones remembers. "Each committee had an hour or two, and each member of the committee got up to make comments after the committee presentation was made. There were a lot of questions and comments from the delegates. It was a long and involved process, but we gained real insights and important intelligence on how the Iraqi elite saw their problems."

The resulting findings were summarized in an American document titled "What We Heard." The paper included twenty-eight points reflecting a litany of Sunni fears and complaints: that Iranian political infiltration would permanently marginalize them in their own country, that the Americans were "unwitting collaborators" in the Iranian effort to dominate Iraq, that the United States "[had] not listened and [had] badly mismanaged the post-war period," and that America "[had] failed to deliver on promises of aid." But "What We Heard" was not the most important document to come out of the conference.

At midday on July 20, Jones and Walker each received a copy of a hand-edited two-page paper from the Iraq National Resistance Council. The paper contained sixteen points. It was the first communication from the insurgency received by any U.S. official. The paper contained three "non-negotiable points" (Iraq should be viewed as one country, the American occupation should be

ended, and the "wealth of Iraq" should benefit all Iraqis);
nonetheless, the "urgent demands" listed by the insurgency's leaders were strikingly reasonable and contained points that both
Jones and Walker believed would be acceptable to the United
States. "I think it was probably the most important document
to come out of the conference," Jones later reflected, "as it was, to
my mind, perhaps the most important piece of intelligence we had
ever gotten on the insurgency. They told us, in plain language,
what they wanted." The paper called for the "replacement of the
American army by the already established Iraqi army," the dis-
banding of private militias, the release of political prisoners, an
end to interference in Iraq by its neighbors, and an end to the depiction of the "Iraqi national resistance as 'terrorist.'"

A final initiative that emerged from the conference would have
crucial long-term ramifications for Iraq's future. The initiative resulted from an informal conversation between Ken Wischkaemper
and Ra'ad al-Hamdani, who suggested to Wischkaemper that
America support the creation of an all-Sunni Desert Protection
Force (DPF) for al-Anbar—a province-wide militia made up of
Sunni citizens and led by professional military officers. The DPF
would be led by former officers of Iraq's army, but its members
would be recruited from al-Anbar's tribes.

Al-Hamdani's unstated agenda in creating the DPF was to provide a shield against any pressures coming from a Shia-dominated
Baghdad government. As Wischkaemper later remembered, al-
Hamdani's idea was not simply to segregate the Sunni population
from radical foreign fighters but also to reconstitute the Iraqi army.
The proposal followed the general outlines of one that al-Hamdani
had prepared in the run-up to the conference. By any measure, it
was a sophisticated and creative look at the challenges and obstacles faced by the U.S. military in the post-April 2003 period. It also
overturned Paul Bremer's decision to disband the Iraqi army—it
was a reversal of American policy.

For General al-Hamdani, Bremer's decision to disband the army ("this was never Saddam's army, or a Baathist army" al-Gaood had argued during the conference, "but an Iraqi institution, an institution of the nation") was a mistake that had fueled the insurgency and transformed the American liberation of Iraq into the American occupation of Iraq. America's ham-fisted conduct of the post-invasion period had turned the Iraqi people against them. The solution, al-Hamdani believed, was a U.S. commitment to a "gradual [five year] withdrawal" from the country, paralleled by the building of an al-Anbar militia led by Sunnis. At the same time, an intensive effort could be made to reduce the "level of the insurgency and influence of terrorist groups, creating a conducive environment for creation of representative government and effective institutions."

Wischkaemper endorsed the plan. "It made perfect sense. It was creative, simple, and it had every chance of working." When Jones read the proposal, he agreed, but he said that it needed to be supplemented by a paper that focused on two pressing issues: Iranian infiltration of Iraq and a plan for responding to the threat of foreign fighters. This supplemental paper was more important to Jones than any specific planning document. It would present the intellectual groundwork for recruiting the insurgency to the American side of the war. It should lay out a strategy not only for Iraq, but for the U.S. war on terror. General al-Hamdani said that he would start on the paper immediately.

AT THE END of the conference, al-Gaood asked a Sunni imam to say a prayer. The delegates then said their farewells. In the lobby of the hotel, al-Gaood approached Walker. "I want you to please be safe," al-Gaood said. "It is dangerous now in Iraq, and perhaps it will even be worse. I do not want anything to happen to you." Walker saw that al-Gaood was genuinely concerned, but he also noted something else in al-Gaood's tone: Despite the conference, the two were still adversaries. Walker thanked al-Gaood, shook his hand, and walked from the hotel.

When Walker returned to Fallujah, he briefed Conway and the IMEF chief of staff, John Coleman, on the conference. Calling the meeting in Amman "the July Surprise," Walker attempted to dampen both Conway and Coleman's enthusiasm. The people Walker had met in Amman had not turned out to be either "dead enders" or "Nazis"—or terrorists. "I am bewildered and touched by the admonishment of Talal, General Ra'ad [al-Hamdani], and others to be careful when I returned to Iraq," Walker said. "Did they mean it? Did they wish their enemy well? I think they did."

CHAPTER THREE

TERRORISTS AND MODERATES

"This is the dark side we're talking to here."
—John Coleman

Reversing a wishful policy already determined is the most difficult and courageous act any senior policymaker can undertake—which is why it is so rare. Although Paul Wolfowitz, Paul Bremer, and Condoleezza Rice would work to undermine the marine opening to the Iraqi insurgency in the months following the July 2004 Amman conference, the most formidable barrier facing Jerry Jones, James Conway, Mike Walker, and John Coleman would prove to be their own government's unwillingness to admit that the policies it had followed in Iraq were not, and could not, succeed.

In the summer of 2004, five governments and movements were shaping the political environment of the Middle East: Iran, Syria, the Islamic Resistance Movement (Hamas), Lebanon's Hezbollah, and Egypt's Muslim Brotherhood. The United States wasn't talking to any of them. That had been the policy, institutionalized as a part of U.S. foreign policy thinking, for nearly three decades—and no one was about to change it. "We don't talk to terrorists," a White House official intoned, "and we don't talk to anyone who does."

Surprisingly, the United States regularly violated the policy of not talking to terrorists. The United States began talking with the Palestine Liberation Organization (PLO), a terrorist organization, in 1989 and to the African National Congress (ANC) the same year. In Iraq, the Bush administration shook hands with officials of the Dawa Party, which had bombed the U.S. embassy in Kuwait in 1983, killing three Americans. Even more extraordinary: Although the U.S. government (and many of its allies) refused to talk to any of the Middle East's most important governments or movements, almost no one outside Europe followed this example. Then too, American and European religious groups, nongovernmental organizations, think tanks, reporters, and retired diplomats ignored the policy and regularly engaged in substantive exchanges with the groups in Cairo, Beirut, Doha, and Amman. Perversely, at the same time the world was undergoing an unprecedented communications revolution—when everyone seemed to be talking to everyone else—the U.S. government was only talking to itself.

When pressed, U.S. government officials readily admitted that this policy was not only harmful to American interests but counterproductive: The very principle that was intended to isolate and marginalize terrorist groups was having the opposite effect, isolating and marginalizing the United States.

The impact of the policy of not talking to terrorists was most deeply felt in Iraq, where the blood of American soldiers was being shed to no good effect because of the failed and futile efforts of American commanders to close the gap between U.S. policies decided in Washington and the realities on the ground in al-Anbar. It was this challenge—to halt the momentum of an accepted idea, to reexamine assumptions—that consumed the lives of Jerry Jones and his colleagues in the summer of 2004.

No amount of planning could have prepared Jones for what he faced when he returned to Washington from Amman in July 2004.

Several days after his return, and in the wake of his report on the Amman conference to Department of Defense (DoD) secretary Donald Rumsfeld, Wolfowitz called Jones to his office. "What the hell is going on, Jerry?" Wolfowitz asked.

Wolfowitz had received a telephone call from Richard Armitage at the State Department complaining about the Pentagon's Amman conference, telling Wolfowitz that neither he nor Jim Jeffrey, the State Department's representative in Baghdad, had been told about the meeting. Armitage was angry: What were Pentagon officials doing in Amman? Why were they meeting with the insurgency? Worse yet, Wolfowitz said, *Washington Post* reporter Robin Wright had learned of the meeting and was writing a story that would say that Pentagon officials had met with insurgent leaders. The report would embarrass Wolfowitz, the Pentagon, and the U.S. government. Wolfowitz raised his voice: "Don't you know these people are Nazis?"

Jones defended himself: Not only had he invited Jim Jeffrey to Amman, but he had asked him to take control of the meeting. Sensitive to the continuing difficulties in the relationship between the State and Defense departments, Jones had gone out of his way to inform the State Department about the meeting. "Paul was angry, there's no question," Jones remembers, "but I don't think he was red-faced. The meeting didn't last that long. He had not yet read my trip report, but he had heard about it and was worried about the leak and how the department would look." Wolfowitz did not order Jones to end his contact with Talal al-Gaood. After all, it was already too late: The al-Gaood initiative was now in the hands of the marines.

Pentagon officials later speculated that Armitage himself had probably leaked information about the meeting to Wright in order to embarrass the Pentagon. But nothing came of the leak. Several days after the meeting between Wolfowitz and Jones, a reporter at a Defense Department briefing asked about reports of a secret

meeting in Amman and was told that the Pentagon had participated in a conference with al-Anbar businessmen. There was
nothing to the report, the Pentagon spokesman said, and the reporter let the matter drop.

Jones was not the only one to be upbraided about the Amman
meeting. U.S. Marine Corps Colonel Mike Walker had a similar
experience. "I was told to report to Jim Jeffrey in Baghdad on my
way back to Camp Fallujah," Walker said,

> and he was very blunt and very cold. He asked me, "Just what do
> you guys in the DoD think you're doing? Who told you you could
> do this? Why is the DoD messing in the DoS's shit?" Those were
> his words. So I told him about the conference and how there had
> to be business development in al-Anbar or we were going to lose
> the whole province, and the insurgency would just get worse,
> and it would cost us more blood. He wasn't having any of it. He
> wasn't interested in solutions; he was interested in what we had
> done that might undermine the State Department. I told him,
> this was about solving problems. This was about not getting
> marines killed. But that wasn't his focus. His focus was on the
> turf war. So I told him, "Listen, this isn't you and me; this isn't
> DoD and DoS. This is about getting this thing right in Anbar."
> And I said that I thought he ought to be able to see that. And he
> looked at me and shook his head. And from that minute on, Jef-
> frey launched an inquisition on me.

COINCIDENTALLY, AS WORD of the meeting between Wolfowitz
and Jones spread, those who had attended the Amman conference
redoubled their efforts to build on the opening they had begun
to shape. In London, James Clad penned a memo to Jones about
the Overseas Private Investment Corporation (OPIC) review of
the Amman conference. "Since we parted on 21 July," Clad
wrote, "I've spoken to some pivotal and prominent Iraqis [whom]

I trust via past Iraqi risk work at OPIC, and asked them both about the people we met in Amman and about those who were not there. These Iraqis say our approach is absolutely on the right track, especially linkage of business opportunities to durable governance and ramp-up of security." The business component was essential. Al-Anbar would need reconstruction money; its security teams would need to be paid; a new Iraqi investment fund would have to be formed. Clad also suggested that al-Gaood's network needed to include an even wider gathering of al-Anbar tribes.

In Baghdad, Walker briefed IMEF commander James Conway and his chief of staff, John Coleman. He recounted his discussions with Dr. Ismail, talked of the creation of an al-Anbar militia, and focused on steps that would end the violence in the province. "I kicked this up the chain of command," he said. "I wanted to be open and transparent and tell them what I had done. John was still very enthusiastic. We thought we could make some headway." From July 25 to July 28, Conway, Coleman, and Walker worked to implement the Samarra cease-fire and open communications with Fallujah's insurgents.

But the channel that Walker had established with Dr. Ismail proved tenuous. "It just didn't work out," Walker recalls. "In the end, we did not agree to stop our routine operations and they did not agree to stop their offensive operations. The agreement was just too ambiguous." Walker and Conway met with a go-between sent to them by Dr. Ismail. The contact was a disappointment. "They were going to pick a rep to meet with us outside of Fallujah, someone who could implement a cessation of hostilities," continued Walker. "So we met with him and we wanted his bona fides and we told him, 'Show us what you can do, if you are from the insurgency show us who you can control.' But he didn't deliver."

In Amman, Talal al-Gaood was desperately trying to get the series of stand-downs implemented. On August 3, he wrote to Ken Wischkaemper that he was planning a follow-on conference to take place in Dubai before the end of 2004: "Our chain of command is in the support camp," al-Gaood wrote of the insurgency leadership. "Hopefully Marine lives will be saved." A second message on August 3 signaled the continuing problems in Ramadi, where a planned cease-fire was being impeded by a lack of communications: "Today Ramadi under siege and house to house search under going [sic]. We will wait and see what is the result of the search." Al-Gaood highlighted the efforts of the insurgency to identify foreign fighters. "We need to continue dialogue to the resistance and separate them from criminals and foreign fighters," he wrote. Five minutes later, al-Gaood sent yet another note to Wischkaemper. "The commanders in Fallujah step-by-step are getting on our side, to fight the criminals and eliminate them, to fight and eliminate the foreign fighters and to stand down the resistance by showing them there are other ways to resolve the issues. It takes a lot of hard work and patience, but I am positive." He was pleading: "It will work. Mark my words. Believe me, it will work."

Wischkaemper responded by warning al-Gaood that the "atmosphere in Washington is highly politically charged due to the forthcoming election [in November 2004], such that few in the current administration have [a] desire to attack tough issues less than 90 days before the election, being afraid that any positive movement will be viewed only as a Bush administration ploy to be re-elected and afraid that any risky movement might turn negative." Wischkaemper told al-Gaood that the Amman initiative could be derailed by the State Department. The solution, he said, would be to recruit State Department policymakers to their side.

Winning over the State Department would be a delicate operation. "There were three problems we were facing after Amman," marine Pat Maloy—who had attended the conference—explained:

The first was what I call NMI—not my idea. With all the turf battles between State and Defense, if it wasn't State's idea, we were afraid they weren't going to embrace it. The second problem was the Green Zone [that is, with the Americans at the CPA in Baghdad]. They didn't want to have anything to do with this. They were working with the people in the Iraqi government, and the government wasn't friendly with the Sunnis in al-Anbar. The third problem was the civilian leadership in the Pentagon. Wolfowitz and his supporters did not have the power they once had, but they could still derail things. They had lots of friends in the White House.

In addition, "We were fighting three wars. We were fighting a war against the insurgents, we were fighting a war in Baghdad, and we were fighting a war against our own people in Washington. I wonder, really, how we ever thought we could win."

In mid-August General al-Hamdani finished his plan for a Desert Protection Force. It called for recruiting 5,000 soldiers, with 1,000 to be deployed to Fallujah and 1,000 to Ramadi. The balance would be used to police al-Anbar villages and the Iraq-Syria border. The plan laid out the weapons the force needed, the cost of salaries, equipment outlays, and a suggested recruiting process. Al-Gaood added details on funding. His figures included a 10 percent "contingency fund" for "unaccounted items" ("payments to related tribal sheikhs") and death benefits to the families of those killed in the line of duty.

Wischkaemper quietly polled responses to the proposal from the Pentagon and then passed their suggestions to al-Gaood in Amman. "The proposal presented appears to be a very workable solution to the security issue," he said. "The number of men, the total funding involved, the equipment needed does not need to be exact, by any means, but rather handled as estimates." Wischkaemper suggested the force be referred to "as something like 'Al Anbar Special Security Task Force' in such manner that it cannot be conceived as a personal militia." He added a final note: "Time appears to be running out."

IN AUGUST 2004, the American military position in Iraq was deteriorating. While the marines of IMEF were focused on fighting the insurgency in Fallujah, American soldiers in Baghdad and in Najaf and al-Qadisiyyah provinces began to feel pressure from Muqtada al-Sadr's Mahdi Army. In a bid for increased political influence, al-Sadr's forces confronted the Americans in Baghdad and then in the Shia south. The sparks of small conflicts spread up and down central and southern Iraq. The final spark, an incident in Najaf in early August, set the conflict alight.

The Battle of Najaf began on August 5, when elements of the Mahdi Army attacked an Iraqi police station. Troopers of the Marine 11th Expeditionary Unit responded. The attacks kicked off an eight-day pitched battle. Most of the fighting took place in one of Najaf's cemeteries and only ended when a cease-fire negotiated by Grand Ayatollah Ali al-Sistani allowed both the marines and the Mahdi militia to withdraw. The bloody three-week engagement was reminiscent of the marines' fight in Fallujah: A small incident escalated into an all-out conflict with large numbers of casualties and no winners. The marines killed scores of Shia militiamen, yet al-Sadr's forces remained intact. Like so many other battles in Iraq, the Najaf fight was indecisive, leaving al-Sadr's militia weakened but still capable of fighting.

As the marines of the 11th Expeditionary Unit battled among Najaf's tombs and crypts, IMEF/Anbar struggled to strengthen the opening with the leaders of the resistance provided them by Talal al-Gaood. But events on the ground did not reflect the pledges made by al-Anbar's insurgent leaders. If anything, the line separating Iraq's "legitimate resistance" and Fallujah's foreign fighters was becoming more, not less, blurred.

During the second week of August, al-Gaood had to reassure Walker and Wischkaemper that "the resistance" was indeed fighting Fallujah's outsiders—and not the Americans. Progress was being made, he argued, but the problem was communication. The marines didn't acknowledge that the insurgency was working hard to keep its end of the bargain; they didn't seem to be getting the message. Al-Gaood pleaded for more time and repeated a frustrating mantra: The insurgents were making great progress; the foreign fighters were being defeated; the criminal elements were being brought under control. His claim was an exaggeration. Marines had begun calling Fallujah "the bomb factory," and every day American soldiers found Iraqi corpses, arms bound behind their backs, in the ditches along the main highways leading out of the city.

Worse yet, resistance leaders in Fallujah had apparently made common cause with a Salafist criminal by the name of Omar Hadid. In early August, Hadid ordered the torture and "execution" of Lieutenant Colonel Suleiman Hamad al-Mawawi, a senior officer of the Iraqi National Guard and a good friend of many senior marine commanders. Abdullah Janabi carried out the order. "He was murdered because he decided to take action against the criminals and insurgents (aka resistance) who kidnapped one of his ING [Iraqi National Guard] officers in the city," Marine Captain Rodrick H. McHaty reported to Dave Harlan in Amman.

Senior marine officers were enraged. Suleiman was murdered by those criminal elements that al-Gaood claimed the insurgency was fighting. "Lieutenant Colonel Suleiman had entered Fallujah alone to obtain the release of his battalion intelligence officer, who had been 'arrested,'" Mike Walker confirms. "The intelligence officer was tortured to death as well. Lieutenant Colonel Suleiman was extremely popular with the marines, and his murder deeply poisoned the well in our relationship with the Fallujah gang." As roadside bombs proliferated, the marines stepped back into the fray, sending U.S. jets against foreign fighter positions. Al-Gaood continued to push for another meeting, but after Suleiman's murder, that seemed unlikely.

In Amman, Suleiman's murder and the deteriorating situation in Fallujah pushed al-Gaood into another furious round of exchanges with Washington. He was desperate to keep his channel alive; at the same time, he knew his credibility as a mediator was eroding. "We had to prove that we could control the resistance, that we had influence on them," a senior adviser to al-Gaood said. "Talal was struggling. He was on the telephone nearly every day, talking and cajoling and screaming. We focused on the tribal leaders. That's the card we played." Al-Gaood was "playing both ends against the middle," this aide admitted, and added, "Talal was really walking a thin line. He was trying to convince the marines that he could deliver the insurgents and he was trying to convince the insurgents that he could deliver the marines. His message was always the same: 'Give me time, give me time.'"

As marine casualties mounted, Conway cautioned his combat commanders to show restraint and respond to the attacks with care, while steeling himself for the possibility that his troopers might have to go back into Fallujah. He was under pressure from his senior commanders and from Washington to respond forcefully. As he had in April, Conway resisted. For him, a full assault on Fallujah would only be ordered if he could be assured that it would have the full backing of the politicians in Baghdad. Nor did he want to make the insurgency stronger. He knew, instinctively, that every time an American soldier shot an Iraqi, the insurgency gained strength. Bing West, a Marine combat veteran, has highlighted the difficult choice facing Conway and his marines—the choice between fighting and making things worse, or not fighting in the vain hope that somehow things would get better. "Every time the Americans launched a raid, bursting into a house to make an arrest—sometimes a genuine insurgent, sometimes not— their actions fueled anger and reinforced the Salafist message that Americans were infidel invaders intent on installing a repressive Shiite regime."

Appointed to succeed Ricardo Sanchez, General George Casey sympathized with Conway. After a midsummer tour of major in-country American units, Casey became convinced that the U.S. strategy of massing men and firepower in response to local crises was fueling anti-American sentiment. The new commander told his senior combat commanders that he was convinced that a large part of the insurgency could be "co-opted." That meant starting a program to peel away the insurgency's less fanatical tribal leaders, who would then turn their guns on Iraq's al Qaeda sympathizers and foreign fighters. Casey's strategy would be flexible, allowing commanders to make decisions without having to defer to Multi-National Force/Iraq headquarters in Baghdad.

Casey was convinced that the U.S. military was facing a far more formidable enemy than it had faced during the race to Baghdad, though President George Bush remained skeptical. He kept urging Casey to "pour it on." During one mid-August 2004 video conference, Bush pointedly ignored Casey's recommendation for a mixed strategy. "How many did we get?" he asked, leafing through the combat returns. Casey shrugged off the question. The war could not be won simply by killing more insurgents, he said. "Every time a soldier meets an Iraqi there's friction, there's trouble," he said. Bush mulled this over. "By that logic," he said, "the insurgency would disappear if we brought all of our troops home." Casey didn't respond.

The logic *did* seem odd: It suggested that the only way to *win* in Iraq was not to *fight* in Iraq. That conclusion contradicted everything America's commanders had been taught about the nature of conflict. Even so, Conway agreed: The marines were not going to kill their way to victory in al-Anbar. But then, hunkering down outside Fallujah wasn't working either. His marines continued to take casualties, with no victory in sight.

In mid-August 2004, the frustration of al-Anbar's senior marines boiled over. During a meeting with Fallujah's religious leaders, General James Mattis, the commander of all of Iraq's marines, exploded. How could they preach hatred? he asked them; why would they so willingly send their worshippers to their deaths? "They're kids," he screamed. "Untrained, undisciplined teenagers. They don't stand a chance." The imams sat quietly, sipping their tea, unresponsive. Mattis looked at them for a moment and then stormed out of the meeting. "The tribes only saw us as the enemy," Mattis told author Bing West. "I needed the real enemy [the extremists] to make mistakes and expose themselves for what they were."

ON AUGUST 17, after week-long consultations with the heads of the insurgency in Fallujah and Ramadi, al-Gaood suggested that the American delegation return to meet with him and a delegation from al-Anbar in Amman on August 30. He envisioned that this "business conference" would be a high-level exchange: He expected General Conway and General Mattis to attend. They would be briefed on General al-Hamdani's rewritten "Al Anbar Security Proposal," which recommended the creation of "an interim auxiliary security force composed of carefully chosen resident men from throughout the province working under the sponsorship and support of the U.S. Marines charged to help restore security." Seed money for the proposal would come from an economic development program creating a "security corridor" that would include "an oil pipeline carrying crude oil from Iraq to the sole Jordanian refinery in Amman." A feasibility study for the pipeline would be funded by the Japan Bank for International Cooperation. Al-Gaood envisioned the briefing with Conway and Mattis as a quiet exchange among a select group. When most of the attendees were "upstairs" talking about economic development, al-Hamdani, Conway, and Mattis would be downstairs talking about a program to transform the insurgency.

There was only one problem. When word of the conference spread, officials inside Baghdad's Green Zone insisted that Iraqi interim prime minister Ayad Allawi be informed. This would head off any misunderstandings of the type that had led to the confrontation between Mike Walker and Jim Jeffrey after the July meeting. The marines agreed and urged that a delegation of Fallujah's business leaders brief Allawi before taking any further steps.

After much debate, seven influential Fallujah officials agreed to meet Allawi in Baghdad on August 22. Prior to the meeting, the seven delegates agreed to tell the prime minister that the insurgency would agree to "stand down and concentrate on dealing with thieves and criminals, and let the government deal with Iranian infiltration in Iraq." The message was communicated from the delegation to Amman and then from Talal al-Gaood to Dave Harlan, who sent confirmation of their agreement in an e-mail to Mike Walker, John Coleman, and Jerry Jones.

Dressed in traditional Arab *thobes*, denoting their tribal loyalties—reserved for only the most important occasions—the Fallujah delegates were brought to Allawi's office under heavy guard on August 22. Among the delegates was Sheikh Khalid Harnood al-Jumeili, an imam representing the areas north and west of Fallujah; Dr. Ahmed Hardan, the head of the Fallujah hospital; and Mohammed Hamed al-Shihan, a high-profile Fallujah city councilman and the chief of police of Fallujah. There was no question whom they represented. Al-Jumeili had regularly preached against the American infidels, Dr. Haran had allowed the insurgents to use his hospital to set up firing positions, and al-Shihan was an insurgency apologist who, just weeks earlier, had looked the other way when Lieutenant Colonel Suleiman was murdered.

At first, the meeting proceeded much as did any Middle Eastern gathering. Coffee was served, and courtesies were exchanged. But Ayad Allawi was only formally polite, as if checking off boxes from the Arab book of required courtesies. Allawi questioned the delegation about the murder of Lieutenant Colonel Suleiman and sat unsmiling as they explained that he had died of a heart attack under interrogation.

After this short discussion, the head of the delegation told Allawi of their plan to hold a business conference for al-Anbar in Amman. Allawi nodded. He was all for business development, he said. Sheikh al-Jumeili smiled. "Do you have any recommendations for us on this subject?" he asked. Allawi thought for a moment. "Yes, I do," he said. His voice took on a harder edge. After a moment he rose from behind his desk. "I think that all of you gentlemen should put all of your weapons on that table over there and surrender. Because you are all criminals. Criminals. Your day is coming, your day is coming—and it will come soon. So get out of my office."

EVEN AS A BOY, Ra'ad Majid al-Hamdani had been obsessed with anything military. He spent every moment reading about the world's great commanders and their battles. He studied war and the mistakes of war. As a young man, he trained as an officer, joined the Baath Party, and rose through its ranks. He was efficient, loyal, and intelligent, and he was a fighter. He became one of Saddam Hussein's most trusted commanders.

As commander of the II Republican Guard Corps, al-Hamdani had made it his business to understand the American way of war. Saddam poked fun at his obsession. He called him "my American General." Such words in the mouth of Saddam Hussein would have been a death sentence for any other Iraqi, but not for Ra'ad al-Hamdani, who took the kidding as a compliment. More than any other of Saddam Hussein's officers, al-Hamdani knew how the Americans fought. Saddam Hussein was convinced the United States would never invade Iraq because they had little taste for blood, but General Ra'ad knew better: The Americans would invade and would try to end the war quickly, taking Baghdad in a coup de main. The way to bleed the Americans, al-Hamdani believed, was to slow their advance. Speed was their strength, but it was also their weakness; it left them vulnerable. Then too, even if the Americans captured Baghdad, he believed, it would do them little good. So long as the Iraqi army survived, Iraq survived. The Americans could have Baghdad—it was useless.

Six months before the American invasion of Iraq, al-Hamdani ordered his aides to prepare a briefing on America's breach of Germany's Siegfried Line in 1944. He culled articles and books for hints about what the Americans would do. Inevitably, he focused his attention on the American assault on the Ludendorff Bridge at Remagen in the waning months of World War II. The bridge at Remagen was the last one standing over the Rhine, but the Germans had failed to destroy it. The Americans captured the bridge on March 7, 1945. They stormed over it, creating a bridgehead, then poured everything they could into Germany. The bridge, had it been destroyed, would have delayed the American advance, allowing the Germans to gather their defenses. Over the next days, realizing their mistake, the Germans launched nearly suicidal attacks to destroy the bridge, but too late. The bridge remained intact, the Rhine was breached, and the war was lost.

Al-Hamdani remembered the lesson of Remagen. He taught it to his subordinates. "Three months before the war, I took the commander in chief of al-Madeena al-Munawara division of the Republican army and his officers and we all stood over a big bridge known as al-Qaed Bridge (the Leader Bridge) in Jurful-Sakhar region over the Euphrates river," al-Hamdani said. "I told them that the enemy would cross this bridge." Al-Hamdani was dedicated to making sure his soldiers destroyed the al-Qaed Bridge. He assigned a force specifically for this purpose and gave them strict orders to destroy the bridge once they spotted the Americans.

Al-Hamdani was summoned to Baghdad from the southern front on April 2. His troops had been fighting since the invasion began, but they were swiftly being overwhelmed. He went to the meeting fearful that, in his absence, the Americans would break through his front. If they did, they would force his depleted units to retreat to Karbala. During the meeting of April 2, he insisted that the major American effort would come in his zone. He was surprised there was disagreement.

> The minister of defense conveyed a message from the high army commander that all what happened was a strategic deception by the enemy, and the attack on Baghdad will be from the north, coming from western front. . . .
>
> I objected, because I was in contact with the enemy [in the south]. So I spoke with the defense minister. He said that no discussion is permitted, because it is a message from the president, and we should start moving the troops starting on 5 a.m. next day, which was April 3.

That night the Americans broke through, crossing the al-Qaed Bridge on the Euphrates River.

Al-Hamdani had ordered the bridge destroyed ten days before, but his orders had been reversed by Saddam, who wanted to leave the bridges intact. After the war, Saddam said, they would be needed to put down the Shia revolt. Losing the bridge was a disaster for al-Hamdani's Republican Guard divisions, and months after the end of the war, he continued to focus on its loss. Eventually, the mistakes made by the Iraqi army became a fading memory, and he became philosophical about the Iraqi defeat. "We all make mistakes, and the best of us are penitents," he liked to say.

Al-Hamdani had that rare blend of qualities that most appeals to military officers: He was not only a fighter; he was a student of history. Being a fighter was important, but it was the intellectual quality of his presentations that impressed the marines. Wischkaemper, Jones, and Walker admired al-Gaood, but they saved their highest praise for al-Hamdani. He was al-Gaood's brain trust.

On the last day of the Amman meeting in July, Jones asked al-Gaood and al-Hamdani to provide him with a paper that gave solutions to two problems: how to stop Iranian infiltration of Iraq and how to separate the national resistance from foreign fighters. On July 27, al-Gaood forwarded al-Hamdani's paper to Wischkaemper and Jones. Its key paragraph provided the intellectual grounding for recruiting what al-Hamdani called "the National-Religious resistance." It put in writing what Jones and the marines had been arguing—that Bremer's decision to disband the Iraqi army had to be reversed.

> The general idea is to separate and distinguish between the National Resistance/Religious and terrorists. To do that the following suggestion could be considered: Recognize the National-Religious resistance according to political and logistical stands and help it to become a recognized institution that works openly in civil society. This must be done based on ethical and logistical guarantees by U.S. and Allied forces. This resistance must be integrated into proper regiments of Iraqi Army which needs to be reformed and re-organized in a manner and form that is efficient and logical. This should take place after sending back (nullifying) the resolution of Dissolving the Iraqi Army taken by [the] CPA. It also must be noted that most of this resistance are [sic] from the dissolved Iraqi Army. The newly formed Iraqi Army should be integrated into the new Army according to various lessons that were learned from WWII.

It was this kind of thinking that so appealed to Walker and his colleagues. It is what pushed them to insist on a second meeting in Amman. In so doing, these few marine officers were not simply seeking to shift the war in Iraq; they were challenging the Bush administration.

Although none of the marines of the 3rd Civil Affairs Group would ever say so aloud, they had decided that the enemies they faced in al-Anbar were not terrorists. They were insurgents; their resistance was legitimate. Al-Hamdani's did not just solidify these convictions; it redefined them altogether—it rewrote the most basic assumptions about the war on terror.

ON AUGUST 22—the same day the insurgent leaders were speaking with Ayad Allawi in Baghdad—Coleman, Conway's chief of staff, wrote to Walker. He agreed to meet with the insurgent leadership in Amman, but he needed a briefing paper as a backup: "Ok, I need an e-mail (short, concise, clear) that articulates why we're going to Jordan, who we're to take/meet, what we expect to accomplish." Coleman's message made it clear that Conway would not come to the meeting. "The last thing we needed was for an American general to be kidnapped in Jordan," Coleman later explained. "That would have been a nightmare."

Walker responded to Coleman's e-mail reassuringly. "This is progress down what looks like a tough road," he said. "It is a road we must travel." But Walker cautioned Coleman about the meeting: "I have become convinced that the resistance we are in contact with is overwhelmingly FRE [former regime elements] and it has become Dr. Frankenstein, it has created a monster it can no longer control and it needs our help (criminal gangs, religious nuts, immature yet violent foreign Arab idealists all trained in deadly warfare, a veritable anarchists stew). [But] the FRE are people we have to reach out to."

On August 23, al-Gaood put the finishing touches on the conference agenda. The meeting would last three days, August 29–31. The first day would be a preliminary session, and the next two would focus on business development. All discussions of the security situation in Iraq would take place under the radar. Dave Harlan in Jordan wrote to Walker that al-Gaood had passed a message to him. The "resistance factions in Fallujah" wanted "no major ground offensive [to] take place in Fallujah until after the meeting at the end of the month," he said. On August 24, Walker wrote to

Conway about the Amman meeting. The two groups Coleman would be meeting, he said, "can roughly be likened to the Sinn Féin and the IRA [Irish Republican Army]. Both oppose our presence. One is attempting to work within the system and the other is fighting us on the battlefield." Walker identified the two groups as the "Public ACF Group" (the anticoalition forces—the equivalent of Sinn Féin) and "the 'Doctor' from the SAR" (the Sunni armed resistance—the equivalent of the IRA).

In the same week, al-Gaood sent Jerry Jones an invitation to attend the conference. Jones declined. "My attendance could be seen by some as U.S. political interference in the security situation in Al Anbar and in Iraq," he wrote to al-Gaood. "While this would not be true, such a claim could be very harmful to your future efforts. You and your colleagues have come too far to have a setback now and my coming is not worth the risk of that. I am working hard to get you and your effort plugged into key officers at the Department of State; and I am hopeful that one or more will come to the meeting on 30 August." On August 25, at Jones's insistence, al-Gaood sent an invitation to Robert Manning and Mitchell Reiss of the State Department. Al-Gaood noted that the proposed conference would take place at Amman's Le Royal Hotel, that it would "discuss a security plan and related issues," and that there would be "some economic and tribal leaders present." Predictably, Al-Gaood underplayed the security part of the meeting. The State Department officials declined his invitations.

Coleman was worried, but he tried not to show it. Prior to his departure from Baghdad, Coleman had a last meeting with Conway. "This is the dark side we're talking to here," he told Conway. The plan was for Coleman to attend the conference in Amman for one day, then fly to Washington, where he planned to meet with a committee of Marine Corps colonels representing all marine commands. It would be a crucial meeting—one such was held every year—and Coleman's attendance was required. "Conway had me going to D.C. as his rep," Coleman said, "but I was to communicate to him what had happened in Amman. He was intensely interested. So we were all set; we even had this thing vetted through the embassy in Jordan. They knew I was coming." Coleman was a career marine officer: dedicated, hardworking, politically savvy. But he had never been in a situation like the one that he faced in Amman in August 2004. "It felt claustrophobic," he remembers. "There was no guarantee that this would work. I didn't know what to expect."

After arriving in Amman late in the afternoon of August 28, Coleman met with al-Gaood and went to dinner with him in downtown Amman. He was the center of attention—the highest-ranking American military officer that al-Gaood had met to date, and a man who could speak directly with General James Conway. "I was very nervous about the dinner," Coleman said. "I had no security and was really on my own. I sat there with al-Gaood in a restaurant and I looked around and there wasn't a female in the room. They were all Sunnis of military age, and they were all looking at me. There was total silence when we were eating. And finally al-Gaood looked at me and he asked, 'Will you meet with people tonight?' And I said that I would."

Al-Gaood escorted Coleman through the lobby of Le Royal Hotel and up one floor to a conference room. "We went into this conference room and every eye turned to look at me," Coleman remembered.

> There were twenty-four chairs around the table, and every one of them was filled except for the chair in the front of the room. Al-Gaood smiled and motioned to the chair and said, "That is where you will sit." I was uncomfortable, very uncomfortable, but I walked through the room and to the head of the table and I sat down. There was a man on my right. He had a mustache, a large man. And he turned to me and he said, "Colonel Coleman, my

name is General Ra'ad al-Hamdani. I commanded the Republican Guards south of Baghdad. My troops fought yours. I have a paper that I want you to have. It is a proposal to bring the insurgents onto the side of the Americans."

AL-HAMDANI'S PROPOSAL was the one that had been circulating in draft form since the July conference; he had worked all through August to perfect it. "The proposal called for the creation of an Anbar military force for twelve months at a cost of 120 million dollars," Coleman remembers. "The provisional brigade would be paid for by the CPA. In exchange for this, they would shut down the insurgency in Anbar." Coleman leafed through the proposal and then looked around the table for a moment. "Gentlemen," he said. "I am very pleased to be here and to talk with you. But I am a low-level person and cannot say that I represent the views of the coalition forces. I cannot commit to this, but I will take it back to the proper authorities." General al-Hamdani smiled at Coleman and nodded. There was no response from around the table.

The meeting went on for another hour. "General Ra'ad was at his best," remembers Walker, who had followed Coleman into the meeting, "very cool and very professional and very articulate. He gave a good briefing. He stood in the front of the room and told us about his plan. But then we went around the room, and we went through pretty much the same thing that we did in July. There was a lot of denunciations of us around the table. But this time we gave back as good as we got. JC gave them hell, and I gave them hell, and we gave it to them with the facts." At the end of one hour, Coleman and Walker left. "We had a meeting with Dave [Harlan] after this," Walker continued, "and we talked it over. We all felt the same way, but Dave was just really pushing hard. He was all for this and kept saying, 'Let's get this done, let's get this done.' We all felt the pressure. There had been a lot of marines killed in Anbar, and we wanted it to end."

The next morning, Coleman and Walker went to the embassy as a courtesy. Coleman had heard about Walker's meeting with Jim Jeffrey in Baghdad, and he knew that the State Department was skittish about any meetings having to do with security. He hoped that a show of openness would help allay these fears. The meeting at the embassy was informal. "There were three guys there," Mike Walker remembers. "The ambassador showed us in and was very gracious, and he introduced us to the chargé d'affaires. There was another guy there. I'm pretty sure he was from the CIA. They were all over this. There was intelligence everywhere. The guy from the CIA didn't have much to say."

Walker assumed there would be few surprises. "I just sat there and let John do his thing," he said, "and he went on and on about business development. And I kept looking at him and thinking, 'Yeah, sure, but . . .' and the ambassador would smile and nod and that was it. JC never said a word about the insurgency." Before he left, Coleman turned to the chargé d'affaires. "I have to go back to Washington this afternoon for twenty-four hours," he said, "but I will be back for the last day of the conference. You're welcome to go over there for yourself and see it. You want me to arrange it?" The chargé smiled; "No thanks," he said.

Walker was stunned by Coleman's presentation. "I kept waiting for John to talk about the insurgency," Walker said, "and it just never came up. He never said a word about it." Had Coleman purposely misled the embassy? Had he purposely remained silent on the import of the conference? Walker was worried. Sensing this disquiet, Coleman turned to him as they left the embassy. "Don't worry about it Mike," he said reassuringly. More than four years after the briefing, Coleman remained nonchalant. "I told them what they needed to know, and no less and no more," he said. "I was told to brief the embassy, and they were briefed. Then I went to the airport and took a flight to Washington." Coleman spent the flight to Washington alternating between elation and worry. "If we could make the Ra'ad proposal work," he said, "it might change the course of the war. It was absolutely revolutionary. It was a breakthrough. But I knew that a lot of people were going to line up against it."

At the Pentagon, Jerry Jones heard about the meeting between Coleman and al-Hamdani, but he remained worried that Coleman's efforts would be undermined by the civilians at the CPA in Baghdad. Still, Jones's plan had worked: The senior marine commanders in al-Anbar were talking with the insurgency. Jones put in a call urging that General Peter Pace, the commandant of the Marine Corps, talk to Coleman. Jones wanted Pace to reassure Coleman that he was doing the right thing. Pace agreed to make the call. There were others tracking Coleman, including officials of the Defense Human Intelligence Service (DHI). "The DHI was all over this, and we were sure they were filing reports," Walker said. "And you don't talk to the Amman COS [chief of station] without them nosing around. We assumed they knew everything that we did. They had everything—our e-mails, our faxes, our telephones. Everything." Coleman attended the colonels' meeting in Washington, but his mind was elsewhere. He was anxious to get back to Amman. At the end of the colonels' meeting, he was told that the commandant of the Marine Corps wanted to talk with him. A secretary escorted him to a private office and handed him a telephone.

"Hey JC, how ya' doin'?" Pace asked.
Coleman hesitated. "Sir," he said, finally, "I think I am out of my lane and over my head."
"Just tell me what you marines want me to do John," Pace said, "and I'll do it."

Coleman briefed Pace on his meeting with al-Hamdani. He told Pace that he would go back to Amman to meet with al-Hamdani a final time, then brief Conway in Iraq. He told Pace that he thought that the paper al-Hamdani had given him was good news for the marines of al-Anbar. Pace told him he was doing the right thing and wished him luck in Amman. Coleman rang off.

AT NEARLY THE same moment that John Coleman was boarding a flight in Washington to return to Jordan, Dave Harlan reported for duty at the U.S. embassy in Amman. Harlan, an enthusiastic supporter of the Jones initiative, was pleased by the progress that Coleman and al-Hamdani had made. He was a "strong believer in Phase IV operations," that is, nation-building, "and a big fan of James Conway." He was certain that al-Hamdani's proposal would save marine lives and transform al-Anbar. Harlan knew that there were obstacles that needed to be overcome, but he thought the marines could do it. "I am a big fan of the marines doing windows," he later said.

Early in the afternoon of August 31, Harlan was called into the office of the embassy's defense attaché (DAT), who said that "he needed to talk with me ASAP." Harlan was unconcerned: The DAT system was used by the DIA to serve as a liaison at U.S. embassies between the military and the State Department. But when Harlan saw the DAT, he knew something was wrong. "The whole room was just filled with tension," he said.

"Lieutenant Colonel Harlan," the DAT said, "you are to proceed to King Hussein International Airport to await the arrival of Colonel John Coleman. He will not be allowed to enter the country." Harlan was stunned. Coleman had been declared "persona non grata"—PNG'd—in Jordan by the U.S. State Department. Someone in Washington did not want him to continue his discussions with insurgents. Harlan hesitated. The DAT glanced at him for a moment before continuing, "I have been told to convey to you that if you do not follow this order, you will be arrested and will stand trial at a general court-martial," he said. Harlan said he understood.

Later that night, Coleman arrived in Amman, just a little over thirty-two hours after he had left. He saw Harlan waiting for him. "I could hardly look at him," Harlan later said. "It was awful. It was one of the worst assignments I've ever had." What happened next, Harlan said, "will always be with me as an indelible part of my experience as a marine officer." As Coleman walked toward him, Harlan put up his hand and shook his head. "I'm sorry, sir, but I cannot allow you into the country."

At first Coleman couldn't believe the order was serious, but when he was told that Harlan had been threatened with a court-martial, he became angry. How could he be PNG'd? He was incredulous: "By the Jordanians? C'mon, Dave." Harlan looked at him and shook his head.

"It's not the Jordanians," Harlan said. "It's your own country.

CHAPTER FOUR

AL-ANBAR AWAKENS

"The turning point . . . wasn't a battle, it was a decision."
—JERRY JONES

PAINFUL EVENTS RECEDE slowly, but for both John Coleman and Dave Harlan the events of August 2004 now seem part of a strange and uncomfortable past. Coleman is almost wistful, looking back on it. He now views the fact that he had been PNG'd in Jordan as something that happened in another era. "It was long ago," he said. "As for our opening, well, that was the end of it."

After Harlan had told him that he was PNG'd, Coleman called a friend in the State Department and received permission to stay in Amman overnight. The embassy acquiesced—so long as Harlan didn't let him out of his sight. "I was RON [room over night]," he said. "I went to a hotel; I had a meal; I slept; I left. I don't think Dave and I talked very much."

Coleman returned to Baghdad the next day. He briefed James Conway and returned to his duties. After returning to the United States, Coleman retired from the marines and went to work for a firm near Richmond, Virginia. He remained unrepentant, but he did not have the star that his years of experience and his spotless record suggest he deserved. Coleman's controversial role in the events leading up to his meeting at the Amman airport with Harlan looked like the ingredients for high drama: The stellar career of a brilliant leader is ended by the shortsighted policies of his own government, sacrificed on the altar of political expediency by less talented men. But "that's not what happened," Coleman said. "I retired because I didn't make general. It's just that simple. Amman had nothing to do with it."

After Harlan confronted Coleman at the Amman airport, the U.S. embassy in Jordan requested he be reassigned. He left his duties in Amman on September 2. Eventually he returned to Washington, where General James Mattis told him to report to the U.S. Army War College in Carlisle, Pennsylvania. The army, Mattis said, was setting up an institute on "phase IV"—nation-building operations. "Go up there and see if you can't help those folks out," Mattis told Harlan. The war college think tank "has one of those really nifty military names," Harlan said—PK/SOI: Peacekeeping and Special Operations Institute. "They've got some good ideas up there," Harlan said. "Some really good ideas." Harlan retired from the U.S. Marine Corps at the end of 2008 and began searching for a new career. He wanted to stay involved in Iraq. "John Coleman is an American hero," he said during one of his visits to Washington, "and Phase IV is the future."

Pat Maloy returned to his family in California, but he made frequent trips to the Middle East. He worked in Kurdistan and continued his attempts to jump start al-Anbar's private sector. "I keep my hand in," he said. "This is important stuff." Maloy is the quintessential marine officer, speaking in coded trooper phrases: "Those with elegant skill sets need to be vectored along the same approach pattern so that the cardinals and bishops in the Vatican can calibrate with alacrity." He means: Soldiers with experience need to work together properly so that senior officers in the Pentagon will have the right information. "Maloy is something, isn't he?" Jerry Jones said. "He's a dedicated marine, a fine man, and a patriot."

Mike Walker also returned to California, where he resumed his civilian life as a math teacher and school administrator. For a time, the events of the summer of 2004 preyed on him, but he put them out of his mind and focused on his work. "I haven't thought about this in a long time," he said when contacted about his role in the Amman opening, "maybe for three or four years. Something like that. But let me go through my files and see what I have." A week later he wrote, "It's all coming back," and he added, "Some of these meetings get confused in my mind. I have to get the chronology right." Walker proved willing to address the tough questions: about General Jassim Mohammed Saleh, General Ra'ad al-Hamdani, and Dr. Ismail, and about the torture and murder of Suleiman Hamad al-Mawawi. When the marines left al-Anbar, they dedicated a tablet to Suleiman on the outskirts of Fallujah. The tough questions kept coming. Weren't the insurgents murderers? Weren't they terrorists? He wrote out answers to the toughest questions and put them in e-mails. At the bottom of one message he wrote: "This is keeping me awake at night."

There were a number of rumors among the members of the 3rd Civil Affairs Group as to why Coleman was stopped at the Amman airport, but they had no definite answer. "No one likes it when the players on a team get off the game plan, or overrule the coach," Maloy said. Harlan said, shrugging, "I wonder, really, what would have happened if we had just kept going, or if I had told the DAT to go to hell." Coleman remains reticent, self-effacing, almost unwilling to talk about the events in Amman. He refuses to blame anyone for what happened. "I was a marine officer, and I was proud to serve my country," he said, "but that never gave me a lock on the truth. There were a lot of Americans who weren't in uniform who were willing to lay down their lives for the people of Anbar. I met them; I know them; I admire them." He hesitates before passing judgment. "If we had been allowed to go forward," he said, "we could have saved a lot of American lives."

Walker remains sleepless, but he is certain of himself. "Our country got a lot wrong in Iraq," he said, "but what we did in Anbar wasn't one of them. And don't let anyone tell you different—the awakening in Anbar began on a hot summer night in Amman in 2004, and a small group of marines from the 3rd Civil Affairs Group did it."

COLEMAN'S TROUBLES BEGAN even before he left Baghdad for the Amman conference. Early on the morning of August 29, Jim Jeffrey told Lieutenant General Henry Stratman—a senior officer at CENTCOM—that John Negroponte was "uncomfortable" with the marine meetings in Amman. Jeffrey was adamant: The marines were not to get involved in politics. All political discussions were to be the sole responsibility of the State Department, he said. Stratman worried about the issue until early on the morning of August 30, when he e-mailed George Casey that Negroponte and Jeffrey were concerned because the military was "working political issues outside Iraq." Stratman added that both Negroponte and Jeffrey knew it was "too late to turn this conference off" but that both of them planned to talk with Casey about their views "the next time you meet."

That should have been the end of it. The State Department's concerns had been laid out, but the conference was on, the marines were there, and the insurgents were talking. But during the morning of August 30, Casey received telephone calls from Jeffrey and Negroponte. Both men said they were getting pressure from interim prime minister Ayad Allawi, who had been working to derail the August conference since his meeting with the Fallujah delegates on August 22. "Casey was in their crosshairs," a senior army officer said, "which was the last thing he needed." By the late morning of the thirtieth, Casey was convinced that Coleman and Walker had stirred up a hornet's nest.

Fearful that the marines were seeking a separate understanding with the Sunnis in al-Anbar, Allawi had complained up and down the civilian and military chains of command. Finally, Allawi called Condoleezza Rice. "Allawi was in a real lather about this," a Pentagon official tracking the events later confirmed.

> He called Negroponte, who called Jeffrey, who called Stratman. I hear that Allawi really laid Jeffrey on the carpet. It was just one question after another: What were the marines doing? Did Casey support it? Was the State Department involved? Was this what the Americans meant when they said they'd support him? It was a pretty ugly scene. Then Allawi called Rice. He was very bitter about the conference and about the involvement of the marines. Rice caved in: She called Negroponte, who called Jeffrey; then she called the American ambassador in Jordan and had Coleman PNG'd. Then she called Allawi and told him not to worry, she had taken care of the problem.

The call to the U.S. embassy had come just as Coleman was on his way from Amman to Washington.

Feeling the ripples of concern from Negroponte and Jeffrey, Casey ordered General Thomas Metz to write to Conway directly. Metz was to provide Conway with "clear guidance on this one," Casey said. Metz provided that guidance to Conway in a brusque e-mail that included a reference to Casey's judgment of what Conway was doing: "The MEF [Marine Expeditionary Force] has no authority in Jordan and should plan no action there. If they have something they want to do there, we should go through the embassy and get the US emb [embassy] in Amman to set it up. Never did find out what happened in July, but that was a goat rope that was poorly coordinated. Bottomline: no meeting outside Iraq unless coordinated through me and U.S. emb."

When Conway read the e-mail, he was furious. "He stewed about it for about two hours and then wrote a reply," one of his officers said. "The only other time I'd seen the general that angry was when he got the order to go into Fallujah. This might have been worse. I thought he was going to have a stroke. He kept repeating 'goat rope' and every time he said it his voice got louder." Conway knew what Casey meant by the term: "Goat rope" referred to the cattlemen's practice of training wet-behind-the-ears boys by having them rope goats instead of cattle. The cowboys would sit nearby and laugh. "General Conway did not like being laughed at," the same senior officer noted, "and he didn't like the implication that his marines were amateurs.

Conway responded to Metz and sent a copy of the e-mail to Casey:

> We are not working what I would call [a] political agenda in Jordan or elsewhere. We have had an effort since our arrival in March to stimulate jobs in the Al Anbar by encouraging local and external businessmen to accept the risk of starting something up. The two business conferences we have hosted in Bahrain and Jordan have had the complete backing of the Embassies there as well as the Iraqi Ministry of Trade (who has had the Deputy speak at both). We were invitees to [the] conference in July—not our "goat rope"—and while there our reps were approached by men who said they spoke for the "resistance" in Al Anbar. We advised our higher headquarters as to the contacts and were encouraged to continue the dialogue. Our object remains to reduce attacks and get at the essence of the insurgency in Al Anbar. I consider the discussions a non-kinetic approach to a military objective and believe we should pursue that option.

Conway's message was as much a reminder as a protest—a reminder to Casey that it was *his* battle plan that had called for "co-opting" the insurgency. The new strategy had promised not only to shift the burden of the war away from the Americans but also to separate insurgents from terrorists. With Casey's new emphasis would come a new way of looking at "who's who in the zoo." Conway had endorsed Casey's program. Furthermore, as Conway was determined to show, the meetings in Amman were not and had never been a secret. The State Department had been invited to send representatives. Conway's staff thought that what had happened with Amman smelled a lot like what had happened during the Vigilant Resolve fight in Fallujah in April: The politicians had lost their nerve. It was okay to strategize about talking with insurgents; it was another thing to actually do it.

Most of all, Conway wanted to keep the channel to the insurgency open. It was a way to get at the insurgency without fighting block by block in Fallujah. His views were confirmed in an eyewitness report given him by Captain Rod McHaty, his staff intelligence officer. McHaty had sound political instincts and an eye for detail. He had traveled to Amman with Coleman for the August conference, but he had remained nearly invisible, allowing Coleman and Walker to take the lead. Conway trusted McHaty's judgment, believing him to be careful, low key, and thoughtful. His briefing paper on the conference reflected this: "My first impression of LtGen Ra'ad al Hamdani was positive," McHaty wrote in a report to Conway, adding, "he seems to be the kind of person able to provide good leadership to any force formed. The proposal submitted by the Iraqis has many merits." McHaty recommended keeping the channel open and argued that the marines should work to bring the Sunni Armed Resistance and the Iraqi authorities closer together. "We cannot undermine the IIG [Iraqi Interim Government], but at the same time we need to push the IIG to recognize and allow the Sunnis in al Anbar some representation in the new government," he wrote. He ended with an endorsement: "We need to continue to engage the people we spoke with in Amman Jordan." Conway had McHaty's memo in hand when Coleman returned from being PNG'd in Amman, but he instead showed Coleman an e-mail he had received from the U.S. embassy in Jordan. The communication was not official and contained advice from a friend; its message was blunt: "Get the hell out of Jordan and stay out." For Conway and Coleman, the e-mail was evidence that the U.S. government would not back Conway or his staff.

In the aftermath of Coleman's experience in Amman, most of Conway's senior staff blamed the State Department for the Amman foul-up. "When it came down to backing either Allawi or the U.S. Marines," one said, "Condi Rice decided to back Allawi. Listen, she could have told him that the marines were doing the right thing and he would have backed off. But she didn't. That's the way we read it, and I don't think we were wrong." James Clad had his own bottom line: "Many people in our system knew this approach had been made," he told a reporter. "They made sure it was slapped down."

In retrospect, Clad is convinced that Rice and the State Department were implacably opposed to the al-Gaood initiative and that, in the end, their opposition couldn't be overcome. "For State, it became a turf war," he said, "and they saw it as the military trying to get round their policy." In truth, Coleman was neither out of his lane nor over his head—he had simply made a mistake. During one of his frequent trips to Washington several months after being PNG'd in Jordan, Joint Chiefs of Staff chairman Peter Pace called Coleman into his office. There wouldn't have been a problem at all, Pace told Coleman, if he had been "a little more forthcoming" during his briefing in Amman.

For Jerry Jones, watching all of this from his office in Washington, what had happened to Coleman was disappointing but not a surprise. He'd seen it before. Policymakers fighting over turf was nothing new. So although Jones was dismayed, he wasn't ready to admit defeat. Neither was Ken Wischkaemper. Of all those involved with Talal al-Gaood, Wischkaemper was perhaps the most enraged over Coleman's treatment. A Republican and a conservative, a Texan and a businessman, Wischkaemper had proudly voted for George W. Bush, believing that he would change Washington. It hadn't happened, and in the summer of 2004, Wischkaemper was starting to believe it never would. For him, Coleman's experience symbolized everything that was wrong with Washington: "Anyone in government who thought that dealing with the Sunnis was the way to go would be facing a C.L.E., a career limiting experience," he said. "So far as I can see, fear of C.L.E. is what drives Washington."

ALTHOUGH CONDI RICE was able to stop Conway, Coleman, and Walker, she couldn't stop Ken Wischkaemper. Through all of September and into October 2004, Wischkaemper was on the telephone or e-mailing al-Gaood. Wischkaemper would then telephone or e-mail Jones, telling him what al-Gaood had to say. In many cases, the information was invaluable: describing the state of the insurgency in al-Anbar, the situation in Fallujah, the Iranian penetration in Basra, or the state of the Iraqi Interim Government. "I was sending Rumsfeld a memo based on Talal's information relayed via Wischkaemper almost every week," Jones said. "I don't know how he [al-Gaood] was getting his intelligence, but it was amazingly accurate, not just on the Sunnis and al-Anbar, but about the Shia leaders like al-Sadr and the rest of Iraq. He was the first to say the Iranians were taking over the south and that the Brits were letting them do it." Inevitably, Al-Gaood's reports made their way to IMEF, which used them to help differentiate between Fallujah's legitimate insurgency and the ever-growing contingent of foreign fighters and al Qaeda sympathizers that had infiltrated the city.

At the same time, Clad also kept a channel open to al-Gaood. In October, he and Jones wrote a letter to CIA director Porter Goss about al-Gaood and the Amman opening. Clad and Jones recommended that the U.S. government build on the opportunity the opening offered. There was no reply. "We were simply trying to get people to pay attention," Clad said. "But the mindset that anyone who took a shot at the Americans was a terrorist was still in place. People were not listening."

Al-Gaood was also busy. He spent an increasing amount of time funneling information to Jones and the marines on Fallujah's penetration by foreign fighters. And he pressed ahead with his contacts in the region. By mid-October he had persuaded the Jordanian government to hold yet another business conference in Amman. The conference took place in November, but without the marines present. Al-Gaood later confirmed that "it really went nowhere." Al-Gaood was frustrated: There seemed little he could do in the wake of the Coleman incident to shape a new opening to the American high command. "We were really cut off," he said. Once again, as in April and August, al-Gaood was desperately attempting to dampen the troubles in al-Anbar. But without an official channel to Coleman and Walker, he knew he wouldn't be able to spare the city of Fallujah a second assault.

When the marines left Fallujah in April, they had made an agreement with the city's insurgents: to separate themselves from the foreign fighters and extremists in the city, or the marines would do it for them. The agreement was confirmation of all that al-Gaood had said: that there was a legitimate resistance, that it was made up of former Saddamists and tribal leaders, and that these leaders (who opposed the American occupation) were willing to come to an agreement with the United States. Al-Gaood believed that such an accommodation would undercut the radical Islamists and foreign fighters, turn the people of al-Anbar against them, and leave the Sunni heartland in the hands of its tribes. The marines had accepted the argument and allowed the legitimate resistance—the Fallujah Brigade—to enter the city. But the brigade had failed. In the six months since the end of Vigilant Resolve, the former Saddamists had proven both politically and militarily incapable of taking on Fallujah's most radical groups, what al-Gaood described as "those angry young men with their beards and brown robes and their talk of Allah and holy war." The evidence of that failure was obvious to James Conway in IMEF's daily casualty reports.

Through all of September and October 2004, Conway's staff had been perfecting plans to reenter the city and destroy the growing power of the foreign fighters flowing into Fallujah from Syria and Jordan. By the end of October, the Fallujah Brigade had ceased to exist altogether, and attacks on the marines were reaching a crescendo. "The city was turning into an Islamist state," an officer on Conway's staff explained. "We were taking a lot of fire, a lot of IEDs, but what was happening in the city was even worse." If anything, Coleman and Walker's end-of-August meeting in Amman was evidence that the forces of the legitimate resistance were on the losing end of the fight for Fallujah. A post-Amman memo to Conway from Walker based on the conversations with insurgent leaders in Amman reflected the worsening situation: The city government (Walker labeled them "the Fallujah Group") was being run by an "Ashura Council," which had recruited "active death squads." The council operated with "a secret membership and proceedings." Walker told Conway that Fallujah's Ashura Council would "probably not allow Lt. Gen. [Ra'ad] Hamdani to make a separate security deal without a fight."

After the meeting between Coleman and al-Hamdani in August in Amman, Walker met with Dr. Mohmad al-Hamadani, an insurgency leader from Fallujah. The doctor painted a grim picture: "Dr. al-Hamadani provided a vivid, if horrific, insight into the reign of terror that al Qaeda had brought to the residents of

the city," Walker remembered. "Our side knew that the planning
and preparations for the November Fallujah fight were well advanced and that if we could not find common ground our offensive would be inevitable." Walker listened to al-Hamadani's plea.
Al Qaeda would be defeated by the insurgents in Fallujah, he
said, if the marines would allow them to do it. But that had been
tried—and it had failed. "I felt the die was cast at that point,"
Walker remembered. "It would now be a military solution to determine who would control Fallujah, and I knew the Marines
would finish the job they could have and should have been allowed to accomplish in April."

On November 8, Conway's marines launched Operation
Phantom Fury. Unlike April's operation, the marines had months
to prepare. In the weeks prior to the attack, city residents were
urged to leave their homes. Conway's intelligence staff carefully
selected their targets, focusing on the command-and-control centers of the city's foreign fighters. By the time the marine offensive
was launched, the city was all but abandoned. Marine officers
later speculated that tens of thousands of people had fled, leaving
a hard-core group of armed al Qaeda militiamen and their supporters, some 2,000 fighters in all, in the city's center. In Amman,
al-Gaood issued yet another plea for a postponement of the attack, saying that he should be given a last chance to shape a political agreement with Fallujah's leaders. But al-Gaood's leverage
with the city's more moderate political officials, including senior
officers of Saddam's military, had disappeared; many of them had
left the city. "One of the untold stories of Fallujah is what happened between July and November," a Pentagon official noted.
"It's not as if there was fighting in April and then again in November. There were huge fights inside the city, heroic fights between Anbar's resistance leaders and the foreign fighters. What
the marines were fighting in November were the guys who won
this battle. They were fighting the jihadis."

Operation Phantom Fury involved 6,500 marines and 1,500 army soldiers (backed by two battalions of newly trained Iraqi troops), who fought through the streets of Fallujah for ten days. The total combat contingent amounted to three times the number as had attacked the city in Vigilant Resolve. In most cases, the fighting was conducted from street to street and from house to house. As in other urban fights, the marines created their own fields of fire, staying out of the street and blowing holes through the walls of private homes to get at their adversaries. After the first seventy-two hours of combat, the Americans abandoned their house-to-house fight and began to reduce enemy strongholds with artillery rounds, bringing down entire buildings.

The northern reaches of Fallujah were nearly obliterated. "There was a lot of close-in combat; these guys were tenacious, fanatical. But this *Saving Private Ryan* kind of stuff is also a bit misleading," a marine veteran of the fight said. "Why sacrifice lives when you've got the kind of firepower we had? We would take fire, return it, then call in the artillery or helicopters and just level buildings on top of these people. They deserved it." Over the course of ten days, the U.S. military killed over a thousand insurgents. The last strongholds of foreign fighters held out until December 23, when a marine unit killed twenty-four insurgents in a short skirmish.

IN THE WAKE OF Phantom Fury, al-Hamdani provided an assessment of the offensive to Wischkaemper and Jones. His review was much less a briefing than a flow of consciousness—and a condemnation of American military actions. He rejected Conway's insistence that Fallujah's militias could be easily divided into "moderates" and "extremists," taking note of a disturbing American tendency to apply the terms after the fact. He had recognized the essential incoherence of America's thinking on the war on terror.

Those the Americans called the "terrorists" of Fallujah were so labeled not because of anything they believed but because they fought the Americans. Likewise, "moderates" were so labeled not because of their political views but because they had acquiesced in America's occupation of Iraq. The Israelis, al-Hamdani argued, did the same thing to the Palestinians; any Palestinian who opposed the Israeli occupation of Palestine was a terrorist; any Palestinian who did not was a moderate. Al-Hamdani applied different labels: Palestinians who opposed the Israeli occupation were different from terrorists because their resistance was legitimate. They were under occupation. They weren't terrorists; rather, they were freedom fighters. So too, those Palestinians who worked with the Israelis were not moderates, but collaborators.

Al-Hamdani's reference to Israel was purposeful; he criticized the Americans for comparing their war in Iraq to Israel's fight in the West Bank and Gaza. He had overheard that comparison made by American officers. "In individual and group consciousness and unconsciousness of Arab and Islamic society, it is an ugly picture for the Israeli behavior in Palestine and repeating such behavior or quoting it by the Americans [is not] compatible between the vision of the American and Israeli soldiers for the Arab and Moslem," he wrote. By occupying Palestinian lands, "the Israelis have changed their big army into miserable police forces" he continued. "Surely this matter is avoidable by wise Americans."

But al-Hamdani also acknowledged that not all violence was legitimate. He too used the word "terrorist" to describe those Fallujah fighters who were not a part of "the national resistance." Terrorists, in his view, were "outsiders" who were interested in a revolution. They were "Salafists" and "takfiris"—"the unsmiling young bearded men in robes" who had come to Iraq from Saudi Arabia, Yemen, and North Africa to fight "the infidel." They weren't interested in Iraq. They were interested in the radical transformation of Muslim society. They wanted to burn it down and start over. They were revolutionaries. General al-Hamdani was not. His recommendation to Conway reflected these views. The United States should "acknowledge the national resistance, encourage it to establish a political leadership able to deal with and negotiate for the interest of all parties and separate them from the terrorist leadership."

Al-Hamdani told Conway that the November assault on Fallujah was counterproductive, as it had undermined the "legitimate national resistance." The attack had created more, not fewer, enemies for the Americans. "Such operations," he wrote, "will not put an end to the resistance . . . but on the contrary will widen the job of those forces." He was making George Casey's argument: Every time an American met an Iraqi there was "friction." Every time an American killed an Iraqi, the American created a "terrorist." After Phantom Fury, he said, "any administration or security leadership appointed by the American authority will find it difficult to stay in Fallujah—or any other [Iraqi] cities when the American forces leave."

To repair the damage the Americans had done with Phantom Fury, al-Hamdani repeated the proposal he had made in Amman: reconstitute the national army in al-Anbar with enough money and training that it could fight the "extremists." He then added some points that had not explicitly been discussed in Amman. The United States, he said, should reverse the decision made by Paul Bremer demobilizing the Iraqi army, should issue a general amnesty for all those who had fought against the Americans as part of the national resistance, should compensate the inhabitants of Fallujah for the damage suffered during the recent hostilities, should outlaw all armed militias outside of the regularly established army, should "decrease their appearance within Iraqi public life," and "should withdraw all armed forces to external camps."

After the scuttling of the Amman channel, al-Hamdani had little confidence that his paper would be read. But it was. IMEF's senior officers actually agreed with many of its points, but remained skeptical that al-Hamdani (or any other al-Anbar leader) could effectively outmuscle al Qaeda. Even the marines, with all their firepower, had failed during Phantom Fury to capture hundreds of al Qaeda fighters who had slipped out of the city and taken up positions in Ramadi and along the Syrian border.

In early 2005, the situation outside al-Anbar was actually worse than it had been in April, just eight months before. Baghdad seemed on the verge of collapse, and Iraq was spiraling further into open civil conflict, with the Iraqi Interim Government unable (or unwilling) to take the necessary steps to open the political system. The U.S. casualty count mounted after Fallujah—with 107 dead during January 2005, nearly the same number as suffered at the height Phantom Fury. After a short breathing spell, the marines in western Iraq were also hit hard. Casualties rose through all of early 2005.

In early May 2005, IMEF launched Operation Matador to root out the remnants of al Qaeda extremists and their sympathizers near the Syrian border. The eleven-day operation netted 125 insurgents killed. But Matador was only a temporary fix. As soon as the marines left the border area, the insurgents reasserted control. Conway's senior commanders were frustrated; they were still awaiting the one event that would tip the struggle against al Qaeda, the one incident that would turn al-Anbar's tribal leaders against the extremists. Back in July 2004, General James Mattis had told Bing West that the key victory in al-Anbar was in the hand's of the province's tribal leaders, who had not yet turned on the foreign fighters and extremists "in their midst." At the end of Matador, al Qaeda's campaign of murder and intimidation was not only continuing, it was succeeding. "The tribes only saw us as the enemy," Mattis had said.

What the marines needed was one miscalculation, one mistake by al Qaeda's leaders. "We needed the real enemy to make mistakes and expose themselves for what they were," Mattis had said. Mattis and Conway had waited, and waited, and waited for that one mistake, that one miscalculation. And nothing had happened. And then they had waited some more.

Finally, on July 23, 2005, al Qaeda's leaders made their miscalculation. Finally, they exposed themselves. And the tribes of Anbar turned.

THE STORY OF the July Surprise ends where it began: with Texan Ken Wischkaemper. At just after noon on July 23, 2005, Wischkaemper received a call on his cell phone from al-Gaood in Amman. Wischkaemper was at home in Shamrock, preparing to take his wife out to celebrate their twenty-fourth wedding anniversary. The connection to Amman was tentative, and Wischkaemper could barely make out what al-Gaood was saying. Still, as Wischkaemper later told the story, he could hear his sense of desperation.

"Ken, we're in trouble," al-Gaood said.

That morning a group of "jihadis" had taken over al-Qaim, near Iraq's border with Syria, and fired on a tribal militia. The jihadis were led by heavily armed al Qaeda operatives, who drove the tribal force into the desert. "It's dark there now," al-Gaood said, "but they've run out of ammunition. If they don't get help, they're going to die at first light." Wischkaemper said he would make a call to Jerry Jones to see what could be done. Wischkaemper called Jones on his cell phone and told him the story. "I could tell from the way that Talal spoke that he was worried, that he thought his friends would be slaughtered," Wischkaemper remembered, "and that's what I told Jerry."

Jones was on the way to Baltimore-Washington International Airport. His marine son, on the way to Baghdad, was in the car beside him. "It did seem somewhat of an irony," Jones recalled. Jones told Wischkaemper that there was little he could do. It was a Saturday, he said, and although the marines might be fighting in

Iraq, most of the Pentagon was empty. Still, he was willing to give it a try. "Let's see what we can do, Ken," Jones said. "Don't worry." Jones then instructed Wischkaemper to stay on the line while he called Coleman, who was on duty in California, as the commander at Camp Pendleton. Jones feared that he wouldn't be able to reach Coleman, but Coleman answered on the second ring.

"I've got Ken on the phone with me," Jones said, "and he's gotten a call from Talal in Amman." Coleman heard them out and then placed a call of his own. "When I got off the phone with Jerry and Ken I called Talal," Coleman said. "He had the cell phone number of one of the Sunni fighters in al-Qaim. I knew who to speak to at the Marine Corps headquarters at Camp Fallujah in Iraq. I called the people who ran operations there and gave them the number of the guy in al-Qaim."

"It was pretty nip and tuck there for awhile," Coleman remembered, "but I had real confidence in the marines at Camp Fallujah. I told them what was at stake, that this was it." Coleman hesitated and laughed: "You know, the U.S. Marines to the rescue, that kind of thing. It is what we do best, I think. I was proud of it."

Less than one hour after al-Gaood had called Wischkaemper in Texas, a "package" of Cobra attack helicopters took off from an airfield 120 miles west of Baghdad. One hour later the helicopters were over al Qaeda's fighting lines outside al-Qaim. "It wasn't the Iraqi Sunni tribes who got massacred," Wischkaemper said flatly. Coleman is not so matter-of-fact. "It was a turning point," he said. "Not Normandy, not the Battle of the Bulge. It wasn't even really a battle, or not much of one. Ironic isn't it. They won't make a movie of it. No one stormed the beaches."

Jones was equally reflective. After calling Coleman, Jones dropped his son off at the airport and waited with him for two hours until his flight left. As the flight lifted off and turned east, marines in helicopters over al-Qaim shifted the American war in Iraq, siding with a national resistance movement against the "dead enders" of al Qaeda. "Just imagine," Jones said, "the turning point in the war in Iraq wasn't a battle; it was a decision. How the hell do you put that in the history books?"

THE FIGHT AT al-Qaim set the stage for a full engagement with the Sunni insurgency in al-Anbar, though it would be many months before the awakening that started in Amman would become "the Awakening" that transformed America's war in Iraq. The transformation would be painfully slow.

Even before al-Qaim, James Clad had convinced Zalmay Khalilzad—the new U.S. ambassador in Baghdad—to meet with al-Gaood. The impetus for the meeting was a letter signed by al-Anbar businessmen that contained a detailed proposal for the "stabilization of Iraq through political and economic initiatives." The letter, written by a committee of businessmen called the Iraq Initiative for Unity and Development, contained four pages of specific recommendations, including a reversal of Bremer's de-Baathification edict. Clad sat with General al-Hamdani and drafted a new plan for al-Anbar called "Winning Iraq, One City at a Time." Al-Hamdani made a detailed and compelling case for "an honest and sustained dialogue" with the United States.

Khalilzad did not officially endorse the recommendations, but he regularized communications with al-Gaood's network. Several months later, in November 2005, U.S. Army commanders held a "breakthrough" meeting with Sunni sheikhs in Ramadi. The sheikhs told army commanders that they would police the province, turn against foreign fighters, and come into the war on the side of the Americans—nearly the same commitments proffered to Coleman in Amman in August 2004. At the center of the Ramadi meetings was Sheikh Abdul Sattar al-Rishawi, an influential Sunni cleric.

Yet even after al-Qaim and the opening to Khalilzad—and even after the beginning of the Ramadi dialogue with Sheikh

Sattar—al-Anbar's tribes remained convinced that they could take on al Qaeda alone. They were deeply mistrustful of the Americans. When Iraqis went to the polls in December 2005 to elect a government, the Sunni heartland boycotted the election. The only good news for al-Anbar's tribes was that Ayad Allawi would be replaced. Through all of early 2006, al-Anbar remained a caldron of anti-American sentiment. "It's hard to blame them," Clad said. "We were working, working, working. But always we faced the same deep mistrust. We were still the occupiers. Even into 2006 we had failed to win their trust. This took a long, long time."

But in mid-2006, the situation in al-Anbar had begun to shift. The opening that had taken so long to build in Fallujah was now repeated in Ramadi, where U.S. Army Colonel Sean MacFarland of the 1st Brigade of the 1st Armored Division attempted to convince the tribal leaders that "sitting on the fence" would only deepen their problems. "We get there in late May and early June 2006, and the tribes are on the sidelines," MacFarland remembered. "They'd seen the insurgents take a beating. After watching that, they're like, 'Let's see which way this is going to go.'"

MacFarland began slowly, one step at a time. He convinced tribal leaders to recruit a local police force for Ramadi. He convinced the military to support his plan, and he convinced officials in the Green Zone to help pay for it. The police force was a part of a grand bargain of the type that al-Hamdani had once proposed: "The way we went about it helped to prove that we were reliable partners, that we could deliver security to the sheiks in a way that broke the cycle of al-Qaeda murder and intimidation," MacFarland wrote later. "In the bargain, the Government of Iraq would assume the burden of paying their tribesmen to provide their security. The situation was a winner any way you looked at it. The tribes soon saw that instead of being the hunted, they could become the hunters, with well trained, paid, and equipped security forces backed up by locally positioned coalition forces."

As the police force gathered strength, Ramadi quieted. Al Qaeda forces that had once dominated the city were killed or arrested. On September 9, 2006, Sheikh Sattar organized a tribal council of fifty sheiks "at which he declared 'the Anbar Awakening' officially underway."

Through October and into November 2006, al Qaeda in Iraq fought a series of running battles with the army, the marines, and Sheikh Sattar's newly empowered police force. They were defeated. Sheikh Sattar's Anbar Awakening Council united forty-two of al-Anbar's clans. Nearly one full year later, on September 3, 2007, a smiling George W. Bush visited with Sattar at the Asad Airbase in al-Anbar. The two shook hands, and Sattar pledged to cooperate with Baghdad's new government. Bush's new commander in Iraq, General David Petraeus, sat in the background as Sheikh Sattar and President Bush faced the cameras. Also in the background were three key officials of the July Surprise. One of them asked Sattar what he had said to Bush. The sheikh smiled: "I told him, 'You know Mr. President, you got this wrong. You got us wrong. We were never your enemy." The questioner pressed him. How had Bush responded? "He didn't say anything," Sattar responded. "I think he knew I was right." Ten days after meeting Bush, Sattar was killed in a car bombing, what Jaber Awad called "al Qaeda's good-bye kiss to the tribes."

The death of Sattar did not derail the Anbar Awakening. "What Sean MacFarland did in Ramadi sparked a revolution in Anbar," Jerry Jones said. "I am convinced that he studied what we did in Amman, that we had set the groundwork for him." Had he lived, Sattar would have agreed: He had been one of the fighters at al-Qaim who was saved by the quick work of Wischkaemper, Jones, and Coleman. If he had been killed there, the Sunni Awakening might never have happened. Wischkaemper had saved his life. MacFarland later wrote of the al-Anbar revolution for a military audience. "We operated aggressively across all lines of operation, kinetic and non-kinetic, to bring every weapon and asset at our disposal to bear against the enemy. We conducted detailed intelligence fusion and targeting meetings and operated seamlessly with special operations forces, aviation, close air support, and riverine units."

Talal al-Gaood did not live to see the transformation. In March 2006, he requested a U.S. visa. He wanted to travel to America to have an operation that would repair a defective heart valve. Jerry Jones argued with the State Department that he should be allowed into the country, but he was denied entry. He had the operation in Paris, but shortly after the procedure he collapsed in a Paris hotel and died. He was forty-four. His brother, Hameed, believes he would have survived if he had been treated in the United States.

When a wake was organized to celebrate his life, Jones called Brigadier General David Reist, who had been the deputy commander of the marines in Iraq. "I told him, 'Dave, you have to be there,'" Jones remembered. Thousands of people showed up in Amman to pay homage to al-Gaood. To accommodate the mourners, the wake was held in a soccer stadium. The man who delivered the eulogy had led the first uprising in Fallujah. "It was the damnedest thing I've ever seen," Jones said. The shock of al-Gaood's death and the on-again, off-again nature of the negotiations he had led left many people embittered. "We were getting some nasty stares," Jones said, "but we were under the protection of the al-Gaood family, and that meant we were safe." Reist met with the tribal leaders during the wake, and the discussions continued in Iraq. "To bring a marine general, to have him there, was another sign that what Talal had started would continue," Jones said.

The dialogue that began in Amman did not end with Sattar. It continues: In February 2008, senior British officers visited General Ra'ad al-Hamdani in Amman. They were seeking his advice on how to deal with Shia tribes in the south. One month later, he was invited to formal talks in Baghdad. On March 23, 2008, he signed a detailed twelve-point agreement with the British and the Americans establishing a "reconciliation committee" that would "seek a quick return of medium and senior military ranks from colonel to major-general to serve as advisors with the ministry of defense and interior and to serve as commanders." After the negotiations were completed, al-Hamdani met with U.S. ambassador Ryan Crocker. Crocker was a supporter of the negotiations and knew al-Hamdani by reputation. "He spoke in Arabic," al-Hamdani said of Crocker, "and was very gentlemanly. He recognized the decision by Bremer to disband the army had been wrong, and he said America had made too many mistakes. He told me, 'We've alienated Iraqis who love their country.'"

More than five years after the July Surprise, the American public extols the transformation of al-Anbar's tribes and praises the efforts of diplomats and policymakers for their courage in supporting America's troops. Former secretary of state Condoleezza Rice is a part of this celebration: A prominent documentary quotes her as saying that she always favored the opening in al-Anbar and supported it from the beginning. That's a lie, of course, but no one will say so publicly.

A number of other publications credit George Casey with reworking the American battle plan by being the first to suggest that al-Anbar's tribes be "co-opted." Casey can well take credit for his plan, but he never implemented it. James Conway did, and when it came time to defend him, Casey was nowhere to be seen.

Our nation's most important military experts believe that our military must determine how we can successfully fight our nation's future wars. The answer to that question, they believe, has been shown by the way we fought the war in Iraq: building a light military machine, trained by counterinsurgency experts, and surging those counterinsurgency troops into a nation's towns and villages to intercept terrorists and kill them. But these new soldiers will not only be able to identify the enemy and kill them; they will also be able to meld with the population—they will speak their language, get to know them, and help them build their communities and their nation. They will build schools, set up waste management plants, establish local governing councils, and train local police. America's soldiers will not just defeat the enemy; they will build new nations. This new counterinsurgency doctrine has now been institutionalized in a new manual on the subject.

But critics of this new dispensation view the doctrine as overly romanticized; it is a deep misunderstanding of what armies do. Nation-building is a long and difficult job, one best done by men and women who do not carry rifles. The criticism is heard most often by soldiers who believe that the job of armies is not to build nations but to kill other soldiers. The most important question facing the military, they say, is not *how* to fight future wars, but *whether* to fight them. The new special operations experts may quote Joseph Conrad and wax philosophical about the meaning of "dark operations," but these highly trained experts were not in Amman—those in Amman were schoolteachers.

Still others, the vast majority, applaud former army vice chief of staff Jack Keane for intervening with President Bush on behalf of General Petraeus and for arguing persuasively that the United States should take a gamble and flood Iraq with a surge of troops to dampen the insurgency and fight al Qaeda. This gamble has now become the accepted explanation for the American "victory" in Iraq; it has been institutionalized by a newly minted COIN (counterinsurgency) clique that has ensconced itself in the Pentagon and in Washington's think tanks.

The truth is quite different. The real gamble in Iraq did not actually take place in Iraq. It took place in Amman. Ironically, it had to do not with a surge in troops but with a surge in thinking. It was the result not of American success but of American failure. It resulted from the realization that America had gotten it wrong—that America's leadership had miscast the enemy in Iraq, had misled its soldiers, and had misidentified the nation's enemies. The fighters in al-Anbar were not terrorists, they were not dead enders, and they were not Nazis; they were the national resistance. They were people who could stand with us against the people who had run our airliners into our buildings. "Al-Anbar was not transformed; we were," Clad said. "We did not teach the Iraqis; they taught us. We abandoned our prejudices; we questioned what we were told; we rejected the easy language of terrorism. We listened. We learned."

The real gamble in Iraq was not in deploying more troops to kill terrorists; the real gamble in Iraq was in sending marines to talk to them.

CHAPTER FIVE

HAMAS

"[This] is not a clash between civilizations;
it is a clash about civilization."
— TONY BLAIR

ON JULY 2, 1994—ten years before the events in Amman, Jordan—
Yasser Arafat arrived in Gaza at the head of a delegation of Palestine Liberation Organization leaders.

Arafat's arrival in Gaza was a triumphant moment for his people. The PLO had once been viewed as one of the world's most violent terrorist organizations. Now that had changed: Less than a year prior to his arrival in Gaza, Arafat and Israeli prime minister Yitzhak Rabin had met in Washington, D.C., to sign a Declaration of Principles outlining steps toward Palestinian self-rule in the Israeli-occupied West Bank and Gaza Strip. In subsequent talks, Arafat and Rabin had negotiated a series of agreements that affirmed the PLO's right to show "symbols of statehood" in the autonomous areas and allowed self-rule under an elected Palestinian legislature. The agreement was followed by a wide-ranging economic accord intended to ensure Palestinian economic growth. Arafat's arrival in Gaza, and his agreement with Rabin, inaugurated an era of hope that the Israeli-Palestinian conflict would end. Palestinians were ecstatic; Israelis were relieved. After decades of conflict, peace seemed at hand.

Yet in the wake of Arafat's arrival in Gaza, the PLO struggled to establish its government. Arafat and the PLO leadership took up residence in Gaza, with Arafat's offices located in a hastily built headquarters on the Mediterranean beachfront. Almost immediately, construction began throughout Gaza and the West Bank on a series of ministries that would disburse the funds made available to the PLO by international donors. Money poured into the West Bank and Gaza, and Arafat and Rabin began the long and difficult process of rebuilding Israeli-Palestinian relations. Arafat delegated much of the everyday work of establishing an autonomous government to his aides, preferring instead to shape the political environment that would meld the PLO leadership with local Palestinian officials. His days were taken up with an endless series of meetings in which he meticulously constructed the contours of a future Palestinian state.

Three weeks after Arafat's arrival in Gaza, Abdul Aziz Rantisi— one of the senior leaders of the Islamic Resistance Movement (Hamas)—arrived at Arafat's headquarters with a group of bodyguards. Rantisi's family had fled Jaffa in 1948 and taken up residence in Gaza. The young Rantisi had been a formidable student and had graduated from Egypt's Alexandria University with a degree in pediatric medicine and genetics. As a student, Rantisi joined the Egyptian Muslim Brotherhood and rose through its ranks, before returning to Gaza as a physician.

In 1987, Rantisi helped found the Islamic Resistance Movement. The movement's earliest days were taken up with organizing social programs for the people of Gaza and the West Bank and building a political organization to rival the PLO. In 1992, Rantisi, along with other Hamas activists, was expelled from the Israeli-occupied territories to southern Lebanon. He returned to Gaza five years later, as a part of a prisoner-exchange agreement. After the assassination of Hamas leader Salah Shehadeh, on July 22, 2002, Rantisi became Hamas's most public spokesman. Articulate, vain, outspoken, and given to bouts of rage, Rantisi was anxious to meet the PLO leader. Rantisi disliked Arafat and thought him a bully, though acknowledging that he was the symbol of Palestinian nationalism. No one, Rantisi believed, had ever really stood up to him. Rantisi was vain enough to believe he would be the first to do so.

The meeting between Arafat and Rantisi was the result of weeks of difficult negotiation. At first, Rantisi insisted that Arafat visit him at his own offices and then, receiving no answer, changed the venue to his home. Arafat refused. As the leader of the "sole, legitimate representative of the Palestinian people" (a formula for the PLO that Arafat insisted Israel agree to prior to the signing of the Declaration of Principles) it was more appropriate for Rantisi to visit *him*. Rantisi refused, believing that his visiting Arafat would place Hamas in a difficult position, as a supplicant to a man that he, Rantisi, believed was plotting with Israel to destroy his movement. Perhaps inevitably—and fearful that there might not be any meeting at all—Rantisi conceded, agreeing to meet the PLO leader at his headquarters. Rantisi viewed this as a concession: He had not wanted it to appear that he actually acknowledged Arafat's standing, and he did not want to be cast as a leader who was congratulating Arafat on his agreement with Israel. The meeting was set for a hot Gaza afternoon in late August 1994, just after midday prayers.

When Rantisi arrived at Arafat's headquarters, the PLO leader kept him waiting. Rantisi was told to sit in the hallway outside Arafat's office until Arafat finished what he was doing. Rantisi reluctantly agreed but viewed this otherwise innocent request as a deliberate humiliation that was intended to keep him in his place. "We're sorry to keep you waiting, Dr. Rantisi," an Arafat aide said, "but the chairman is quite busy now."

Rantisi paced the hallway for twenty minutes, his anger rising, before Arafat emerged to greet him. Arafat was smiling broadly and kissed Rantisi on both cheeks, in a traditional greeting between friends, but he did not apologize for keeping the Hamas leader waiting. Arm in arm and exchanging pleasantries, Arafat and Rantisi entered Arafat's office and closed the door behind them. What happened next is now a part of Palestinian political lore, related again and again by Arafat's aides as proof of their leader's strength and patience.

According to an Arafat aide, Rantisi began to shout—his voice coming through the door and into the hallway. "You are traitor to the Palestinian cause," Rantisi shouted, "and you have betrayed the Palestinian people." For a seemingly interminable amount of time, Rantisi ticked off Arafat's crimes: He had come to an agreement "with the Zionist entity"; he had "made friends with criminals"; he had "sold the birthright of the Palestinian people"; he had "divided families and tribes" and "ensured the permanent dispossession of our nation." According to Arafat's own account of the meeting, he sat impassively and without emotion behind his desk throughout this tirade, eyeing Rantisi with disdain. Eventually, Rantisi ended his condemnation and fell silent.

Arafat leaned back in his chair, digesting what Rantisi had said. But then, leaning forward, he asked him a simple question: "What is it that you *want?*" Rantisi thought for only a moment: "Forty seats in the Palestinian legislature," he said.

THE EXCHANGE BETWEEN Arafat and Rantisi raises the single most important question about terrorist organizations: Are they political parties capable of political engagement? Or are they intractable and uncompromising networks bent only on exacting pain and promoting violence? Are terrorist organizations worth talking to?

In Amman in 2005, Ra'ad al-Hamdani argued that the al-Anbar insurgency was not a terrorist network but a national resistance movement answering to a well-defined Sunni constituency. The "terrorists" in Iraq, he said, were "outsiders" interested in the revolutionary transformation of Muslim society. The national resistance movement had legitimacy, he said, whereas the terrorists were "Salafists" and "takfiris"—"the unsmiling young bearded men in robes" (as Talal al-Gaood described them) who were intent on fighting "the infidel." These outsiders weren't interested in democracy or Iraq; they were interested in following the dictates of their version of Islam.

The difference between insurgents and terrorists, he argued, consisted simply in this: National resistance movements were political, defensible, legitimate, and constituent-based. Terrorist organizations, on the other hand, were interested in only one thing: the radical transformation of society. They wanted to burn it down and start over. The key was not only to separate insurgents from terrorists but, as al-Hamdani argued, to "reject the easy language of terrorism."

In his influential book *A Fundamental Fear*, Dr. Salman Sayyid, a research fellow at the University of Leeds, questions the premises underlying the war on terror and writes eloquently on "the language of terrorism." As he notes, "By establishing a frontier between the 'international community' on the one hand and terrorists and rogue states on the other, the 'war against terrorism' becomes close to being 'a war without limits,' since those who are not members of the 'international community' cannot be considered its peers, and thus they have no legitimate right to exist."

Sayyid argues that the current relationship between "the West" and Islam is actually a repetition of the colonial relationship the United States and Europe have maintained with the peoples of the Middle East. "The articulation of an 'international community' in opposition to (Islamist) terrorism replays the colonial discourse of a world order that is organized in terms of civilization and barbarism," he says. "By defining the opponents of the current world order as external to that order, the 'war against terrorism' can be waged with a savagery similar to that used by the colonial powers to pacify their 'savages.'" Sayyid articulates the assumptions about "terrorist organizations" promoted by Western policymakers: that terrorist organizations use violence for political ends, that they oppose "modernity," that they seek to overthrow the rule of law, that they advocate erasing the line between church and state (or mosque and state), and that they support the overthrow of the world order. Because of this, Sayyid argues, Western policymakers believe that terrorist organizations lie outside the protections offered by both natural law and civil society.

There is also, as Sayyid implies, a racial component to the war on terror. Terrorists are not simply outside of the pale of civilization; they are savages. Thus, advocates of talking with terrorists are deluded. There is nothing to talk about, because terrorists have nothing to say.

This characterization is reflected in the words of prominent Western leaders and policymakers. The case was best put by former Spanish prime minister José Maria Aznar during a visit to the White House in May 2002. "But [what] I would like to say once again is that we can establish no differences among terrorists," he said. "They're all the same. They're all seeking to destroy our harmonious co-existence, to destroy civilization. They're seeking to destroy our democracy and freedoms." For Aznar, terrorism was not simply a temporary political threat; rather, it was an existential danger. He agreed with Paul Wolfowitz: Terrorists are Nazis. The events of 9/11, Aznar said, "threw down a calculated challenge to the values of our core humanity, freedom, moral decency, compassion and respect for the lives of others."

Aznar was not the only political leader to draw stark contrasts between uncivilized terrorists and "those with values." On February 6, 2004, Russian president Vladimir Putin endorsed Aznar's views: "But the commonly accepted international principle of fighting terror is an unconditional refusal to hold any dialogue with terrorists, as any contact with bandits and terrorists [encourages] them to commit new, even bloodier crimes," he said. These views have formed the basis of America's war on terror, where talking with terrorists was viewed as negotiating with them—and thus giving them "legitimacy."

"Terror must be stopped," President Bush said in the immediate aftermath of the 9/11 incidents. "No nation can negotiate with terrorists. For there is no way to make peace with those whose only goal is death." The administration never softened this stance, even when urged to do so by friends and allies. As late as May 15, 2008, Bush characterized discussions with terrorists as an endorsement of evil. Once again, terrorism was compared to Nazism: "As Nazi tanks crossed into Poland in 1939," Bush said, "an American senator declared, 'Lord, if only I could have talked to Hitler, all of this might have been avoided.' We have an obligation to call this what it is—the false comfort of appeasement, which has been repeatedly discredited by history."

Bush's views met with broad support not only by policymakers but also by academics. Professors John Bew and Martyn Frampton—in a paper for the Jerusalem Center for Public Affairs—point out that those who argue against talking to terrorists do so because there are "clear pitfalls to negotiation, as much as there are potential benefits. In some instances, the willingness of the state to negotiate might encourage the terrorists to believe that their opponents are ready to concede—even when this was not the case. It can also strengthen the perception that it is their violent campaign that has delivered results." Bew and Frampton's reflection of these policymaking arguments rests on their view of "legitimacy": that talking alone confers legitimacy, whereas not talking denies it.

Other academics, however, chipped away at Bush's notion. In a seminal paper on the subject, scholar Stacey Pettyjohn provided an exhaustive analysis of the reasons why mediators, practitioners, or states (in particular) might open discussions with terrorist organizations—among them: that there are no "alternative groups" that can provide a solution to a conflict, that the organization has abandoned the use of violence to achieve its political aims, that the terrorist organization is openly seeking a compromise solution to a conflict, or that the terrorist organization is in a weak position and is seen as malleable. Pettyjohn constructs a useful matrix of when governments might negotiate with terrorists, noting that although it might be difficult to assess a terrorist organization's motives for wanting to talk, judging a nonstate actor's intentions remains the single most important factor in making that judgment.

In his book *Making Peace*, George Mitchell reminds us of perhaps one of the most useful reasons for talking with terrorist organizations: because not talking to them will not end a conflict. As he notes, an earlier set of negotiations that attempted to resolve the conflict in Northern Ireland—talks that took place in 1991 and 1992—ultimately collapsed because they did not include armed organizations: "Those negotiations failed, in part . . . because they did not include the political parties associated with the paramilitary organizations; as a result, the negotiations were not accompanied by a cessation of violence."

The decision of whether or not to talk to terrorists begs an even more important question: Which terrorists should governments talk *to*? Mediators can answer the question of *whether* to talk by gauging the "legitimacy" of a terrorist organization. After all, the standard argument of those who believe that talking with terrorist organizations is always wrong (because it offers "the false comfort of appeasement") is that talking to terrorists confers on them a legitimacy they do not already have. Political scientist Robert Nozick has suggested that legitimacy is not conferred, but earned. Using this standard, terrorist organizations have legitimacy if they represent constituents—if they have political support in the first place.

Applying this test yields interesting results. Those who would talk to Hamas, Hezbollah, the Muslim Brotherhood, or Pakistan's Jamat i-Islami would be able to argue that doing so only confirms these organization's claims to political legitimacy—the four groups actually represent robust constituencies and all of them have participated in democratic elections. The same would not be true for al Qaeda, Lebanon's Fatah al-Islam, the German Red Brigades, or the Abu Nidal Organization, which are not political organizations answering to a well-defined population but political networks answering to no one. Assessing legitimacy remains the core means of determining not only whether to talk to terrorists, but when and for what purpose.

But even though the intellectual foundations for the war on terror have been progressively chipped away in the years since 9/11, Western policymakers continued their defense of their views well into the final years of the Bush administration. In the January 2007 issue of *Foreign Affairs*, then British prime minister Tony Blair endorsed the hard-line view shared by Aznar and Putin, writing that the war on terror "is not a clash between civilizations; it is a clash about civilization. It is the age-old battle between progress and reaction, between those who embrace the modern world and those who reject its existence—between optimism and hope, on the one hand, and pessimism and fear, on the other." To this day, Blair's views have been echoed by senior U.S. policymakers, including former presidential candidate John McCain, whose 2008 defense of the invasion of Iraq was structured in terms of a war between those who have "Judeo-Christian values" and those who don't: "This just wasn't the elimination of a threat to Iraq—this was elimination of a threat to the West, part of this titanic struggle we are in between western Judeo-Christian values and principles and Islamic extremists."

During the Bush years, these views were regularly communicated to and parroted by those whose job it is to implement Middle East policy. In the summer of 2005, a State Department official in the office of the undersecretary of public diplomacy and public affairs stated that the "war on terrorism" was being conducted "to end violence." When it was pointed out that the United States was using violence at that very moment (in Iraq and elsewhere) and that the prosecution of a "war" on terrorism implied the use of violence, the official was puzzled. "What is it you're saying?" she asked. Upon hearing the answer—that in the war on terror the United States and its allies had made violence a central part of its strategy (including the questionable invasion of a nonbelligerent state whose leader said that he too opposed terrorism)—the official was dismissive: "That's different," she said. "Terrorists use violence because they don't have values; we use violence to spread democracy." That is to say, as Sayyid notes, it is perfectly defensible to wage a war without limits against terrorists, because they lie outside those protections offered by God and government. We have values; they do not. Our violence is good; theirs is bad. When they kill us, it's "terrorism"; when we kill them, it's self-defense.

That terrorists are barbarians and have nothing to say is an established tradition of Western thinkers. Paul of Tarsus likened nonbelievers to "barbarians" who lived in darkness: When he spoke of "Christ crucified" they refused to listen; when they spoke of "the gods" he refused to hear: "Therefore if I know not the meaning of the voice, I shall be unto him that speaketh a barbarian, and he that speaketh shall be a barbarian unto me." Paul refused to listen not because the pagans could not be heard but because they had nothing to say.

Western officials have, at times, adopted Paul's language, describing those they label as terrorists as a class of new barbarians whose words are without content. When an FBI counterterrorism official was asked for his views on a video of Ayman al-Zawahiri, a prominent al Qaeda leader, he responded with a shrug: "It's the same old jihadist rigmarole," he said. Thus, terrorists not only have nothing to say, what they say is meaningless.

Do TERRORISTS HAVE anything to say? In August 2004—just one month after the first meeting between the marines and the Iraqi insurgency in Amman, Jordan—a delegation of Americans and Europeans traveled to Beirut to meet with the leadership of the Islamic Resistance Movement (Hamas) and the Lebanese Party of God—Hezbollah.

The purpose of the trip was to provide an opening to Islamist political organizations listed as terrorist entities by the United States. Delegation members believed their effort would begin a process that might persuade Western governments to open discussions with political movements whose legitimacy was derived from a broad base of popular support in their own communities and who were participating in or had agreed to participate in democratic elections. The delegation included Bobby Muller, a well-known American veterans' advocate and an activist recognized for his leadership of the international landmines campaign; Dr. Beverley Milton-Edwards, a professor at Queens College, Belfast, and an expert on Palestinian security issues and Hamas; Alastair Crooke, who had served the British government in numerous overseas assignments from South Africa to Afghanistan; and the author of this book, who has served as an unofficial adviser to the Palestinian leadership and has worked with Muller on the landmines campaign and with Milton-Edwards and Crooke in the West Bank and Gaza.

The delegates knew their meetings would be controversial: Both Hamas and Hezbollah were on U.S. and E.U. lists of proscribed terrorist organizations, both had been accused of participating in the targeting of and killing of civilians, and both had vowed enmity to Israel, which maintains close ties to the United States and its European allies. Each of the members of this delegation believed that opening discussions with Hamas and Hezbollah and other Islamist political movements in the Middle East could provide a way out of the present morass. Since the tragedy of 9/11, the delegates believed, the West had adopted policies that undermined its goals in the war on terror. Western policies reflected not only an undifferentiated view of Islamist organizations, but a mistaken conflation of moderate, pro-democracy groups with the network of radical Salafists that had attacked the United States.

Are Hamas, Hezbollah, and the Muslim Brotherhood terrorist organizations (in the same sense as al Qaeda or its network)? Or are they more moderate groups open to political dialogue and change? The public statements of Hezbollah and Hamas reflected a desire to reinforce their political legitimacy by participating in elections and shaping programs to meet the needs of their constituencies: Hezbollah was engaged in a national parliamentary campaign in Lebanon in which its candidates were gaining increasing support, and Hamas was then considering entering candidates in the planned Palestinian parliamentary elections of January 2006. Both organizations had condemned the events of 9/11, both had publicly stated their willingness to open contacts with the United States and its allies, both had committed to providing broad support to their constituencies, and, though both maintained that their conflict with Israel was legitimate, they had not ruled out a political resolution of that war. Both movements argued that their fight with Israel had nothing to do with the West, that neither the United States nor its European allies were their enemy.

The delegation was one of the first to seek an opening with these groups and work to reassure its interlocutors that it was not their intention to engage in lectures or to present ultimatums in advance of discussions. They told the leaders of both movements that it was their intention to listen—not just talk—and proposed that they describe the meetings as "an exercise in mutual listening."

After several preliminary meetings, the group convened two larger engagements, bringing to Beirut a group that included former senior U.S. and British diplomats and retired officers of Western intelligence services. These meetings took place with both groups in three-day sessions in March and July 2005. Every one of the visiting delegates had served in the Middle East, often in conflict situations. All of the American and European delegates knew the history of the groups they would be speaking with, and all were familiar with those groups' senior leaders and political goals. Many on the delegation had served in high-level positions as ambassadors, military officers, or senior officials in Western intelligence services. Although the talks with the leaders of political Islam were not a secret, the meetings themselves were private. Because of the sensitivity of the topics covered, a number of the Western delegates preferred that their participation not be highlighted and that statements made during the more informal sessions that occurred between sessions not be publicized. The delegations included the original four organizers of the conference, plus three former officers of the CIA, a well-known television producer, a former member of the Mitchell Commission, a former ambassador, two Middle East activists, and the head of a U.S. foundation focused on the Middle East.

In no sense could it be said that any member of the American or European delegation arrived in Beirut sympathetic to the groups with whom they were speaking. A number of delegates were anxious to confront their interlocutors over their use of violence. A number of others were skeptical of any of the groups' claims for engagement with the United States. Nearly all of the Western delegates had lost close friends in the region's conflicts.

The exchange began by forgoing formal presentations by the U.S. and European delegates. Instead, the leaders of the movements were asked to address a specific topic: "How do you view the current situation in the Middle East and what would you like the region to look like twenty-five years from now?" The conveners of the exchange also believed it was important that the organizations be comfortable with the meeting's format, which was specially designed so that the organizations would (to use practitioner David Steele's phrase) "feel heard."

The meeting was held on neutral ground in a Beirut hotel, and the format for the meeting reversed the standard model used in negotiations, where presenters and hearers were equal participants. In the Beirut meetings the delegations were not viewed as equal; the leaders of the movements were given prominence. "We made it clear from the beginning that we were there to listen to what they had to say," a participant confirmed. "They could dictate the pace of the meetings and the focus of the discussion. They were the presenters, our role was to ask questions." Other mediators have used the same technique; during the first Amman meeting with the Sunni insurgency in July 2004, for instance, the American delegation spent the first hours of the meeting listening. The effect of this, particularly in the Beirut exchange, was that the "terrorists" were made to feel that this was their meeting, and not the Americans'.

Because language is a tool of power, the arrangement of the March and July conferences in Beirut in 2005 (as well as the meetings in Amman in 2004) reversed the power equation, so that the organizations represented could express their identity, as well as their political and social views, without interruption. But the underlying, and real, purpose of the arrangement was to allow the leaders of the "terrorist organizations" in attendance to define *themselves* and so to answer the specific questions posed by their critics: Did they "use violence for political ends"? Did they "oppose

'modernity'"? Did they "seek to overthrow the rule of law"? Did
they wish to "erase the line between mosque and state"? Did they
seek to "overthrow the world order"? The answers to the questions
were not predictable and resulted in an exchange on the nature of
government, society, culture, and religion that was at once complex and differentiated.

"Our discussions were blunt, touching on nearly all the subjects
sensitive to the groups and to the West: suicide bombings, attacks
on Israel, the compatibility of democracy and Islamic law, philoso-
phies of governance, the compatibility of Islamic economics and
globalization, their views on al Qaeda and radical Islam—as well
as issues of particular interest to them," Geoffrey "Jeff" Aronson—
the director of research and publications at the Foundation for
Middle East Peace and an important participant in the March and
July meetings—later noted.

The exchanges in Beirut in March began with a presentation
by the Islamic Resistance Movement.

THE ISLAMIC RESISTANCE Movement traces its roots to Egypt's
Muslim Brotherhood or, more properly, to the *al-ikhwān al-muslimūn*
(Society of Muslim Brothers). The Muslim Brotherhood, founded
in 1928 by Hassan al-Banna, an Egyptian schoolteacher, grew into a
significant political movement throughout the region over a period
of two decades, and it still ranks as the single most important political movement in Egypt. Less important in other parts of North
Africa, the Muslim Brotherhood remains immensely popular in
Egypt, Jordan, the West Bank, and Gaza and has a presence in
nearly all Muslim societies. Although the movement's adherents
have been censured in the West as "radical Islamists" and in Egypt
as "unrepentant jihadists," al Qaeda's Ayman al-Zawahiri actually
sees the group as an enemy of Islam and condemns it for participating in the democratic process in Egypt, for "luring thousands of
young Muslim men into lines for elections . . . instead of into the

line of jihad." Al-Zawahiri's condemnation is particularly interesting: Now al Qaeda's number two leader, he was once the "emir" of Egypt's Islam Jihad, whose goal was the overthrow of the Egyptian state and the establishment of a caliphate.

The leadership of the Egyptian Muslim Brotherhood has been condemned by the Egyptian government over the last four decades as intransigent (the head of Egyptian intelligence, Omar Suleiman, told one American audience that they were "incapable of change"), but it has responded with a "testament" on the movement's beliefs and its commitment to peaceful reform under the rule of law. This testament, written by Egyptian Muslim Brotherhood deputy chairman Mohammad Ma'mum el-Hudaibi, remains the most articulate exposition of the movement's goals. In it, el-Hudaibi defends the brotherhood as being "afflicted by an overwhelming assault which has portrayed them as savage and primitive people devoid of sensitivity, rational capacity and practical experience of the means of development and progress and of denying others the right to life, liberty and freedom of thought. This depiction has caused the World to negatively suspect almost every Muslim and Islamic person, institution, etc."

Although the Muslim Brotherhood is widely viewed in the Middle East as a credible political movement dedicated to working within a democratic framework, most American and European officials and journalists claim otherwise. Their view mimics that of the Egyptian government, which has worked to undermine the movement since the mid-1950s, when it accused the movement of being a fundamentalist and revolutionary organization. The Egyptian government continues to harass the movement and regularly jails its leaders. Veteran journalist Douglas Farah dismisses the brotherhood's claim to democratic principles as "a charm offensive," current White House Middle East adviser Dennis Ross claims the brotherhood uses violence to promote its political agenda, and former White House counterterrorism chief Juan Zarate describes the brotherhood as "a group that worries us not because it deals with philosophical or ideological ideas but because it defends the use of violence against civilians." British scholar Azzam Tamimi, perhaps the foremost thinker on the Muslim Brotherhood and Hamas, disagrees with the portrait, saying that the movement is rooted in its commitment to constituent services. The Muslim Brothers of today are noted for their roots among Egypt's poor, and it is this that gives them their popularity, he notes. Through the years, the Muslim Brotherhood has either given birth to countless other Islamist movements in the region or has served as a model for political action for other organizations. This is particularly true for the Hamas—the Palestinian Islamic Resistance Movement.

The Islamic Resistance Movement was created in 1987 in Gaza as an offshoot of the Egyptian Muslim Brotherhood in response to Israeli military actions resulting from the First Intifada. Like the Muslim Brotherhood, Hamas takes pride in its network of social programs, which include the establishment and operation of schools, clinics, social and athletic clubs, women's organizations, day-care centers, orphanages, tutoring services, mosque-centered programs, and universities and colleges. "The Brothers are always the first on the streets after any disaster," an Egyptian official notes with chagrin, "while our government makes sure the military is there, with their guns, to protect property. The difference between the responses is significant, I would think." Like that of the Muslim Brotherhood, the Islamic Resistance Movement's primary social and political focus is noncontroversial: It is constituent-based, though it has clearly undergone periods of extreme militancy.

The leadership of the movement, Tamimi notes, is not unlike that of any other mainstream political movement. It is governed by a political bureau that mixes leaders from constituent political organizations with grassroots labor, women's, and social groups. The organizational leadership is popularly elected from polling among small neighborhood groups that takes place during regular organizational meetings in schools, mosques, and community centers. It is not unknown for the top leadership to be replaced—as happened when Musa Abu Marzouk, the head of Hamas's political and military bureau, was defeated in an election by the movement's current leader, Khalid Meshaal. Additionally, unlike the Egyptian Muslim Brotherhood, Hamas derived at least a part of early senior leadership cadre from disaffected members of a rival political organization (in this case from Fatah—the Palestinian mainstream organization of Yasser Arafat).

A thumbnail sketch of Hamas's current known leadership provides some illuminating examples of a central truth: The best-known members of its political committee are well educated and politically sophisticated. Few of the leaders of Hamas can be considered "street captains" in the ordinary sense of the term. The political committee of Hamas is headed by a physicist (Khalid Meshaal), who is assisted in his leadership role by a doctor, a chemist, an engineer, and two leaders with degrees in Arabic literature. The initial cluster of Muslim Brotherhood activists around Hamas's founder Sheikh Ahmad Yassin were student activists. Ibrahim al-Maqadmah, Isma'il Abu Shanab, Abd al-Aziz Awdah, Fathi al-Shiqaqi, and Musa Abu Marzouk were all student activists. The Hamas leadership that has emerged in the wake of the January 2006 elections in Palestine mirror this trend. Palestinian prime minister Ismail Haniyeh has a degree in Arabic literature, Mahmoud al-Zahar (the Palestinian foreign minister) studied medicine in Cairo, Hasan Yousef and Jamila Shanti (a woman) have advanced degrees. The other core leaders of the group are as well educated: Omar Abdul Razeeq is a professor of economics, Mariam Salah has a master's degree in Islamic law, Nayef Rajoub is a poet (and beekeeper), Yusuf Rizqa is the president of the College of Arts of the Islamic University, and Atif Adwan (the head of refugee affairs) is a political scientist and the author of eighteen books.

Strangely, perhaps, the rank and file in Gaza contains not simply a sprinkling of those whom we ("we" in the West) would consider militants, but also a large number of businessmen and women as well as shopkeepers, lawyers, pharmacists, and leaders of service organizations. This is not reflective of an organization or an organizational leadership that "rejects modernity."

THE HAMAS LEADERSHIP present for the first meeting of western delegates in March 2005 included Sami Khatar, Musa Abu Marzouk, and Usamah Hamdan—all senior members of the Hamas leadership. Khatar was soft-spoken, but articulate, the apparent philosopher of the three and one of the most controversial member of the Hamas leadership. He freely criticizes Israel and the United States and was outspoken in his condemnation of American policies. His radicalism is well known. Musa Abu Marzouk and Usamah Hamdan were the best known of the Hamas representatives. Born in Gaza, Abu Marzouk—an engineer educated in the United States—is the deputy head of the organization's political bureau and was indicted in the United States for conspiring to violate U.S. laws prohibiting the funding of terrorist organizations. He spent time in a U.S. prison before being expelled first to Jordan and then to Syria. Usamah Hamdan is the head of the organization's bureau of external affairs and has a Ph.D. in chemistry. Tireless, even tempered, and with a quick sense of humor, Hamdan is the most recognizable face of the Islamic Resistance Movement, appearing often on international news channels.

The three began their presentation with a statement of Hamas's political beliefs and goals. "We will continue the struggle to provide national unity, to stop Israeli aggression. We will participate in Palestinian elections, we will establish the framework for rebuilding the Palestine Liberation Organization to represent all Palestinians, we will offer a truce with Israel, and we will continue our work to make certain that Israel abandons the West Bank, Gaza, and Jerusalem," Abu Marzouk said. "We do not endorse murder, but we do support resistance."

Abu Marzouk's statement was significant: His formula—that Hamas would fight Israel until it "abandons" the West Bank, Gaza, and Jerusalem—was the first indication that the movement had rethought its goals of establishing a Palestinian state on all the lands of the former British Mandate and of destroying the Jewish state. His statement contradicted the movement's charter, which was explicit in calling for Israel's destruction. "The charter is not the Koran," he said. "It can be amended." The offer of a truce (*hudna*) was also new, though the Hamas delegation argued that their offer of a truce to Israel had been a position of the organization since 1993. "We are willing to resolve the differences we have with Israel that are the easiest to resolve," Usamah Hamdan said, "and those most difficult problems we can wait to resolve. There is much blood between us and perhaps in a generation we can return to those questions, after tempers have cooled. A long-term solution can wait for a later time, but now perhaps it is enough that, if Israel will withdraw to its borders, we can live in peace with them for a generation."

The idea that Palestinians could live in peace with Israelis for a generation—effectively postponing the most intransigent of issues between them—is based on a well-established principle in Islamic history. A kind of cease-fire, a *hudna,* lies somewhere between outright war and total peace. It allows tempers to cool during a period in which there would be no conflict. "The idea for a *hudna* began in 1993," Sami Khatar explained. "Hamas proposed a *Hudna* before Oslo although after the signing of the Oslo Accord the concept of *hudna* became outdated. In 2001 the opportunity to issue a *hudna* arose again after the Camp David talks failed. We felt then that it was nearly impossible to use the Oslo process as a way forward. We said that Sheik Yassin [would] announce the *hudna* because he was the founder of Hamas. We offered a long truce—a ten-year truce—if Israel would make concessions. This would end violence, and it would be good for the Palestinian people. It would leave hope for our future." He concluded: "We believe that the *hudna* reveals two things in particular. The first is that Hamas and Palestine are ready to discuss practical ideas with the Israelis. The second is that we are still committed to the *hudna* despite Israeli aggression, but we cannot guarantee that this will always be the case."

Abu Marzouk's statement about democracy was also one of the first indications that Hamas would agree to run candidates in upcoming 2006 Palestinian parliamentary elections. "We believe in democracy and we are a democratic organization," Sami Khatar said. "We are confident in our support from the people and we will serve in any government that is elected, whether we win or lose." Later, in a private conversation, Usamah Hamdan confirmed that—should the movement gain a majority of seats in the Palestinian parliament—it would present a name to be considered for prime minister. "The decision will be made by consensus among the leaders of the organization," he said. Abu Marzouk presented Hamas's decision to participate in the elections as a natural result of the movement's principles: "We are a democratic organization and are confident that we will gain the support of the people," he said, "and there is no question in our minds that we will win."

Sami Khatar was outspoken in his view that, should Hamas win the parliamentary elections, the United States would not accept the results: "The Palestinians decide their leaders, and the international community must accept that. And when we win those elections, it will be a great problem for the Americans, I am sure. Is the international community going to ignore these elections, the results of the elections?" The leaders noted that although they believe that "Islam is comprehensive," they understand that the Palestinian people are diverse "and the people have to decide who will lead them and what [type] of government we will have. And we must respect those differences and we *will* respect those differences." He went on to note, "We want a democratic process. We want to be part of the political reality in Palestine, but not to have all the power. The resistance of Hamas will continue as long as occupation remains. Hamas is both progressive and moderate. We have no problem with communicating with the E.U., U.K., or U.S."

Hamas's long period of targeting Israeli civilians in a series of bloody bombings of cafés and buses during the Second Intifada was the topic of the most detailed exchange during this March discussion and was the subject that required the greatest premeeting preparation on the part of the attending Americans and Europeans. "Our goal was not to talk about morality, or to condemn," Jeff Aronson said, "but to explore the political reason behind the decision—to draw out the decision-making process."

Because of the importance and sensitivity of the issue, it was the final subject of the exchange. Even so, the discussion on the topic took several hours, with long periods of silence between questions and answers. "It was fascinating, and painful, and uncomfortable" an American delegation member noted, "but it was necessary." Initially, Hamas leaders defended their actions by citing their right to lawful resistance, but as the discussion progressed, the organization's leaders propounded an increasingly assertive defense of their tactics, noting at one point that their decision had not been made lightly or without reflection and that it had only been undertaken after it became clear that Israel refused to reciprocate a Hamas offer to end the targeting of civilians.

"We are against targeting civilians," Abu Marzouk said,

and we did not do so until 1994—after the Hebron Mosque massacre [perpetrated by Israeli settler Baruch Goldstein]. And they built a shrine to him [Goldstein] in Hebron. And at that point, since we were never attacked in that way before, we determined that Israelis kill civilians. But no one asks about Palestinian civilians. In the last five years, 347 Palestinian civilians have been killed. The numbers you see are exactly reversed for Israeli and Palestinian deaths. What about the targeting of civilians who are Palestinian? And the homes and the farms of Palestinians that are destroyed? The Israelis have rejected our offer, and we have made the offer, that both sides should stop killing civilians. But they rejected that offer.

When pressed on their targeting of civilians, Hamas leaders expressed their conviction that there is no distinction between Israeli civilians and soldiers. "Every Israeli is a soldier," one of them said. "Settlers are armed." When asked whether, in their view, terrorism worked—that is, whether it yielded political benefits—the Hamas delegates answered that it served to unite their people and to gain support for their political program.

Aronson pressed the point: "How did you make the decision?" he asked. "And after you made the decision, did it keep you awake at night?" Aronson's dual questions were disquieting: If the Hamas leaders answered that the decisions kept them "awake at night," then the next logical questions would have been, would you like to sleep better? If, on the other hand, the decision did not keep them awake at night, then the next logical question would have been, what kind of people are you?

There was only a slight hesitation, though the answer was carefully framed:

If our tactics work, then Palestinians feel they are defending themselves. It wasn't so easy losing our founders, our people, our leaders, and our friends. When all channels are closed to us, we use violence. We don't have jets; we don't have tanks. So we made the decision. It is one of the ways we resist; it is not the only way. We don't agree to be considered terrorists by the U.S. administration. We didn't wage war on the United States, not even verbally. Why did the U.S. administration take such a decision to make us terrorists? We have never ever expressed a link with Osama bin Laden, and we don't support him.

The discussion ended. "Their description of terrorism," one of the delegates noted, "convinced me that we are not dealing with genetically encoded monsters, but hard-headed—albeit brutal—political actors who carefully choose their tactics and attempt to manage the effects of their actions. Just as we do."

At the time of the meetings with Hamas, there had been no suicide bombings in Israel since August 2004. Hamas leaders signaled that this unofficial calm would be maintained, so long as it was reciprocated by Israel. Even in the wake of the collapse of the Palestinian unity government and the Hamas takeover of Gaza, the calm persisted—and persists still, despite the December 2008 Israeli attack on Gaza, which claimed 1,430 Palestinian lives. Yet Hamas leaders said that they retain the right to respond to "Israeli aggression," just as (as they pointed out) Israel said that it had the right to continue targeting Palestinians it viewed as ticking bombs.

THE ISLAMIC RESISTANCE Movement won the January 2006 Palestinian parliamentary elections and moved to form a Hamas-led government. But within days of their electoral victory, Hamas leaders expressed a willingness to unify their ticket with the defeated Fatah movement in order to form a unity government that could "represent all factions of the Palestinian people." The Bush administration responded to the Hamas victory with surprise, though then secretary of state Condoleezza Rice had been warned of the impending victory through a number of channels.

Within weeks, the Bush administration was pressuring Palestinian president Mahmoud Abbas [Abu Mazen] to refuse all participation in any unity effort. The pressure was explicit: During a meeting with Abu Mazen at the United Nations, Bush said that Fatah could expect the United States to withhold funding from his movement if there were any unity talks. The resulting paralysis in the Palestinian political environment threatened to spark an open war between the two organizations. But as the situation worsened throughout 2006, Saudi Arabia stepped in to mediate the dispute. In March 2007, during a meeting convened by the Saudi's King Abdullah in Mecca, Hamas and Fatah leaders agreed to govern together.

In the aftermath of the Mecca meeting, President Bush signed a "finding" directing the CIA to fund an armed opposition movement that would unseat Hamas leaders in Gaza. Millions of dollars were poured into the Fatah security services, and Egypt became a launching point for an American-funded initiative that would confront Hamas throughout the Gaza Strip. Although reports circulated in the region that U.S. Lieutenant General Keith Dayton, who continues to oversee the training of the Palestinian Security Services, was in favor of the program, a senior officer at CENTCOM headquarters who knows Dayton and is familiar with the operation denies the claim: "This was a CIA operation," this officer said; "Dayton had nothing to do with it. He thought the idea was stupid." Dayton was not alone. Senior Israeli officials refused to provide heavy arms to the CIA-funded Palestinian militia, believing that Fatah was not politically credible enough to win the support of the Palestinian people. "We told the CIA that this wouldn't work," an Israeli politician said. "You can hurt Hamas, you can bloody Hamas, but you can't destroy Hamas. We knew that." In June 2007, fearing the increased strength of Fatah gunmen in Gaza and faced with a deterioration of security, the Hamas militia struck first.

In the United States, this "Hamas coup" is still viewed as stark evidence that the Islamic Resistance Movement represents an extremist current that is uncompromising and opposed to democracy.

But the claim is not believed in the Arab world, where America's role in the "coup" is viewed as evidence that, despite its rhetoric, the United States is committed more to the defense of Israel than to its own democratic principles. In truth, the role of the United States in undermining Hamas in the wake of the 2006 elections that gave them a majority in the Palestinian parliament remains a deep stain on America's avowed support for democracy. It places us on the side of the Arab dictators.

Hamas remains on the State Department list of proscribed organizations, a fact that has long enraged Hamas's leadership. "We knew we were going to be put on the list, and so, in 1996, we tried to communicate with [then secretary of state] Madeleine Albright to find a way to object—to talk with her about the decision," Usamah Hamdan says. "We were told that she was unavailable to talk with us and that we should call back. We were then put on the list and we made our second call, and we were told, 'We're sorry, but secretary Albright doesn't talk to terrorists.'"

CHAPTER SIX

HEZBOLLAH

"That is their nature."
—Shimon Peres

In a dramatic scene from the 2005 movie *Syriana*, George Clooney—playing a CIA officer named Bob Barnes—visits his contact in southern Beirut. Making such a visit can be treacherous. Not everyone has the courage of Bob Barnes, but then Bob has a job to do and college tuitions to pay. He takes a cab from the airport into southern Beirut, where men with guns stand on street corners and eye him from the rooftops while crowds of people jostle in the markets. Suddenly, the cab is stopped at a gate, and a group of men grab Bob and hustle him into another car. He is thrown into the back seat. A black hood is yanked over his head and the car speeds off, wheels squealing. Later, in a quiet, air-conditioned room, Bob faces his contact, a man of stature, named Sheikh Hashimi. He has a business proposition for a friend, Bob tells Hashimi. That is the only reason he is in Beirut. "I thought it would be prudent to say," he intones, "I have no interest in Hezbollah. This is business and it doesn't concern Hezbollah." Hashimi nods: "If what you say is true," he responds, "consider yourself welcome in Lebanon."

Unfortunately, as it turns out, Bob has crossed some kind of line. Following his reassurance to Sheikh Hashimi (after a few complex plot turns), Barnes is kidnapped from his hotel and driven to a seedy warehouse in southern Beirut. There, his hands are duct-taped to a chair. The "friend" Bob was attempting to contact, a man named Mussawi, enters the room, pliers in hand. "Bob," he says, "you're going to give me the name of every person who has taken money from you." When Bob refuses, Mussawi yanks out one of his fingernails. "You're a P-O-fucking-W," Mussawi shouts; "give me the names." As Mussawi puts a knife to Bob's neck—and just in the nick of time—Sheikh Hashimi enters the room. The sheikh is offended by Mussawi. Is this the way that we treat our guests? This implied criticism, and the sheikh's very presence (as a man of great learning), is enough to save Bob.

Although in the film the sheikh is named Hashimi, he is the spitting image of a young Mohammad Hussein Fadlallah, who some American policymakers claim was once (and others claim is still) the spiritual leader of Hezbollah. So Bob is saved, but as he passes out from the pain inflicted by Mussawi, his eyes focus on a postcard advertisement for an orphanage. The postcard is propped against a bottle of Mecca Cola: "Consider a donation on your way out of Beirut," it reads.

Syriana was one of the more popular movies of 2005, and Clooney's characterization of Bob Barnes won him an Oscar. For those familiar with the region and its history, the film remains memorable—a conflation of three or four well-known stories about the CIA, American policy, oil, Hezbollah, and the rise of al Qaeda. The film is also winkingly subversive, implying that America itself is responsible for its own mess in the region.

That heresy was not lost on conservative commentators, who excoriated Hollywood for promoting an anti-American message. *Washington Post* columnist Charles Krauthammer viewed the film as worse than typically liberal. "Most liberalism is angst- and guilt-ridden, seeing moral equivalence everywhere," he said. "Syriana is of a different species entirely—a pathological variety that burns with the certainty of its malign anti-Americanism. Osama bin Laden could not have scripted this film with more conviction."

Syriana repeats a number of well-worn clichés: the rich emir with fast cars, the high-tech CIA situation room, spy satellites that can see into pocketbooks, the naive but well-meaning young oil wizard (played by Matt Damon), the tough but bighearted CIA veteran who is struggling to pay the bills. And, of course, Beirut itself: Where gun-toting Hezbollah *shabab*, the "boys," live among impoverished hovels and billboards celebrating the martyrs of the resistance. When not plotting against Israel (or "the West"), these boys spend their time guarding the neighborhood or snatching Westerners who just happen by. They are guileless, tough, and ripe for recruitment by well-meaning men of stature like Hashimi. From time to time, the boys are called on to use techniques that are as brutal as they are effective.

Syriana resonates because its clichés tap into deeply felt and widely accepted beliefs about terrorism, Beirut, and Hezbollah. So it was not surprising that when, in the spring of 2007, a group of high-profile neoconservatives were invited to meet with Hezbollah officials in Beirut, each of them turned down the offer. "Why would I talk to them," one said, "I know what they have to say, and it's not worth listening to." Another was more forthright. "I don't like Arabs," he said. "I never have." One senior scholar at a major conservative think tank thought for a moment about attending, but then retreated. "You know, I'm actually a little afraid of doing this," he said, his voice lowered. "I mean, are they going to pull a black hood over my head?"

LEBANON'S HEZBOLLAH—"Party of God"—is viewed by the United States as one of the world's most dangerous terrorist organizations. In 2003, then deputy secretary of state Richard Armitage called it "the A-team of terrorism," more dangerous even than al Qaeda. The movement is blamed for the bombing of the U.S. Marine barracks in 1983, the kidnapping of some thirty westerners in Lebanon in the mid-1980s, the torture and killing of Marine Colonel Rich Higgins, the kidnapping and death of CIA station chief William Buckley, and the TWA 845 hijacking and murder of Robert Stethem. This is the baggage of the past—events that the United States says must be cleared up before any official relationship can be established. For the United States, this baggage is the primary reason why America continues to perceive Hezbollah as a "bad actor" in the region.

Baggage aside, the United States continues to treat Hezbollah as an intransigent terrorist organization and an uncompromising enemy of the West. In 2008, former director of national intelligence Michael McConnell said that Hezbollah retains the ability "to attack almost worldwide with little warning" and added that the organization has "sleeper cells" in the United States that are capable of carrying out terrorist operations. McConnell did not provide evidence for his claim: He was reporting about Hezbollah, so no evidence seemed necessary. That said, Hezbollah has maintained a strong relationship with some of America's adversaries, including the Tehran regime—though it is not clear whether, as many policymakers suppose, it acts on Iran's behalf. The movement receives millions of dollars in subsidies from the Iranian government, but there is little evidence to suggest that the movement is Iran's puppet. Rather, the relationship is far more complex. Much like the United States and Israel, Hezbollah and Iran have built a foundation of mutual support and trust. But Iran is in no position to dictate to Hezbollah, and Hezbollah is certainly in no position to dictate to Iran.

America's primary concern with Hezbollah is that it is an enemy of Israel—America's most important strategic ally in the region— and a threat to American interests. Hezbollah and Israel have fought continually since the mid-1980s. The most recent conflict occurred in July and August 2006, when Hezbollah fighters turned back an Israeli invasion of Lebanon after kidnapping and killing seven Israeli soldiers. But Hezbollah has a history at variance with American and European stereotypes. It runs the most comprehensive and competent network of social service programs in Lebanon and is a willing and trusted participant in the nation's confessionally based democratic system. A visit to southern Beirut reflects the reach, power, and popularity of the movement. Modern high-rises have replaced the bombed-out section of the city, schools are open, roads have been repaired, and community centers are operating. The movement is both deeply rooted in the community and directed by capable leaders.

Hezbollah's leader, Hassan Nasrallah, is considered one of the most articulate and sophisticated of the region's political voices, and the movement reflects his immense stature: Its leadership is educated, thoughtful, and forward looking. Nasrallah is a fiery orator, but he seems far removed from a report that described him as "a round and rather jovial individual who wears a black turban." Hezbollah's leadership is focused on careful and incremental change that eschews radical steps that might threaten its popularity among Lebanon's Shia population or that would alienate large segments of the country. In the wake of the 2006 war with Israel, Nasrallah's personal popularity soared (as did that of Hezbollah), and Secretary of State Condoleezza Rice complained to her staff about television reports showing Hezbollah leaders passing out American dollars to Beirut's homeless. She called the practice outrageous, which drew a retort from one of her more outspoken aides: "Well, maybe that's what we should do."

Hezbollah leaders openly confirm their strong relationship with Iran. But they are well known for taking a more independent line when it suits their purposes. When, in the spring of 2005, Iraqi Shia parties under Iranian influence busily positioned themselves as the leading edge of a new and powerful regional Shia resurgence, Hezbollah decided to go in the opposite direction: They downplayed their ties to their Iraqi Shia brethren and tied themselves more closely to Lebanese nationalism.

Lately, the movement has also subtly distanced itself from Syria, a longtime ally. As a result of the assassination of former Lebanese prime minister Rafiq Hariri, the Syrian government—which had an internationally mandated presence in Lebanon—was forced to withdraw its troops from the country. Huge anti-Syrian demonstrations underscored the popularity of the anti-Syrian position and symbolized the outpouring of grief for the martyred leader. To show its own strength, Hezbollah organized pro-Syrian rallies, but without criticizing Hariri himself—with whom the Hezbollah leadership had had a strong working relationship. Hezbollah admirably straddled this midcourse position, showing support for its erstwhile ally without damaging its reputation as a domestic Lebanese political force. Still, there was little doubt that although the movement viewed Syria as its friend, the movement's leaders did not fight to retain Syrian influence in the country. As a former CIA officer who served in-country noted,

> Hezbollah clearly understood the delicacy of its political situation; it was committed to playing out its relationship with Syria carefully as the latter decamped from Lebanon, intent on letting Syrian president Bashar Assad down gently without appearing disloyal to an old supporter. I never garnered any notion that Hezbollah was interested in the Syrians remaining in Lebanon. Rather, their mass demonstrations of solidarity with Syria seemed more a parting wave of thanks before they set about the tricky process of defining their own autonomy, and balancing the elements in the complex political process that is Lebanon in the Spring of 2005.

In the wake of the Syrian withdrawal, Hezbollah set out to redefine what it meant to be Lebanese, shaping a national identity that, though not splitting from the past, provided a political vision for Lebanon recognizing its diversity. It was a breathtaking program and seemed to imply that Beirut was neither a "suburb of Paris" (a common criticism of Beirut's Christians) nor a "suburb of Tehran" (the standard retort of Beirut's pro-Christian café class). The movement's basic message was clear: Hezbollah's Lebanon would be different from Shia Iraq, where Shia militias were enjoying a season of ethnic cleansing against the Sunni minority. Lebanon would be Shia, to be sure, but it would also be Christian and Sunni and, above all, Arab. The message provided a welcome reassurance to Lebanon's population, particularly in the wake of the Hariri assassination—when Beirut's streets were filled with people eager to celebrate Hariri but nevertheless worried about a return to the violence of the 1970s.

HEZBOLLAH IS ALLIED with Iran, but the organization views itself as a distinctly Lebanese political movement with deep ties to local communities. Its relationship with Iran has as its first premise that both Iran and Hezbollah are led by Shias, but Hezbollah's status as a defender of a minority population requires a different set of calculations from those formulated in Tehran. Nowhere is this tyranny of geography more apparent than in Hezbollah's relationship with Israel.

Although the movement is intransigently and vocally opposed to Israel's influence in the region, it regularly engages in indirect exchanges with that nation, primarily through the auspices of the German government. In addition, in Israel (particularly in the wake of the 2006 war), there is a quiet recognition that Hezbollah is popular and capable of defending itself and that its leadership is powerful and respected.

Finally, although the United States regularly warns against Hezbollah's desire to dominate the government of Lebanon, the movement has consistently recoiled from any government take-over. It prefers to remain a part of a broad coalition, in opposition, with a veto over government initiatives it does not like. Even in extremis, as it believed it was in May 2008 (the government had shut down the movement's telecommunications capabilities and removed the Hezbollah-supported airport security chief in order to pressure the movement politically), Hezbollah acted with purposeful restraint, sending its gunmen into central Beirut to prove its strength—but without any intention of overthrowing the government.

Hezbollah is satisfied to remain a permanent opposition party in Lebanon at least in part because the movement has always prized its independence. Hezbollah leaders are outspoken in their defense of their rights, while making it clear they will not be pressured by movements or political parties that they believe are working to attack them. "Everyone talks of Iranian interference in Lebanon through Hezbollah," one Hezbollah partisan noted in the wake of the May 2008 events. "But Iran had nothing to do with the May crisis. This was an unnecessary crisis that need not have happened. We did not want it to happen. And when it was over, we agreed to try to find a new working relationship with the different political movements. And we are still working to build that relationship." Another senior official was more direct about Hezbollah's domestic political goals. "We are prepared to work hard to maintain Muslim unity and avoid *fitna* [division]. We wish to avoid sectarian divisions, which is why we are prepared to make such overtures to other parties. . . . We are born here and will die here. We are a part of Lebanon's future; we participate in elections; we make our case to the people; we win seats in the parliament."

In this sense, then, Hezbollah's long-term political strategy is both practical and defensive. It is more interested in protecting its position as Lebanon's most influential and powerful political movement by serving its broadly based constituency than in undertaking the arduous task of ruling a diverse and divided national establishment. Hezbollah's leadership promotes a domestic agenda that is supported by almost every confessional group, arguing that the nation's national resource-allocation priorities, its property system, and its banking establishment are all in need of genuine reform. The movement also calls for a fairer distribution of governmental monies, pointing out that few of the national social service organizations serving the southern part of the nation enjoy government monetary support.

Hezbollah is also willing, when necessary, to reach across Lebanon's sectarian divide to recruit allies. In February 2006, Hezbollah signed a "memorandum of understanding" with General Michel Aoun—the leader of Lebanon's Christian Free Patriotic Movement—which set out a set of principles that confirmed its commitment to the strengthening of Lebanon's independent judiciary, reinforced its adherence to the fight against government corruption, gave voice to its belief in the independence of Lebanese political institutions, and institutionalized its principle that Lebanon should be free of outside interference. The memorandum also confirmed Hezbollah's right to maintain its arms as a part of Lebanon's defense against outside aggression. Aoun was pleased with the agreement. "They are a trustworthy partner," he said in early 2009. "They stand by their word."

If anything, America has as much baggage with Hezbollah as Hezbollah does with America. In the wake of the bombing of the Marine barracks, the CIA initiated a presidentially approved covert operation to train pro-American gunmen to assassinate Hezbollah officials. President Ronald Reagan ended the program two years later when, on March 8, 1985, a group of these agents set off a car bomb that killed eighty Muslims, many of them women and children. Sheikh Fadlallah, thought by the United States to be the most influential figure of the movement, was their target. He survived the attack. The United States denies involvement in the bombing, but former Reagan national security adviser Robert McFarlane has admitted that those who set off the bomb may have, in fact, been trained by the CIA. In *Veil*, his book on the CIA under William Casey, Bob Woodward reports that the ties between the CIA and the assassination team were established through the help of Saudi Prince Bandar bin Sultan, who was close to Casey. Both the Saudis and the Americans considered Fadlallah a threat. The CIA and Bandar, Woodward reports, contracted an English operative who organized the Fadlallah assassination attempt: a car bomb that was packed with explosives that could destroy Fadlallah's residence, which was close to a mosque. The bombing was timed to coincide with Friday prayers, when the mosque was crowded and the explosion would have a maximum impact.

American views of Hezbollah have been sharply influenced by the events of the 1980s, and Hezbollah leaders themselves understand that the *Syriana* portrait of their organization is nearly impossible to dispel. Then too, the kidnapping and killings of the 1980s (though Hezbollah leaders have consistently denied any responsibility for them) are a permanent, and sensitive, part of U.S.–Hezbollah history—it is as if the events happened yesterday. And for large numbers of Americans, the baggage of the 1980s is more than simply baggage: Hezbollah leaders, U.S. policymakers insist, must be held accountable for their actions, which include random murders and kidnappings and an intransigently inflammatory language that condemns the United States as a colonial and imperial power.

Even so, the Hezbollah of the twenty-first century is quite different from the movement that found its roots in Lebanon's Shia community nearly thirty years ago. In many respects, Hezbollah is no longer simply a movement, or even a state within a state.

Rather, it is a statelike actor within a nonstate—an entity without which Lebanon itself would not exist.

NAWAF AL-MOUSSAOUI, the head of Hezbollah's department of external relations, loves cigars and is always pleased to offer one of his best to those Americans who share this taste. "It is from Cuba," he says, smiling. "You are not able to get them in America." As if any explanation is necessary, he will sometimes add, quite purposely, "Of course, that's not true here." He shrugs and laughs, driving home the point, pointing at the cigar: "From Cuba," he says. Moussaoui also enjoys American television; he watches *Comedy Central* and instructs his family to never bother him while he's watching *Malcolm in the Middle*. But Moussaoui's attraction to American television is belied by his reading habits.

In early 2005, the Hezbollah leader was engaged in a detailed study of American neoconservatism, reading primary source material on the thinking of Norman Podhoretz and William Kristol and delving into the political philosophy of Leo Strauss. When asked whom he planned to read after Strauss, his answer was immediate: "Karl Popper." Popper was an eminent British thinker and scholar at the London School of Economics who authored a stunning critique of logical positivism in the 1930s (*The Logic of Scientific Discovery*) before becoming one of the world's most renowned scholars on the scientific method. But Moussaoui was interested not in Popper's philosophy of science or his "evolutionary epistemology" but, rather, his defense of liberal democracy in his 1945 book *The Open Society and Its Critics*—a bible for neoconservatism. His reading was part of Moussaoui's goal: to understand the foundational beliefs motivating the Bush administration. "He knows more about neoconservatism than a lot of neoconservatives," a colleague reflected.

Moussaoui speaks French in addition to Arabic, but though he understands English, he does not readily speak it in public, as he feels uncomfortable with his command of the language. Thus he is able to answer questions put to him in English without translation, but he then carefully chooses his own words in Arabic and then corrects his translator, finger raised: "Not complicated," he says, "complex." A European who has visited with him several times in recent years said, "He is one of the brightest and most careful speakers I have ever met," and an American noted that "Mr. Moussaoui, I am convinced, understands English perfectly well, but uses an interpreter as a tool to help keep himself disciplined and sharply focused in his responses." Moussaoui will sometimes repeat a phrase in Arabic, emphasizing the most important words. "Language," he says, "is important." So it was not a surprise when he interrupted his translator often during a series of meetings with American and European delegates in March and July 2005, which were held in a large room in a restaurant in Christian Beirut. Moussaoui was comfortable in the restaurant, with no security personnel evident. "Beirut for me is home," he said. "I am perfectly safe."

The delegation of Americans who visited with Hamas in March 2005 spent time in a detailed exchange with Moussaoui just one day later. Included in the delegation of those visiting with Moussaoui were Americans who were familiar with Hezbollah's activities in the 1980s, including one former senior military officer who knows Lebanon well and who monitored the effort to free U.S. Marine Corps Colonel William R. "Rich" Higgins. The delegation also included two retired senior intelligence officers with decades of experience in the region. They too were concerned about the baggage—particularly the Higgins kidnapping.

Higgins was kidnapped from a Beirut street in February 1988. He was taken captive, as his wife Robin Higgins said, "by Hezbollah radicals." Higgins was tortured and killed, and his body was dumped on a Beirut street in December 1991. American officials said at the time that Higgins had been killed six months after his kidnapping. A videotape of his torture and pictures of his body hanging by a rope were then made available to American officials. "It was horrific," an American who viewed the videotape said. Since that time, U.S. policymakers have worked to piece together the Higgins murder. They say that the evidence that Hezbollah was responsible is "overwhelming," and they point to "Hezbollah intelligence operative" Imad Mugniyah as the man responsible for supervising Higgins's torture. Mugniyah, who was assassinated under mysterious circumstance in 2008 in Damascus, is also blamed by American officials for planning and carrying out the 1983 bombing of the U.S. Marine barracks, the hijacking of TWA flight 845, and the subsequent murder of Robert Stethem. Simply stated: Mugniyah was Hezbollah's dark presence—a latter-day "Carlos the Jackal," a notorious international terrorist, who loomed in the background of the organization.

When Moussaoui appeared in March 2005, he knew he would be faced with questions about the barracks bombing and the Higgins kidnapping and murder—and Mugniyah—but he ignored these topics in his opening remarks. He focused instead on "Hezbollah's necessary defense of Lebanon and its opposition to Israeli aggression," while remaining careful to make a distinction between disagreeing with U.S. policies and considering the United States an enemy. "We do not underestimate the American [Bush] administration," he said, "but we are not their enemy. We simply oppose their policies in the Middle East." At one point in his remarks, Moussaoui allied his movement with the fight against terrorism, making a plea that the United States make an effort to distinguish between its enemies and its friends and between terrorist networks and national liberation and resistance movements: "For the world to succeed in fighting terrorism, America has to realize what exactly it is and how it is different from national liberation movements," he argued. "One shouldn't be hostile towards the Muslim Brotherhood simply because they are the Muslim

Brotherhood, or Hamas simply because they are fighting Israel, or Hezbollah. Once again it is important to differentiate between these movements. To continue isolating Hezbollah, Hamas and the Muslim Brotherhood, all of which have widespread popularity, does not assist the fight against terrorism."

Moussaoui was well prepared for the exchange with the delegates. His focus on Israel was an attempt to anticipate questions he knew he would be asked on Hezbollah's insistence on maintaining its independent status as an armed organization in Lebanon. "When it comes to Israel, the international community is weak, and therefore we understand that the duty here is to defend ourselves. No one else will," he said. "There is also the contradiction between the Israeli and Lebanese state. In Israel there is a religious domination and in Lebanon a pluralist society based on cooperation and coexistence. It is our belief that this contradiction is a threat to Lebanese unity. We have had to use our arms to liberate ourselves. We also have to find the formula to protect our country." Moussaoui then emphasized Hezbollah's condemnation of the events of 9/11, adding that the movement also condemned suicide attacks in Iraq, which were then reaching a crescendo. "Following 9/11 we condemned an act of terrorism: in the same way that we consider the bombs in Najaf, Karbala, and Riyadh as acts of terrorism."

Moussaoui's explanation of why Hezbollah must retain its arms seemed distinctly unsatisfying to his American and European listeners. It might be possible, one of them advised, for Hezbollah to come to an agreement with the Lebanese government to integrate its militia into the national army. Moussaoui did not dismiss the idea. "We would study any and all programs that might make that possible," he said. Later, during a meeting of Americans and Europeans with Moussaoui on this specific topic, John Alderdice—a member of the House of Lords and the head of Northern Ireland's

Alliance Party—laid out just such a program, using the model that had helped advance the peace process in Northern Ireland. Moussaoui listened intently for many minutes without interrupting. He then carefully thought through his response. "This is certainly an interesting proposal and one we would take seriously," he said, and he asked Alderdice for an outline of such an initiative. But, he said, the prospect of Hezbollah's disarming (which the United States would require before establishing any contact with the group) was more a distant goal rather than an immediate possibility, despite his interest in Alderdice's model.

"I believe that to have a fruitful policy in the region, Israel must be confronted," Moussaoui explained. "Political settlement demands equity of power. Israel holds all the cards. So there is a demand that we disarm, which is the same as a demand for our surrender. But we will not surrender, and we will not give up our arms." For Moussaoui, Hezbollah's arms were not simply a means of, as he said, "defending our movement." The question was also political. In this sense, Moussaoui is a political realist and, as he describes himself, "a student of history." He noted, "As far as we are concerned, it is not in anyone's interest to leave the Arabs weak. Also in the past there has been a stability in Lebanon. Hezbollah's arms have delivered this. We know how the world works, and we are not naive about it. We know that the weak never deal on an equal basis with the strong. That is a sad but true reality. We want to deal with our adversaries from a position of strength. America feels the same way; every nation and every movement knows this."

During the course of the discussions, Moussaoui maintained that his movement's "military actions" against Israel were justified. "We do not target civilians," he said during the March 2005 meetings. "Even when Israel was occupying southern Lebanon, we were absolutely diligent in making certain that our actions did not endanger Israeli civilians, and we even stopped operations

where Israeli families of military personnel would have been en-
dangered by our actions. You cannot say the same for Israel."

In 2007, in the wake of the Lebanon War of 2006, Moussaoui
maintained this view:

> We were fighting a war, and so we fired missiles at Israel, and this
> is known by everyone. But we did not purposely target those mis-
> siles on civilian population centers, as our technology would
> have not made that possible. In fact, the success of our conflict
> was not because we threw missiles into Israel; it was because we
> defeated the Israeli army on the ground, soldier to soldier, and we
> did it without tanks. We defeated Israel because we killed their
> soldiers and drove them out of our country. Even the Israelis
> agree with this.

At this point, Moussaoui leaned forward.

> Would you ask this same question to Israel? Would you ask them:
> Did you target civilians in southern Lebanon and in Beirut? And
> ask them about Operation Grapes of Wrath. They did it then
> too, but the international community did not pay attention.
> And if they told you, "Well, this was not intended"—would you
> still condemn them as you are condemning us? We do not target
> civilians. We did not burn down cities. We did not lay waste to
> their homes. But come with me to south Beirut and I will show
> you what they have done. They brought down blocks of apart-
> ments. There were hundreds and hundreds dead. You can check
> the casualty figures for yourself.

INEVITABLY, MOUSSAOUI WAS asked about his movement's baggage. His answer is always the same. "We have no blood on our
hands," he says and then is silent. Was Hezbollah responsible for

the Beirut barracks bombing? "We have no blood on our hands," he says again. And the murder of Rich Higgins? "We have no blood on our hands," he repeats.

In March 2005 the questioners were surprised by the response, expecting that Moussaoui would give the by-now formulaic construction that is predictable for such politically charged meetings: The past is the past, and mistakes were made by both sides; it is now time to begin anew. Moussaoui's answer was so blunt, so certain, that it came as a surprise: Hezbollah has no blood on its hands? "These are very sensitive and very important questions," one of the delegation's interlocutors said at the time. "Is that your answer—that you have no blood on your hands?" Moussaoui remained unruffled, even when asked again—and then again. "We have no blood on our hands," he answered.

When pressed once again, for one final time, he faced his accusers. "If we open every file on the [Lebanese] Civil War, then the Americans would not set foot in an office of any political party in Lebanon," he responded, and then added,

> Everyone in the U.S. [Bush] administration knows we are not a terrorist organization or a threat to America. We are a national resistance movement. This is about politics. It is not even about America. This is about Israel's psychological headache, and we are that headache. We are not raising our children to hate America. America is not our enemy. Israel is our enemy, but not the Jewish people—Israel. This is not a religious war against the Jews. We have nothing against the Jews. Our war is against the Israeli occupation of our lands—that is it.

Moussaoui's audience remained skeptical. "The movement seemed keenly interested in establishing a key dialogue with the West and in particular with the United States," observed retired intelligence officer Milt Bearden, who attended the 2005 meetings in Beirut, "and Mr. Moussaoui is right to say that if we open every file then everyone will look bad. Certainly, there is much to answer for in Beirut in the 1980s. Then too, Moussaoui spoke with the usual Hezbollah caginess on a variety of subjects, including on the early years of the Lebanon conflict, on the period of 1982 to 1985, and on Imad Mugniyah." Later, in the interests of precision, Bearden wrote out his impressions of the Hezbollah leadership's discomfort with their past, noting that movement officials quietly admitted that in the early days of their organization's formation there had been many "controversial and mistaken acts." These leaders accept that Mugniyah was guilty of the litany of charges made against him by the Americans, Bearden added, but they continued to claim that Hezbollah had "no American blood on its hands." The clear implication from the answers of Hezbollah's leaders is that Mugniyah, a movement icon (his portrait still hangs prominently in Hezbollah offices), is not so easily erased from Hezbollah's history. "I always came away with the impression that Mugniyah was always some kind of freebooter in the world of terrorism," Bearden later wrote. "They can't just airbrush him out of the picture. He is more like a Hezbollah Colonel Kurtz; he operated on the margins."

Hezbollah is no more willing to admit to or renounce its past associations than the United States is willing to admit to or renounce its own operations of the mid-1980s, when the Reagan administration and its allies in Lebanon fought a nearly open war with the nation's Shias. Just as Hezbollah will not turn its back on Imad Mugniyah (who, in the wake of his assassination in Syria, is viewed as a martyr), so the United States will not turn away from Samir Geagea, its ally in Lebanon during that country's Civil War. Geagea's Phalange militia is held responsible for the murder in September 1982 of hundreds—and perhaps thousands—of Palestinian refugees in the Sabra and Shatila refugee camps. In 1994,

Geagea was arrested and found guilty of ordering the assassinations of former Lebanese prime minister Rashid Karami, National Liberal Party leader Dany Chamoun and his family (his wife and two young children), and former Lebanese Forces member Elias al-Zayak. Geagea has also been implicated in the murder of Lebanese political leader Tony Frangieh (and his wife and baby daughter) and of Ghaith Khoury, the head of Lebanon's Kataeb militia in Jbeil. Geagea was punished for his crimes by being held in solitary confinement for eleven years in the basement of the Lebanese Ministry of Defense and was released as a part of the general amnesty announced following the Cedar Revolution; he was released on October 25, 2005. Geagea's close association with the United States is unquestioned: He visited the White House in March 2008 and met with Secretary of State Rice and National Security Adviser Stephen Hadley. When Geagea was welcomed in Washington, the Hezbollah leadership remained silent, but spokesmen for Michel Aoun's Free Patriotic Movement were enraged: "The man is a convicted murderer," one of Aoun's senior advisers said. "So the United States will not speak with Hezbollah, will not meet with Aoun, but is willing to shake this man's blood-drenched hand."

The most serious claim leveled against Hezbollah, however, is not its alleged bombing of the Marine barracks, not the murders of Buckley, Stethem, or Higgins, but its reported "virulent anti-Semitism"—an allegation that is of continual interest to a small but influential number of U.S. commentators and political analysts. The claim is significant because it is rooted in Hezbollah's conflict with Israel.

During the July 2005 meeting and in subsequent discussions with Hezbollah in Beirut, the claim of anti-Semitism—complete with a presentation by one of the American delegates of television footage showing Islamists marching on Jerusalem (which was aired on Hezbollah's al-Manar television station)—became a source of discussion and dispute. Moussaoui rejected the charge that the movement and its communications network are anti-Semitic: "We are an enemy of Israel," he repeated, "we have nothing against Jews. They are not our enemy." In fact, a number of Jewish Americans have met with Moussaoui and have been members of delegations holding discussions with the Hezbollah leadership. None of them have ever claimed to have overheard any Hezbollah leader issuing what might be considered an anti-Semitic statement.

During the March 2005 discussions, however, one of the American delegates pointed out that al-Manar had aired a documentary on "The Protocols of the Elders of Zion," one of the most vicious anti-Jewish smears of modern history and one of the most defamatory and scurrilous claims ever made against an entire people. The documentary portrayed the "Protocols" as an accurate depiction of how "worldwide Jewry" conspires to influence events: undermining governments, controlling international banking, and assassinating world leaders. Moussaoui was clearly taken aback by the claim and noticeably sagged when confronted with the al-Manar incident. "This is true," he said, "and I am embarrassed to admit that it is true. This show should not have appeared. I noticed that it was on al-Manar only after it had begun. It is deeply embarrassing to me and to our movement. I apologize, unreservedly, for this. I wish it had not happened." A participant later observed, privately, that he accepted Moussaoui's word and his apology: "But that doesn't make it right," he added. "The program aired because someone inside the organization, and at a high level, wanted to influence its audience. An apology is an apology, but it doesn't make what happened right."

The most prominent critic of Hezbollah, and a commentator who repeatedly claims that Hezbollah is virulently anti-Semitic, is former *New Yorker* reporter and current *Atlantic* correspondent Jeffrey Goldberg. Goldberg has met with the leaders of both Hezbollah and Hamas and has spent considerable time in the Middle East. His most important report on Hezbollah came in the October 14, 2002, issue of the *New Yorker*, in which he wrote that Hezbollah "is, at its core, a jihadist organization, and its leaders have never tried to disguise their ultimate goal: building an Islamic republic in Lebanon and liberating Jerusalem from the Jews." Strangely, Goldberg seems tone deaf to the arguments of those he critiques and is, oddly, less careful in his characterizations than those he condemns. His articles are filled with "telltales." Does Hezbollah want to build "an Islamic republic in Lebanon"? In fact, Hezbollah has very carefully stated that this is precisely what is does *not* want to do. Does Hezbollah seek to liberate Jerusalem "from the Jews"? Hezbollah, Hamas, and the Palestinians all want to liberate Jerusalem. But Jerusalem is occupied not by "the Jews" but by the Israelis. There's a difference, and the difference is one that thoughtful Muslims are careful to make. Thus, Goldberg signals his own prejudices: Anyone who opposes the occupation of Jerusalem opposes "Jews."

Goldberg's primary claim is that Hezbollah is no different than al Qaeda, the world's preeminent "jihadist organization." The allegation is disputed by Hezbollah leaders, who point out that al Qaeda has condemned the movement and that extremist organizations affiliated with al Qaeda have targeted the Hezbollah leadership for assassination. Al Qaeda's leaders argue that by participating in Lebanon's elections, the movement has abandoned Islam. Privately, Hezbollah's leaders are outspoken in their condemnation of Goldberg's claim: "The bin Ladens and Zarqawi's of the region pose a greater threat to us than do the Americans," one of these leaders said in 2005. "Twenty thousand Shias have died at the hands of these outlaws, these al-Kawaraj." The Kawaraj were the first Muslim group to sanction (within the first century after the death of Mohammad), on theological grounds, the murder of fellow Muslims.

To claim that someone is Kawaraj is to claim that they are advocating an inter-Muslim civil war, a prospect that, more than any other, Hezbollah works to avoid.

Goldberg paints a grim and not altogether unconvincing portrait of the Middle East, claiming that anti-Semitism has been on the rise in Muslim countries since 9/11. To support his point, he gives examples of anti-Semitism in the region, instances that are pernicious but that remain below the level of the "malignancy of genocidal anti-Semitism," of which he says Hezbollah is guilty. Oddly, none of his examples are from Hezbollah itself, deriving instead from an imam in Saudi Arabia and a sheikh in Gaza. During the Lebanon War of 2006, Goldberg made the same claim about Hezbollah's anti-Semitism during a television interview with CNN's Anderson Cooper. Cooper introduced Goldberg by noting that Hezbollah's "obvious anti-Semitism" was one of the untold stories of the war. Goldberg vigorously agreed. Anti-Semitism, Goldberg said, is "embedded in the core of Hezbollah ideology."

Goldberg quotes, as an authority on anti-Semitism in the region, first, Martin Kramer, a scholar at the Washington Institute for Near East Policy, who has written a book on Hezbollah and Sheikh Fadlallah—though apparently without having ever traveled to Lebanon or interviewed the sheikh. Kramer's opinions on Hezbollah (and Hamas) are well known in policy circles in Washington, though not because they are held in any great esteem. Rather, Kramer is among those who continue to get the region wrong: supporting and predicting an American victory in Iraq and predicting the same, in August 2006, when he said that Israel's military would defeat Hezbollah. Israel's current president Shimon Peres is the second authority on anti-Semitism cited by Goldberg. Peres sees anti-Semitism everywhere, but particularly among "religious people"—who presumably populate the world of Israel's political opponents. "These are religious people," Peres said, speaking of Hezbollah. "With the religious you can hardly negotiate. They think they have supreme permission to kill people and go to war. That is their nature."

ONE OF GOLDBERG'S most outspoken critics is Ken Silverstein, a former reporter for the *Los Angeles Times* and now the Washington editor for *Harper's*. Silverstein journeyed to Beirut in 2006 to meet with Hezbollah leaders, spending weeks in the country and attending Hezbollah rallies. He came away with an impression of the movement different from Goldberg's. "There is no question that Hezbollah opposes Israel, views itself as being at war with Israel, and is proud to call itself the defender of Lebanon," Silverstein says. "But I found no overt anti-Semitism in any of the language of its leaders—who were intent to make a clear distinction between their war on Israel and their feelings on Jews. They continually said that they had no argument with Jews and were not at war with them." Silverstein, however, adds a well-considered caveat: "Listen, I cannot read a person's innermost thoughts. I am sure there must be anti-Semites in the Hezbollah movement; it would be foolish to think otherwise. But I am also sure there are Arab-haters in Israel. But I don't think that should be our focus. I guess my main belief is that the conflict is certainly marked by religious hostility on both sides, but the conflict is not about religion; it is about land and national identity—and reducing it to a religious conflict is an oversimplification."

Upon his return, Silverstein submitted his article on Hezbollah to his editor in Los Angeles. Then trouble began. In an article he later wrote for *Harper's*, Silverstein recounted the problems he faced in getting his reporting into print:

The primary problem, it soon became clear, was fear of offending supporters of Israel. At one point I was told that editorial changes were needed to "inoculate" the newspaper from criticism, and although who the critics might be was never spelled out, the answer seemed fairly obvious. I was also told in one memo that "we should avoid taking sides," which apparently meant omitting inconvenient historical facts. Over my repeated objections, editors cut a line that referred to "Israel's creation following World War II in an area overwhelmingly populated at the time by Arabs." That, I was told in an email from one editor, David Lauter, "was the Arab view of things. Israelis would say, with some justification, that much of the area wasn't overwhelmingly populated by anyone at the time the first Zionist pioneers arrived in the first part of the 20th century and that the population rose in the mid-decades of the century in large part because of people migrating into Palestine in response to the economic development they brought about."

But that argument, which in any case doesn't refute what I wrote, was long ago rejected by serious Mideast scholars, including many in Israel. It also avoids confronting a root cause of the conflict. According to the Jewish Agency for Palestine, the original Zionist governing body in what was to become Israel, there were roughly 1.1 million Arab Muslims living in Palestine at the time of partition—twice the number of Jews. "Perspective is everything," I replied in an email to the editors. "If my name was Mostafa Naser and I grew up in the southern suburbs of Beirut, I seriously doubt I would be an ardent Zionist. If we can't even acknowledge that Arabs have a legitimate point of view—and acknowledge what the numbers show—we caricature them as nothing more than a bunch of irrational Jew haters."

The debate, Silverstein said, "reached the point of the absurd." David Lauter, whom *Los Angeles Times* editors viewed as an expert on Hezbollah, had never met anyone from the movement. Even so, Silverstein was told, the newspaper viewed his (Silverstein's) reporting with skepticism because "Hezbollah had a history of inviting reporters to Lebanon and controlling their agenda." The implication was that Silverstein had been "duped" by Hezbollah. They told him they weren't anti-Semites, and he actually *believed* them. The fact that Silverstein ran across no evidence of their anti-Semitism meant nothing: Hezbollah, a clever and sophisticated organization (as *New Yorker* writer Goldberg noted), was perfectly capable of deluding its Western guests—that is, of actually not saying anything anti-Semitic. Indeed, the fact that there was no evidence of Hezbollah's anti-Semitism was in itself convincing evidence that the organization was, in fact, anti-Semitic. "If we can't even acknowledge that Arabs have a legitimate point of view . . . we caricature them as nothing more than a bunch of irrational Jew haters." In truth, the stronger Hezbollah (or Hamas) becomes and the more rational and commonsensical their arguments, the greater the need to view them as anti-Semites. Hezbollah and Hamas are not enemies of Israel because they are anti-Semites, they are anti-Semites because they are enemies of Israel—or, as Goldberg would have it: They are not enemies of Israel, they are enemies of "the Jews."

Eventually, Silverstein pulled his story ("I decided to pull the piece rather than 'inoculate' it to the point of dishonesty," he later said), left the *Los Angeles Times*, and joined *Harper's*. The story appeared in that magazine, as part of a larger article on political Islam. Silverstein's "Parties of God: The Bush Doctrine and the Rise of Islamic Democracy" included a straightforward portrait of Hezbollah and of Nawaf al-Moussaoui. Silverstein confronted Moussaoui directly on the charges of anti-Semitism, and particularly on the claim that Islamists are Holocaust deniers. "We are not denying that European racists persecuted an entire people or belittling the suffering of the Jewish people, and we say this with utter frankness and without compliment," Moussaoui responded. "But Europeans committed those crimes, and then we were made to pay for them with our land."

HEZBOLLAH IS NOT the Democratic Party. It is not the American Civil Liberties Union. The movement is not committed to non-violence. Hezbollah has trained and deployed the most sophisticated military force in the Middle East—a force that handily defeated Israel in the Lebanon War of 2006. The rhetoric of the movements and its leaders is often filled with clichés about the West and the "dangers of Zionism," and its television station airs between-program political messages that show young men marching on Jerusalem. All of this sparks unease among both Americans and Europeans. But uncomfortable as we may be with Hezbollah's image and rhetoric, the organization is far removed from the Jacobin dead enders of Osama bin Laden or Ayman al-Zawahiri. Of course, it could be that Hezbollah's leaders are lying, that behind all of their talk of democracy and the justice of their cause, they are intent on creating an Islamic Republic in Lebanon and liquidating the Jews. But there is no evidence for this. Even so, Americans remain unconvinced, as shown by an exchange with a young Lebanese American student during a private briefing given at a prominent Washington think tank on Hezbollah.

"You spoke to the leaders of Hezbollah?"
"Yes."
"And to Hamas?"
"Yes."
"And they said that they wanted democracy?"
"Yes."
"And you *believed* them?"

Such skepticism is intended not simply to cast doubt or to spark controversy, but to empty any exchange with political Islam of its content and so translate it into a form that reflects U.S. policies: Hezbollah says they believe in democracy, but what they really mean to say is. . . . Or, more properly: When we talk about democracy, we're telling the truth, but when Hezbollah talks about democracy, they're lying. A more persistent question for critics of Hezbollah suggested itself in the answer to the questioner at the Washington think tank. Do we oppose Hezbollah because we believe they are incapable of telling the truth, or do we claim they are incapable of telling the truth because we oppose them?

CHAPTER SEVEN

ISRAEL

"God has nothing to do with it."
—KHALID MESHAAL

IN THE SUMMER of 2007, an Israeli man explained his views of what it means to be Jewish and Israeli. "I am both," he said. This is an accomplished man who served in the Israeli military before becoming a political activist. He was driving from northern Israel to his home on a kibbutz near Jerusalem, one of the few left in the country. As the long slope that defines Israel from north to south stretched out before him, he spoke in loving terms of his country. "In the IDF we spent many hours discussing whether Judaism is a nation or a religion. And it's both. We, the Jewish people, have a home now called Israel. And we will defend it. Israel is where we can practice our beliefs and live together as Jews. I think it is important to keep the Jewish character of our state. The Jewish people have done much for humanity in the thousands of years of our existence, so we can have a state. It is not so much to ask. We have a distinct culture; we have made real contributions. We have not only earned the right to have Israel; we fought for it." These views reflect those of a vast majority of Israelis: "We, the Jewish people, have a home now called Israel. And we will defend it."

Another man—of roughly the same age—has the same view, though he comes from the opposite end of the political spectrum. And his remarks, although from more than twenty years ago now, also reflect those of the vast majority of Israelis. His fellow citizen, from the kibbutz, would not disagree with them. Ze'ev "Benny" Begin is the son of the first Likud prime minister of Israel, Menachem Begin. He's much like his father: mistrustful of compromise, with a readiness to fight Israel's enemies regardless of what the world may think. "It is very easy to sit in America and write about the peace process and have your articles appear in the newspapers, because really it is not happening to you" he said in an interview.

> It is easy to say "we must push Israel to sign a peace agreement with its enemies because this will ensure stability," but it is not your land and your future that is being bargained with. So make no mistake, when Americans discuss peace in the Middle East they are discussing the prospect of our national annihilation. They are discussing extermination. We are not a nation of victims. We were not given this land out of pity, we fought for it by force or arms and we won it. I say that we have put our heads in the ovens already once and we will not do it again. Ever.

It is difficult for an Israeli to discuss what it means to be an "Israeli." The answer is both personal and complex. A westerner walking down a street in the Old City of Jerusalem might be approached by a Palestinian with a simple question. The question is not, who are you? but, *what* are you? Palestinians in the Old City of Jerusalem—or in the West Bank or the Gaza Strip—do not want to know who one is as much as they want to know where a person is from. The answer for an American, a Brit, a Canadian, a German, or anyone from "the West" would be predictable. "I'm an American," or "I'm a Canadian," or "I'm a German." It would be extremely unlikely for any American or Brit to answer the question by saying, "I'm a Christian" or "I'm a Jew." We do not define ourselves that way. Neither do Israelis. Although a poll published by the Israeli Democracy Institute in May 2008 seems to show that Israelis are divided in their description of themselves (47 percent of the Israeli public view themselves as Jews first and Israelis second; 39 percent "consider themselves first and foremost Israeli"), the authors of the poll conclude that the broad consensus among Israeli Jews is that it is necessary to meld traditional religious belief with the requirements of living in a secular state. Israeli Jews have a strong Jewish identity, but they are committed to creating a free and democratic nation. They are also anxious to segregate themselves from Orthodox and Ultra-Orthodox Jews. Only 10 percent of those Israelis polled based their identity on their religious affiliation. The pollsters were then told by 51 percent that they wanted separate secular and religious neighborhoods.

Israelis are sensitive to this difference: When confronted with the question, what are you? they are as unlikely to answer "Jewish" as an American or a Brit is to answer "Christian," "Hindu," "Muslim," or "Buddhist." Just as Israelis do not use the words "Israeli" and "Jewish" interchangeably, neither do Americans. We would be shocked to see a *Washington Post* headline that read, "Jews, Hezbollah Vow Wider War." Yet at key moments during Israel's more controversial military actions (the bombings of Lebanon in 2006 and of Gaza in 2008), policymakers and commentators in the United States—and especially Israel's most outspoken and public advocates—have conflated the two. It is precisely for this reason that America now finds itself embroiled in an ugly public debate on how to fight and win the "global war on terror" and settle the Israeli-Palestinian conflict. What is important about this

debate is not simply that it is about words (in some sense, all de-
bates are about words), but that the words used in this debate are
crucially important. For if it is true, as some in the American Jewish community allege, that opposition to Israel means opposition
to Jews (and is therefore a reflection of anti-Semitism), then anti-
Semitism is growing. And Israel is in trouble.

WHEN JOHN MEARSHEIMER and Stephen Walt's book *The Israel
Lobby and U.S. Foreign Policy* first appeared in print in 2007, its
authors were subjected to what they called "various personal attacks." The criticisms ranged from claims that the two were exag-
gerating the Israel lobby's impact on American foreign policy
decision-making to accusations that the two were "anti-Semites."
The latter was intended to be the most damaging, as Mearsheimer
and Walt themselves admit: "The charge of anti-Semitism is one
of the most powerful epithets one can level at someone in America, and no respectable person wants to be tarred with that brush."
The Anti-Defamation League (ADL), for instance, called Mearsheimer and Walt's views "a classical conspiratorial anti-Semitic
analysis invoking the canards of Jewish power and Jewish control."
    Mearsheimer and Walt said that they understood the sensitiv-
ity of the charge of anti-Semitism and so were especially careful
in dealing with it in their book. They rejected the allegation and
then spoke directly to the fears of American Jews:

> The accusation is likely to resonate among American Jews, many
> of whom still believe that anti-Semitism is rife. Not only does
> the history of Jews in the Diaspora provide plenty of cause to
> worry, that tendency is magnified by the role that the Holocaust
> plays in the attitudes of a significant number of Jewish Ameri-
> cans. . . . It defines how many American Jews think about the
> world around them, and not surprisingly, it has fostered a power-
> ful sense of victimization for some of them. Despite the great suc-

cess Jews have achieved in America, many Jewish Americans still worry that virulent anti-Semitism could return at any time.

It may well be because of this admission—and their insight—that the charge of anti-Semitism leveled at the two seemed to make no difference to America's readers. Not only did *The Israel Lobby* find itself on the *New York Times* bestseller list, but it received favorable treatment from many critics, including commentators who might otherwise be viewed as Israel's friends. The *New York Review of Books*, the *Financial Times*, and the *Chicago Tribune* all praised Mearsheimer and Walt for "raising interesting questions" about the influence of the lobby and about American foreign policy in the Middle East.

Mearsheimer and Walt have said that they are gratified by their book's success and by "encouraging signs" of a deeper discussion of the American-Israeli relationship. Yet despite their book's popularity and influence, and in spite of the sometimes vicious attacks it sparked, the critique of Mearsheimer and Walt did not come as a surprise to policymakers, scholars, and the loose network of Middle East thinkers in Washington who have been dealing with the Israel lobby for years and who recognize its power. In fact, in the wake of the rising criticism of the Israel lobby (the result not only of Mearsheimer and Walt's book but also of the publication of former president Jimmy Carter's book *Palestine: Peace Not Apartheid*), a loose coalition of American Jews banded together to establish J Street—an advocacy organization that promotes political views antithetical to the voices more commonly heard from the powerful American-Israel Public Affairs Committee (AIPAC). AIPAC and J Street differ markedly not so much on their views of Israel (both believe that Israel is America's most important strategic ally in the region and must be defended) as on their views of the Israeli-Palestinian peace process. J Street is pro-Israel and pro-peace; AIPAC is pro-Israel.

The emergence of J Street, when coupled with that of the Israel Policy Forum (another moderate pro-Israel organization), holds out hope that the Israel lobby can become more diverse in its views than it has been in the past, when they insisted that support for Israel should come at all costs—even, or perhaps especially, when such support is not in America's interest. The acceptance of Mearsheimer and Walt's criticism (that support for Israel should not be unconditional) is now viewed as a given among Middle East policy circles, and particularly among policymakers in the new Obama administration. Even so, Mearsheimer and Walt say, recasting the American-Israeli relationship will take more time and will necessitate adopting some painful positions. They recommend that the U.S. government shape a new relationship with Israel that treats Israel as a normal state, that the United States act decisively to end the Israeli-Palestinian conflict, that the public force a more open discourse about Israel's role in the Middle East, and, finally, that new and more moderate voices for Israel redirect the Israel lobby's agenda.

But Mearsheimer and Walt's critique—that the pro-Israel lobby will support Israel, even when it is not in America's interest—is not universally accepted even among vocal critics of Israel. A number of influential voices in the U.S. policymaking establishment believe Mearsheimer and Walt's portrait is overdrawn, particularly in their view of the causes of the U.S. war with Iraq. Although Mearsheimer and Walt admit that pressure from Israel and the Israel lobby "was not the only factor behind the Bush administration's decision to attack Iraq in March 2003," they argue that the war "was motivated at least in good part by a desire to make Israel more secure." They make a compelling case, pointing out that key U.S. officials cited Israeli security as a reason for the attack and citing "abundant evidence that Israel and the lobby played crucial roles in making that war happen." Their conclusion is that without the efforts of Israel and the Israel lobby, "America probably would not be in Iraq today." The authors go on to provide reasons why Israel would want Saddam Hussein removed, show how "a small band of neoconservatives" who supported Israel pushed America into the war, detail how the lobby then provided a drumbeat of support for the war, summarize the work done by Israeli supporters in the press, and demonstrate how a small clique of Israel supporters in the administration manipulated the intelligence on Iraq through the Pentagon's Office of Special Plans, which was headed by and filled with officials who were avowedly pro-Israeli.

Much of this is true. Mearsheimer and Walt are right to draw a link between the march toward war in Iraq and the supporters of Israel. But there is often a stark difference between what Israel's supporters in America want and what the government of Israel desires. In early 2003, as the Bush administration was beginning to make the case for invading Iraq, a team of senior Israeli intelligence officials came to Washington to talk about the Iraqi threat. Paradoxically, a very influential retired senior Israeli intelligence official accompanied the team to lend his reputation to their briefing. This official, who remains prominent in Israeli political affairs, talked hesitantly but firmly about his own recommendations in the wake of his American trip. "I knew when I came to Washington that there was nothing that I could do about the American invasion," he said during a luncheon in Jerusalem in 2005. "I thought the invasion was a mistake. But I didn't focus on that. Instead, I said that if the U.S. was absolutely committed to doing this then they should remember two things—don't break up the Baath Party and keep the [Iraq] military intact." He laughed and shook his head: "Of course, as you know, that's not what happened."

ISRAEL DOES NOT speak with one voice. There were many in Israel who believed that the American invasion of Iraq would be good for their country. But many others believed that America's adventure in Iraq would only complicate Israel's foreign policy problems.

"There was a consensus view in Israel that Saddam Hussein was not a threat to Israel," the former Mossad senior official says. "So if that was the case, how could he possibly be a threat to America?" The tale told by this former official points up one of the more salient truths about the Israeli-American relationship: that many supporters of Israel in the United States are more Israeli than the Israelis. Some Israelis in very influential positions in Israel might not have thought that Israel needed protection from Saddam Hussein, but its supporters in America were convinced otherwise. This is a fairly common state of affairs, and not just for Israel. The Palestinian diaspora is, on key issues, more outspoken than many moderate Palestinian leaders. Many of them, as senior Fatah official Hani al-Hassan says, "are a lot more radical than we are." The same is true, in varying degrees, for Cuban Americans and for Irish Americans. But each of these diaspora communities is powerful and wields considerable influence in Washington. This is particularly true for the Israeli lobby. Israeli leaders, then, must not only listen carefully to what the American government says, but must also pay particular attention to those of their supporters who claim to know what is best for them.

This pattern of events emerged strikingly during the 2006 war with Hezbollah. Israel's friends in America unstintingly supported Israel's attacks in Lebanon, but some also went one step further: White House supporters of Israel, including neoconservative Elliott Abrams (a senior National Security Council staffer and adviser to President Bush) and his group of adherents inside both the White House and the Pentagon, urged Israel to expand the war into Syria.

When pushed by the Bush administration to expand the war, however, the Israeli government balked: "One Israeli source said [US President George] Bush's interest in spreading the war to Syria was considered 'nuts' by some senior Israeli officials, although Prime Minister Ehud Olmert has generally shared Bush's hard-line strategy against Islamic militants," reporter Tom Regan wrote in the *Christian Science Monitor*. "After rebuffing Bush's suggestion about attacking Syria, the Israeli government settled on a strategy of mounting a major assault in southern Lebanon aimed at rooting out Hezbollah guerrillas who have been firing Katyusha rockets into northern Israel." Israel's decision to limit its war to an attack on Hezbollah was not greeted warmly by Israel's most ardent supporters in America, who wondered why Israel was holding back. But Prime Minister Ehud Olmert was adamant. Israel did not want to turn its limited war with Hezbollah into an unfettered regional war.

This was not the first time that an Israeli prime minister had rebuffed Israel's U.S. supporters. After winning election as Israel's prime minister in 1992, Yitzhak Rabin traveled to the United States to meet then president Bill Clinton and to speak with Israel's supporters in the Jewish community. The groundwork for Rabin's American trip was laid by Israeli newspapers, who emphasized the Israel lobby's support for Rabin's opponent in the Israeli elections, Yitzhak Shamir. The Israeli press criticized AIPAC for its support for Shamir and called for the resignation of AIPAC leader Tom Dine. An aide to Rabin was blunt: "American Jews sometimes think that they know what is better for Israel than Israelis do, but what is really at issue for them is not Israel, but money. They have spent so long selling Israel as a nation under attack that the prospect that peace might break out scares the hell out of them. Let's be real honest about this: every time that we're threatened they end up padding their pockets."

During his trip to the United States, Rabin was, if anything, more outspoken when he addressed those who had supported Shamir—and had opposed his announced goal of seeking peace with the Palestinians. In August 1994, Rabin faced off against the AIPAC leadership in a meeting in Washington. "You've aroused too much antagonism, you keep too many enemies for yourself and your record is poor," he told them. "We decided in a democratic way what are our priorities. It's we, the Israelis that will decide it." Rabin's message was clear, startling, and almost insulting. "You have damaged Israel," he intoned. An AIPAC supporter, listening in the audience, characterized Rabin's remarks in the following terms: "He told us that the government of Israel resides in Jerusalem, and not in some lobbyist's office in Washington."

The leaders of the Israel lobby resented Rabin's message. "He told us that he did not need our permission to act as prime minister," one of them said. "That was pretty much the gist of it." She went on to note, "It was a real shocker. I can understand his sensitivity, but to say that we damaged Israel. Really, it's too much." Yet the lobby should have seen this coming. Prior to Rabin's arrival, Matti Golan, a leading Israeli commentator, wrote about the Israel lobby and Israel's supporters in America in *With Friends Like You*, a book popular in Israel. Golan slammed the lobby and Israel's Jewish supporters as being "more harmful to Israel than the PLO" (this was prior to the Oslo Accords). One of the reasons for this, Golan claimed, is that although Israel's Jewish friends in America give money to the lobby and to Israel, they give little else: They do not live in Israel; their children are do not serve in its military; they make none of the sacrifices that Israeli Jews make. They stay on the sidelines, applauding when Israel does what its American friends want, criticizing it when it doesn't.

At the core of Golan's argument is an imagined exchange between an Israeli Jew and an American Jew. The Israeli is harshly outspoken in his condemnation of Jews who support Israel for their own purposes: "What you feel for me is a special connection of belonging to the same people. But there's a catch here, too. Do you know why? Because your feeling of affection depends almost entirely on what I can do for your own self-image. That's why you had genuinely warm feelings for me [when] I triumphed over the combined armies of half-a-dozen Arab countries in my War of Independence. I was the good little David vanquishing the big bad Goliath against all odds and expectations."

The Israeli then turns to the sacrifices made by his country during the 1967 war. The American is overcome with emotion, remembering Israel's great victory: "I remember dropping everything to sit glued to the radio and television around the clock. And to pray. Nonstop. With tears in my eyes. And to pray some more. Physically I was in America, but my heart was with you." His Israeli friend responds:

> Yes. That's precisely the point, isn't it? I can tell you quite categorically that your heart helped me very little in those days. I was staring destruction in the face. I—you—the whole world—saw it as more than just a possibility; it seemed almost a certainty. And what did you do about it? You cried and prayed and sent me your heart. But your body stayed in America. Do you know what would have happened if all the predictions had come true? You would have cried and prayed for my soul a little harder, but you would have gone on living while I would have been dead.

Not much has changed in Washington in the years since Golan wrote these words in 1992. If anything, matters have gotten worse. In the midst of Israel's war with Hezbollah, in the late summer of 2006, Israel's strongest supporters in the United States urged the Israeli government to "take off the gloves" in their war. That Israel might actually lose the conflict—or that, as some argued, its attack was out of all proportion to the threat it faced—was not even considered. Writing in the *Los Angeles Times*, conservative Max Boot (a senior fellow at the Council on Foreign Relations and a widely published columnist) implied that the United States was holding Israel back. "To secure its borders, Israel needs to hit the [Syrian] Assad regime. Hard," Boot wrote. "If it does, it will be doing Washington's dirty work. Our best response is exactly what Bush has done so far—reject premature calls for a cease-fire and let Israel finish the job."

Boot implies that Israel couldn't wait to attack Syria but that the White House was counseling caution. Just the opposite was true. Israelis were actually more moderate in their expectations of what they could do than the United States. Surprisingly, Boot's words brought little protest from the American Jewish community, as if they agreed that that is what Israel was for: to do Washington's "dirty work." Boot's imprecation was repeated by Irving Kristol, who wrote of the war as if he were an Israeli. "Our focus should be less on Hamas and Hezbollah, and more on their paymasters and real commanders: Syria and Iran," he wrote in the July 24, 2006, edition of the *Weekly Standard*. "For that matter, we might consider countering this act of Iranian aggression with a military strike against Iranian nuclear facilities. Why wait?"

"Who's *our*? Who's *we*?" a Jewish American activist responded. "It just goes to show—the United States will fight the war on terror to the last drop of Israeli blood."

Golan complains that American Jews believe that Israel should do *their* bidding, Mearsheimer and Walt complain that the Israel lobby believes America should do *Israel's* bidding (even when it's not in America's interest), and Boot and Kristol complain that America is timid (we should stop "holding them back"). For Golan, "the problem" is with American Jews; for Mearsheimer and Walt, it's with "the Israel lobby"; for Boot and Kristol, it's with the cowardly American government. But maybe "the problem" isn't with American Jews (who are hardly united in their views of Israel) or the Israel lobby (after all, advocates for Israel have a right to exercise their influence) or the American government (which certainly didn't hold Israel back when it came to bombing Gaza). Maybe "the problem" is with America's (and the West's) view of Israel. Maybe Israel isn't what we think it is.

FOR NEARLY ALL Americans, Israel is "the Jewish State." But that's only nominally true. Of the 7.3 million people of Israel, approximately 2.5 million of Israel's citizens are not Jews; they are Arab Muslims and a smattering of other religious denominations. Put simply: credible claims put the population of Israel at about 4.8 million Jews and 2.5 million Muslims, Christians, Druze, and Samaritans. In fact, according to this figure, "the Jewish State" is a bit more than 34 percent non-Jewish, a very sizable minority. That is a controversial figure, however, and is disputed by the Israeli government. Yet, even in the best instance, in a figure cited by the Israeli Central Bureau of Statistics, of a total population of 7,411,000, 20.2 percent of all Israeli citizens are Arabs and another 320,000 are non-Jewish immigrants. This is a very sizable minority. If the same proportions held for the population of the United States, 60 million people would be non-Christians. Such a large number would almost certainly have a significant impact on American policies, viewpoints, and culture: It is already difficult to describe the United States as a "predominantly Christian state"; with 60 million Muslims and other non-Christians it would be nearly impossible. Even now, given America's vast diversity, Osama bin Laden and his cohort's description of the American invasion of Iraq as a part of the Christian "crusader program" sounds ludicrous. For the most part, Americans and their coalition partners viewed the invasion of Iraq not as a part of "Christianity's war on terror" but as a part of "America's war on terror," or (if we were to include Europe) as part of "Christian civilization's war on terror." So too, it is nonsensical to say that Jerusalem is occupied by "the Jews," as if those who attend temple services in Milwaukee or New York or anywhere in America are as responsible as the Israeli government for the occupation of the West Bank or the assault on Gaza.

Israelis are much more sensitive to this conflation of "Jew" and "Israeli" than are Jewish Americans. According to Israeli commentator and journalist Yossi Melman, the Israeli public prefers that they be described as "Israeli," not "Jewish." Melman speaks of "the Israeli public" (not the "Jewish public") and the "Israeli military"—not the "Jewish military." For Melman, although Israel has hardly settled on a unitary identity, it is clearly more than simply "a Jewish state." A national identity has emerged in Israel that Jewish Americans are not a part of. In truth, Israelis think of themselves as more than just Jews who happen to be living together in the same country. They are distinctively different from other Jews. They are Israelis. Even so, Israelis see themselves as representing what Israeli historian Walter Laqueur calls "the new Jew"—the Jew who is not a victim, who is tied to the land, to a new nation, to a national Jewish project.

Laqueur's *History of Zionism* remains a touchstone for those who are engaged in attempting to define what it means to be a Jew, an Israeli—or a Zionist. As early as 1972, Laqueur identified the transformation that Israel had wrought on the world Jewish community and on the way that Israeli Jews think about themselves. For Laqueur, the crucial question was no longer whether the Jewish people would survive (a question that was very much on the minds of the first Zionists in the late nineteenth and early twentieth centuries), but whether *Israel* would survive. The romanticism of Zionism, of creating a state, was beginning to wear off. Laqueur implied that whereas Judaism remained vibrant and robust, the idea that Jews had created a "Jewish national home" was "limited." That is, Israelis were beginning to think of themselves as something different than just an extension of the world Jewish community: "While esteem for Jewish determination and prowess has increased as the result of the creation of the state, the position of Jews—contrary to widespread hope—has not become more secure," he wrote.

The Zionist sense that Israel's claim to be a "spiritual lodestone, a redemptive model, a centre of humanity" has waned in Israel, Laqueur argued. Being Jewish is an integral part of being

Israeli, but it is not the only way that Israelis define themselves. How do Israelis separate their Jewish identity from their national identity? The simple answer is that they don't. Yossi Melman has made this clear in posing a series of seminal, if uncomfortable, questions:

> I am aware of the special, often confusing, problem we face con-cerning the question of our identity: Who, as Israelis, are we? We are born and nurtured in a free, democratic, and westernized society—but many of our institutions are intensely bureaucratic and reach into private life. . . . The state of Israel defines itself as a Jewish state, but what does this mean? Are we Israelis or are we Jews? Which identity takes precedence? What is our nationality—Israeli or Jewish? Does our Jewishness express itself in national terms, or rather, in religious ones? And what about the terms "the Jewish people" and "the Jewish state"? Do they exclude Arabs who live in Israel? Finally, what is our mainstream culture—European or Middle Eastern?

The idea that there is an emerging Israeli identity that is dis-tinct from a Jewish identity is everywhere apparent in Israel. So it is that Israelis draw clear distinctions between Jewish religious beliefs and the Jewish program for establishing a homeland for Jews and are careful not to speak of a "Jewish occupation of the West Bank" or a "Jewish war with Arabs." For Israelis, it is impos-sible to think of Judaism as a religion that condones the occupa-tion of a foreign land, that relegates another people to the status of second-class citizens, that would condone the use of white phosphorous shells against a civilian population. This dichotomy is what Melman means by "the special, often confusing, prob-lem." Judaism would never do these things. Israel has. It is no wonder that Israelis recoil from saying that "the Jews" treat Arab Israelis as second-class citizens, that "the Jews" lay siege to Gaza, or that "the Jews" occupy Jerusalem. Such a description sounds like what it is: blaming the entire Jewish people for the policies of a nation-state that contains a Jewish majority. It's anti-Semitism. The question of Israeli identity resonates throughout the Middle East and poisons the already poisonous Arab-Israeli conflict with a religious component that it need not have. This central truth is obvious to anyone who has engaged in political exchanges with Israelis, Palestinians, and Jewish Americans.

There are any number of Islamist leaders who understand that there are differences between Jews and "the Zionist national project," as the early Zionist settlers called their program to establish a homeland for Jews. These Islamists have no problem in meeting and speaking with Jews (and have met with them continually over the past few decades), but they hesitate to meet with Israelis. "We have no problem with the Jews," Hezbollah's Nawaf Moussaoui said. "Our argument is with Israel." And he added, "There's a difference." Senior Hamas official Usamah Hamdan agrees: "We are facing an Israeli occupation, we are dodging Israeli bullets. This is not a Jewish occupation, these are not Jewish bullets. I meet with Jews all the time. But they are not occupying our land. The Israelis are."

For Moussaoui and Hamdan, the hesitation over meeting with Israelis is purely political. It is not because they are Jewish. The contention with Israel is not religious; it is national. In the spring of 2008, a prominent activist who has worked for Israeli-Palestinian peace for many decades visited Hamas leader Khalid Meshaal in Damascus. He spoke with him about the Israeli-Palestinian conflict and about the religious fight over the land of Israel. Both peoples—Muslims and Jews—cite their holy books in attempting to argue their points, this activist said. Both peoples believe that God promised them the land. In the Torah, the "land of Israel" is reserved by God for the Jews; in the Koran, the *wafk* (literally, "endowment") is reserved for Muslims. But the contention over who was promised what cannot be decided now, this activist said. Rather, the issue would be decided by God in "redeemed time"—when God would make his wishes known to all. Until then (in our "unredeemed time"), this activist concluded, Jews and Muslims, Israelis and Palestinians could agree to divide the land between themselves.

Meshaal thought for a moment before responding. He said that he found the argument compelling, but he disagreed with it. "This is an argument among men," he said. "God has nothing to do with it."

IS IT POSSIBLE to be against Israel but not be an anti-Semite?

On December 27, 2008, Israel launched an air assault on Gaza. Israeli warplanes targeted the leaders of the Islamic Resistance Movement in an attempt to destroy Hamas's infrastructure, police force, security services, and weapons stores. Israeli leaders defended the assault by saying that the attack was in response to continued rocket fire into southern Israel. The assault followed the end of a fragile six-month cease-fire that had expired on December 19. Hamas defended its rocket fire on Israel by pointing out that Israel had not lived up to its promise to end the economic siege of Gaza, which had been in place since the summer of 2007, when Hamas forces had waged a bitter battle against their Fatah rivals. Israel had spent many months planning for the attack, and their opening aerial bombardment of Hamas positions was very successful: After the first twenty-four hours of the assault, Israeli officials said that 227 Hamas fighters had been killed and over 700 had been wounded. Thousands of people protested the attack worldwide, but Israel enjoyed support in its assault from the United States and the European Union.

American newspapers supported Israel; European editorialists were more circumspect. "Israel's air offensive against the Gaza Strip yesterday should not have been a surprise for anyone who has been following the mounting hostilities in the region," the lead editorial in the *Washington Post* intoned on the day after the start of the Israeli attack, "least of all the Hamas movement, which invited the conflict by ending a six-month-old ceasefire and launching scores of rockets and mortar shells at Israel during the last 10 days." The *Times* of London, however, said that the Israeli attack followed numerous cease-fire violations and "breakdowns"—a mounting escalation that had begun (the *Times* pointed out) in July. As the conflict worsened, the American government, and a large portion of the major American press, continued its support of Israel, while European nations began to distance themselves from the Israeli offensive.

By the beginning of January, the United Kingdom began drafting a UN resolution calling for a cease-fire. At first, the U.S. government supported the British call, but by January 8 the Americans were having second thoughts, and a discernable gap over the cease-fire issue began to open between the United States and the United Kingdom. On the night of January 9, after the United States vetoed the British resolution, Secretary of State Condoleezza Rice explained the American change of heart: "Here you have a terrorist organization and a member-state, Israel, and there isn't any equivalence here. Israel was defending itself because of these (Hamas) rocket attacks. Yet, we are concerned about the suffering of the people, the humanitarian situation, and we're doing everything we can to alleviate that, as well."

According to press reports, the shift in the American position came after Prime Minister Olmert called President Bush urging him to veto the resolution. Bush complied. Several days after the telephone conversation, Olmert chortled about the call: "When we saw that the secretary of state, for reasons we did not really understand, wanted to vote in favour of the U.N. resolution I looked for President Bush and they told me he was in Philadelphia making a speech," Olmert said. "I said, 'I don't care. I have to talk to him now.' They got him off the podium, brought him to another room and I spoke to him. I told him, 'You can't vote in favour of this resolution.' He said, 'Listen, I don't know about it, I didn't see it, I'm not familiar with the phrasing.'" Olmert then told Bush, "'I'm familiar with it. You can't vote in favour.' He gave an order to the secretary of state and she did not vote in favour of it—a resolution she cooked up, phrased, organized and maneuvered for. She was left pretty shamed and abstained on a resolution she arranged."

As Great Britain, France, and other European countries continued to work to end the fighting, Bush defended Israel and placed the blame for Israel's attack on the Islamic Resistance Movement: "The situation now taking place in Gaza was caused by Hamas," he told reporters. "Instead of caring about the people of Gaza, Hamas decided to use Gaza to launch rockets to kill innocent Israelis. Israel obviously decided to protect herself and her people." Israeli leaders and their American and European allies universally condemned Hamas for breaking the cease-fire, but Hamas leaders claimed the facts were otherwise. "We told the Israelis in Cairo that we would extend the ceasefire if they would end the economic blockade," a Hamas leader said within hours of the beginning of the assault. "Israel broke the ceasefire on November 4. They came into Gaza and killed six people and wounded dozens more. It was a clear violation, and we protested it. But no one paid attention. Still, we held back. It was Israel that wanted this fight."

Although Israel's violation of the cease-fire went virtually unmentioned in the major American press, Israel's press reviewed the mounting tensions between Hamas and the Israeli government. *Haaretz*, Israel's prominent English-language newspaper, editorialized at length on Israel's November violation of the cease-fire. *Haaretz*'s editorial staff, in fact, placed the responsibility for the attack on both Hamas and Israel. Their comments were balanced and thoughtful. "The inherent desire for retribution does not necessarily have to blind us to the view from the day after. . . . Israel's violation of the lull in November expedited the deterioration that gave birth to the war of yesterday. But even if this continues for many days and even weeks, it will end in an agreement, or at least an understanding similar to that reached last June." *Haaretz*'s commentary urged the Israeli government to dampen its military attacks and begin searching for a way to call a cease-fire:

> Hamas's terms for calm have not changed: a cessation of the attacks on Gaza and the organization's activities in the West Bank, a reopening of the Gaza border crossings, and a release of Palestinian prisoners. Israel's demands will also remain as they were: a halt to rocket attacks on its towns. It would behoove both sides to enlist every possible mediator—from Egypt to Qatar to the United States and Europe—to implement those terms. One may assume that the military message Israel sent was fully understood. It would be best not to turn it into a disaster that would preclude a future agreement.

Senior correspondents for *Haaretz* were even more outspoken than the newspaper's editorial staff. They seemed to place the blame for the cease-fire on Israel. "Six months ago Israel asked and received a cease-fire from Hamas," Zvi Barel wrote at the beginning of the attack. "It unilaterally violated it when it blew up a tunnel, while still asking Egypt to get the Islamic group to hold its fire." Another *Haaretz* writer, Gideon Levy, went even further: "Israel embarked yesterday on yet another unnecessary, ill-fated war. On July 16, 2006, four days after the start of the Second Lebanon War, I wrote: 'Every neighborhood has one, a loud-mouthed bully who shouldn't be provoked into anger. . . . Not that the bully's not right—someone did harm him. But the reaction, what a reaction!'" Historian Tom Segev, an admired public figure in Israel, asked whether the Israeli government's decision to launch the offensive was wise: "The assault on Gaza does not first and

foremost demand moral condemnation—it demands a few historical reminders. Both the justification given for it and the chosen
targets are a replay of the same basic assumptions that have
proven wrong time after time. Yet Israel still pulls them out of its
hat again and again, in one war after another."

IT TAKES COURAGE for Israelis to criticize the Israeli government,
particularly when a war waged by that government is so popular.
The Israeli public overwhelmingly supported the Israeli Defense
Force's attack on Gaza. *Haaretz*'s editorial writers and their colum-
nists, however, questioned the wisdom of the attack and were outspoken in raising doubts about whether it had been necessary. But
American commentators, a large number of whom have been vocal
in their support for Israel, could not find the same courage. Their
support for Israel was outspoken, the language they used inflammatory. They seemed filled with an almost obsessive hate for Hamas,
for the Palestinians, for Arabs, and for Muslims. The outpouring began on January 1, 2009, in the pages of the *Washington Post*.

Robert Lieber, a professor of international studies at Georgetown
University, began the onslaught with a commentary that accused
Hamas of transforming Gaza into "a military base for Iran." He
stated that Israel's attacks on Gaza were justified and that early figures from the attacks showed that Israel was targeting the Hamas
military infrastructure, that only a few civilians had died. He quoted
anti-Hamas Palestinian officials as condemning the Islamic Resistance Movement for sparking the conflict. "PLO and Fatah officials
fault Hamas for the deaths in Gaza," he wrote, "and an adviser to
Palestinian President Mahmoud Abbas, Nimr Hammad, told the
Lebanese newspaper *Al-Akhbar*: 'The one responsible for the massacres is Hamas, and not the Zionist entity, which in its own view
reacted to the firing of Palestinian missiles.'" He described Hamas
as "a radical, terrorist, adventurist, Islamist organization" and noted
that it enjoyed little support by Muslim governments—aside from

"Iran and its surrogates." Lieber's conclusion left little doubt about where he stood: "Egypt and Jordan have made peace with Israel, not because they embraced the ideas of Theodor Herzl, the founder of modern Zionism, but because they concluded that the effort to destroy the Jewish state had failed and that refusing to come to terms with it was harmful to their national interests. Ultimately, peace will be possible only if most Palestinians and their leaders become convinced that terrorism and violence are a dead end and that they cannot under any circumstances prevail over Israel through the use of force."

Lieber's views were moderate in comparison with those expressed by Charles Krauthammer, whose column the next day ("Moral Clarity in Gaza") dripped with sarcasm. Krauthammer implied that Hamas's goal in firing rockets into Israel was not to kill Israelis but to kill Palestinians. As he wrote, "For Hamas, the only thing more prized than dead Jews are dead Palestinians." This decidedly odd view is actually not without precedent. Golda Meir had said essentially the same thing—with a twist—at the National Press Club in 1957, long before her celebrated tenure as Israel's prime minister. "We will have peace with the Arabs when they will love their children more than they hate us." Meir implied that "Arabs" were willing to sacrifice their children if it meant Israelis would die. She once said this directly to Egyptian president Anwar Sadat. "We can forgive you for killing our sons. But we will never forgive you for making us kill yours." That is to say, if an Israeli pulls a trigger and an Arab dies, it is not the Israeli's fault. It is the Arab's fault.

Krauthammer repeated this perverse mantra: "For Hamas, the only thing more prized than dead Jews are dead Palestinians. The religion of Jew-murder and self-martyrdom is ubiquitous." He went on to note, "At war today in Gaza, one combatant is committed to causing the most civilian pain and suffering on both sides. The other combatant is committed to saving as many lives as possible—

also on both sides." According to this reasoning, when Arabs kill Israelis (or "Jews," as Krauthammer says), it is the Arabs' fault. When Israelis kill Arabs, it is also the Arabs' fault. No matter what happens, no matter who dies, no matter who pulls the trigger—it can never be the fault of the Israelis. Their sole purpose in attacking Gaza was self-defense. And Hamas's purpose? Why, it wasn't even to kill Jews. It was to kill Palestinians—because they hate their children more.

This drumbeat continued (on the same page) in a commentary written by Michael Gerson ("Defining Victory for Israel"). In his column, Gerson compared Hamas's attacks on Israel to the attacks on London during "the Blitz," in World War II. "There is no question—none—that Israel's attack on Hamas in Gaza is justified," Gerson wrote. "No nation can tolerate a portion of its people living in the conditions of the London Blitz—listening for sirens, sleeping in bomb shelters and separated from death only by the randomness of a Qassam missile's flight. And no group aspiring to nationhood, such as Hamas, can be exempt from the rules of sovereignty, morality and civilization, which, at the very least, forbid routine murder attempts against your neighbors." Gerson went on to claim that Israel's attack on Hamas was an integral part of America's war on terror. Israel is facing a military test, he said, but America is facing a test in identifying who is good and who is bad. "America, in turn, faces a test of its moral judgment," Gerson wrote. "This conflict is not a contest between shades of gray in mist and fog. It is a matter of distinguishing between murderers and victims—and of supporting an ally until a clear victory against terrorism is achieved."

Although there were few responses to Lieber, Krauthammer, and Gerson in the pages of the *Washington Post*, their comments raise questions. If, as Lieber claims, Gaza is "a military base for Iran," then why is the Hamas militia so poorly armed? Where are its tanks, it rocket-propelled grenades, its surface-to-air missiles?

If it is true that Israel is not responsible for the deaths of Palestinians in Gaza (some 1,430 by Hamas's count), then why were there all those corpses in the streets of Gaza City? Is it really rational to believe that Hamas purposely killed its own people in order to bring down international opprobrium on Israel? Lieber calls Hamas "a radical, terrorist, adventurist, Islamist organization." He has a right to his opinion, but how many Hamas members has he met or spoken with? He might be right in his views, but the Palestinian people don't think so. They voted for Hamas in January 2006 in overwhelming numbers. It wasn't because they viewed Hamas as "radical, terrorist, adventurist, Islamist"— it's because they thought Hamas could provide good government. They still do.

Is Krauthammer right? Do Palestinians hate their own children more than they hate the Israelis? Does that even make sense? Did Israel attack Gaza because Israel is "committed to saving as many lives as possible"? If Palestinians die, is that, as Gold Meir implies, their own fault? When do dead Palestinians become the responsibility of Israel?

And what of Gerson? Simple arithmetic might add perspective to his claim that living in Israel is like living in London during the Blitz. Thirteen Israelis died from Hamas rocket attacks before Israel's November onslaught. That is hardly comparable to the London Blitz, in which 48,000 people were killed. Then too, and more insidiously, in making the comparison he makes, Gerson implies that Palestinians are like the Germans during World War II or, as Paul Wolfowitz might have said, that they are Nazis. And yet if a Palestinian brigade were loose in Tel Aviv, would we say that the Israelis must disarm? If Israeli corpses were piled high on Dizengoff Street, would we say that their deaths were their own fault? If Israelis were fighting in their own streets, would we say that for Israelis, the only thing more prized than a dead Palestinian is a dead Jew? And if we did make that claim, what would that make us?

During his campaign for the presidency, Barack Obama visited Sderot—a town in southern Israel that had been regularly hit by Hamas rockets. "If somebody was sending rockets into my house where my two daughter sleep at night, I'm going to do everything in my power to stop that," he said at the time. "And I would expect Israelis to do the same thing." We agree. We all agree. But do Palestinians have the same right? If Barack Obama were living in Gaza with his two daughters and Israeli shells were landing on his home, would he say, "I'm going to do everything in my power to stop that?"

AMERICANS NEED TO begin to sort through their feelings about Israel. We must begin to see Israel for what it is. Israel is not "a Jewish national project." It is a nation-state. As such, it is capable of waging a war in which innocent people die. It is capable of making mistakes. We do violence to our understanding of Israel, and to what Israelis think of themselves, by continually and purposely conflating the moral dimension of Judaism with the moral concerns of the Israeli government. Jews, Christians, Muslims, Hindus, and Buddhists are all members of religions that place the human being at the center of human history. For all of them, human life is sacred—and has been breathed into our species by a power greater than any of us. That is not true for nation-states. Our "Judeo-Christian values" created societies that extol the rights of the individual and created nations and people that gave us profoundly moving works of art, literature, and music, that gave us Beethoven, Bach, and Brahms. But those same societies, those same "values," gave us something else too: They gave us Buchenwald, Bergen-Belsen, and Auschwitz.

The failure to make the distinction between Judaism and Israel will lead us not to "moral clarity" but to the kind of muddled thinking that is reflected in the most extreme defenses of Israel—and that leads to hate speech. But if we begin to make the kinds of distinctions that Israelis are making about themselves—if we separate the foundational humanist beliefs of Judaism from the political goals of Israel—we will be able to answer the more important questions that crowd in on us in the war on terror: are Hezbollah and Hamas enemies of Israel because they are anti-Semites, or are they called anti-Semites because they are the enemies of Israel?

CHAPTER EIGHT

TALKING TO TERRORISTS

"Here the answer is always yes."
— A PALESTINIAN FRIEND

I HAVE SPENT twenty years traveling to and from and living in the Middle East. I have been to Israel, the West Bank and Gaza, sometimes for weeks at a time. I have been to the region over forty times. I have been to Lebanon, Jordan, Syria, Egypt, and Tunisia. I have visited Saudi Arabia.

On my first flight to the Middle East, I met a group of German Masons, from a lodge in Hamburg. They were traveling to Jerusalem to measure "the greater house" of Solomon's Temple. It is a part of their Masonic rite. In the back of the plane, teenagers returning to Israel from America were singing Israeli songs. They were happy to be going home. Later in the trip I was invited to attend the reunion of officers of the British army who had served in Israel during the Mandate era of the late 1940s. They sang army songs and talked of "Jewish and Arab terrorism."

On one trip I met an elderly Israeli woman, going from Tel Aviv to Paris to be with her daughter and son-in-law. She told me she was leaving Israel to live with them and spend time with her grandchildren. "Israel has always been my dream," she said. "My husband is buried there. But I cannot stay there now. It is too diffi-cult for me, at my age. My daughter needs to care for me." She was crying.

In all my travels to the Middle East, I befriended some of the finest people I have ever known. I became friends with an elderly man in Amman, in his nineties and nearly blind, who once told me a good story. "I was a translator for the king," the elderly man said when I visited him in his home in Amman. "I met Churchill."

Once, he remembers, he sat between Winston Churchill and the future king, Abdullah, at a table in a dark room in Amman. The light shone only on their faces, with people standing in the dark in the room, watching. This was in 1921. "It was a long time ago," the man said, his voice filled with age. "It seems like another lifetime." He sat for a moment, remembering. The man translated for the two officials. Churchill told the king, "In consideration of your service to His Majesty, we are pleased to award you the King-dom of Transjordan." The man hesitated, trying to shape the Ara-bic words for "in consideration of." He told me, "I just couldn't find the Arabic." A voice in the back of the room found the words and said it aloud for him. The man nodded and gave the trans-lation. The old man remembered every part of the story. "Later, during the reception, I looked for the face that went with that voice, and I saw the man, a British officer standing in the corner by himself. So I went to him and I said, 'You are the person who knew the translation of 'in consideration of'—your Arabic is very good. I would like to know your name. The man smiled and told me, 'My name is Lawrence.'" The man blinked behind his thick glasses. "That is my story," he said.

I became friends with the Palestinian owners of a hotel in East Jerusalem and with a senior official for a kibbutz in Israel. The Palestinian hotel owners suffered greatly during the Second In-tifada. The hotel is a hotel for pilgrims, who come in great crowds from England and Germany and Tanzania and Greece. They are Greek Orthodox and Copts and Catholics and Lutherans. The pilgrims pray in the lobby, where great soft sofas are pushed end to end. The pilgrims fold their hands and sink to their knees and cross themselves as the Palestinian boys standing at the bar watch with interest. During the day, huge buses come and take the pilgrims to Nazareth, in northern Israel, where they visit the birthplace of Jesus. On Friday nights, the hotel puts on a dinner that features Palestinian dancers. All of this ended for the four years of the Second Intifada. The hotel was virtually empty, and on many nights, I was the only guest. I would get up in the middle of the night and wander through the hallways and make myself coffee and write on the only computer in the hotel. "When will this end?" the owners would ask me. And I would always answer, "I don't know." At night, because of the Israeli checkpoints, the Palestinian waiters would stretch out on the couches and sleep. They would try to go home every week.

Once, while driving from Amman to Aqaba, I spotted an American fast-food restaurant. I was overjoyed. There were camels tethered to stones in the parking lot. It was a unique sight, one you do not see often now in the Middle East. I marveled at it. I wished I had a camera. The desert was bare and went on forever. It was the real desert, with only a small plant here and there amid the orange and yellow and red. The sun shimmered off the desert and waves of heat rose at the horizon. The road was as flat as an Iowa highway, following the contours of the land. Thousands of years ago our ancestors came this way, looking for a place to live, following the melting ice. They went up the highway and then down into the Jordan Valley to Jericho, building one of the world's oldest cities. The Palestinians built a casino in Jericho, where the Christian boys of Bethlehem had good jobs. Israelis would come, speeding down the highway from Tel Aviv and Jerusalem, to play Texas hold 'em at the casino. A group of Muslim elders came to Arafat to protest. He told them to go away. The casino was closed during the Second Intifada, and it has never reopened. A stone could have been rolled down that highway all the way to Aqaba.

My friend from the kibbutz—one of the few remaining communes in Israel—invited me to his home, where he introduced me to his family. That night, they escorted me to a kibbutz dinner, where all the families gathered. The entire crowd sang patriotic songs of Israel. They laughed and talked together. They were a proud people and proud of their work, of what they had created. The man told me a little about himself and his family. During the dinner, the man's youngest son asked me about Hollywood. He said he wanted to be a producer. His father, my friend, looked at me and rolled his eyes. I told the boy that Hollywood was not all it was cracked up to be. "It's a lot of work," I said. "It sounds romantic, but it's not so easy to do." He told me that he would do it "for sure" and that he knew just the kind of films he would make. He talked about Al Pacino. "The best actor there is," he said. He asked me if I knew him. No, I said, I had never met Al Pacino. I later asked his mother if she was upset that her youngest son didn't want to stay in Israel. She smiled. "I don't worry," she says. "He won't go." He didn't.

The family's oldest son was the commander of a tank unit in Gaza. His family was worried about him, but they didn't say anything. He had been home on leave the week before. The family was still talking about it. "He is doing his duty," his father said. "He is serving his country." On another day, my friend and his wife took me to dinner. There was an Arab restaurant they liked, just north of the kibbutz. "It has some of the finest Arab food in the Middle East," my friend said. He was right.

IN 1993 I was privileged to introduce Yitzhak Rabin to a group of Arab American reporters in Washington, but after my introduction, Rabin was angry. "You made two mistakes," he said.

The first was that you called Israel's 1948 war the War of Independence. If you want to make friends with Arabs, you have to be sensitive to how they view things. For us it was a great triumph, the realization of our dream. But for them, it was a catastrophe. Second, and most important, you called me "a man of peace." I want you to know, I am not a man of peace. I am an Israeli patriot and I am a soldier. I would do anything to help Israel. If making peace will help Israel, I will do that. If making war and killing Palestinians will help Israel, why, then I would do that too. I will do anything for the country I love.

Just months earlier, over coffee, I had asked Rabin whether he would ever negotiate with Arafat. He said he would never do so. He said it seven times: "I will never, never, never, never, never, never, never negotiate with Arafat." Years later, it came to me: When he had said that he would "never" negotiate with Arafat, he knew that Shimon Peres was in Oslo, negotiating with Arafat. Less than one year after saying "never," he was shaking Arafat's hand on the White House lawn.

I was first taken to the city of Tunis in North Africa by my friend Tom Martin, who worked tirelessly for many years in Washington helping the Palestinians and who had been based in that city since leaving Lebanon in 1982. In Tunis, Tom introduced me to Bassam Abu Sharif. Abu Sharif was a vibrant man, filled with life, who was then tasked with assisting Arafat with coordinating Fatah's external relations. I would meet him in his office in Tunis, which was in a large room in his home. "Where is the organization's foreign ministry?" I once asked him. He pointed to a file cabinet: "In those drawers."

Abu Sharif's left hand was gnarled, and there was a long scar on the side of his face. One of his eyes was clouded and sightless. Ironically, *Time* magazine once described his scarred face as "the face of terror." As a senior official of the Popular Front for the Liberation

of Palestine, he had organized the 1970 hijacking of four international airliners—from Swissair, TWA, Pan Am, and El Al—all on
the same day. The hijackers of the El Al flight were overpowered,
but the rest of the aircraft flew to Dawson's Field in Jordan, where
the passengers were freed and the aircraft destroyed. The "Dawson's
Field hijackings" were a legendary moment in Palestinian history.
In 1972, in Damascus, Abu Sharif opened a letter, which blew up.
He lost four fingers and was deafened in one ear and blinded in one
eye. During my first visit to Tunis, he told me the story of the hijackings and the letter bomb. "But that is all in the past," he said.
"Now we have to have a different strategy." He told me that he had
contacted an acquaintance who was friends with Ariel Sharon.
"Tell him, please tell him, it is time to talk," Abu Sharif told his
friend. The man was skeptical, but he promised to pass the message
on to Sharon. Several months later, the man returned. Abu Sharif
was anxious to hear Sharon's reply. "Did you pass on the message?"
The man said he had. "Well, what did he say?" The man looked at
his shoes: "He said, 'Ask Abu Sharif: Didn't he get my letter?'"

In 1990 I met Yasser Arafat in his office in Tunis. He asked me
if I was hungry. The question was rhetorical. He got up from his
desk and did something that made me uncomfortable but that, after a time, I grew used to. He took my hand in his and squeezed it
and held it, and we walked, hand in hand, down a stairway and
across a courtyard to a two-story building. In the basement of the
building was a cafeteria, filled with Palestinian boys and girls of
all ages, from very small children to older teenagers. All of them
were orphans, children of those who had died fighting in Lebanon. They were all milling about, and there was a lot of noise.
When Arafat entered they scrambled for their seats.

He walked me down among the tables, still holding my hand,
and placed me between a boy of about eleven and a little girl of
about eight. The boy, wearing a big smile, was happy to be sitting
next to me; the little girl was indifferent. I remember that her

face was freshly scrubbed and someone had put a red ribbon in her hair. The children stood as Arafat addressed them. The little girl next to me, however, suddenly sat and started sipping her soup. The boy, a smile in his eyes, nudged me with his elbow and in perfect English said, "She couldn't wait." The girl looked at me when the boy talked, and she also smiled and then turned in her seat and pointed at Arafat with her pudgy index finger: "Daddy," she said and then went back to her soup. She made a lot of noise eating, but no one seemed to mind. Arafat's message was simple and, as he told me later, always the same: "Study hard, respect your teachers. Someday you will be in Palestine." He was right.

I met a group of "Arafat's children" in Ramallah thirteen years later—in Palestine. Six of them were living in a new apartment complex that had been built with international donations. They shared one room with a bathroom and a small kitchen. They slept on mattresses on the floor. Two of them were in college. "We have nothing," one of them told me. "But we are here." They had once lived in the orphanage I visited with Arafat, in Tunis.

At times I would sit with Arafat in his headquarters in Ramallah, and in his later years, during the Second Intifada, we would sometimes be there long into the night. He would read from memos and reports, turning over the pages, occasionally pushing them toward me. Coming to see him was not easy. To get to his headquarters from my hotel in Jerusalem, I had to go through or around Israeli checkpoints. Sometimes it would take me hours to travel only a few miles. When I arrived outside his compound—the streets around it were deserted—I would stand behind the façade of a ruined house and look up and down the street. I would sprint to the headquarters' gate, timing my dash to dodge the Israeli tank that drove in circles around and around the compound, occasionally stopping and swiveling its turret. The tank was a behemoth. It rocked and churned as it ground the street outside his offices into a fine powder. It scared the hell out of me. Inside, I would sit and talk with Arafat as the tank circled. I told him once that I was afraid he would be killed. "Don't worry. It is not so bad," he told me. "I am under siege, yes, but I am here among my people, in Palestine. And I am only eight miles from Jerusalem."

To his last days, on his desk, Arafat kept a small picture of Yitzhak Rabin. "I could always call him, with this phone," he said one day. "He would always answer. If they had not killed him, there would be peace."

On his lapel, Arafat wore an Israeli flag crossed with a Palestinian flag. He wore no other ornamentation, no medals, no commendations. Sometimes he would arrange his kaffiyeh, taking great care with it. I never saw him without it. He always dressed the same, but impeccably. Everyone says he was corrupt. That he had millions. Billions. I never saw any evidence of that. Others cared about money. He cared about Palestine.

On my last visit with him, two months before he died, he announced that he wanted to show me a "present" he had gotten from a friend. He was overjoyed with the gift. He went to get it. "Wait here," he said. When he returned, he was holding a digital camera in his hand. "Truly," he said. "It is like magic." We stood in the hallway that ran from his office to the building that housed the Palestinian legislature. The sun was pouring in from the west. He aimed the camera and pointed into the far distance. He snapped a picture and then looked at the digital image and shook his head in wonder. He then turned back to the window and pointed. "Look," he said, "you can see the tall buildings of Tel Aviv." And there they were, shimmering in the distance, sixteen miles away.

I have spoken with the leaders of Hamas and Hezbollah; I have exchanged stories with ambassadors; I slept for a night on the dirt floor of a Palestinian home in Beach Refugee Camp in Gaza. The Gaza family fed me and gave me tea and talked with me into the night. The next day I tried to pay them. They wouldn't take it. The father looked at me and shook his head. "To even offer is a great insult," he said. I mingled with Israelis in Herzliya; I went with my friend Dan to a rock-and-roll bar in Jerusalem. There we met a young Israeli woman who had come from South Africa. "You are from America?" she asked. "Why would you come here? I would never come here. I would stay in America." I stood in the lobby at the Ritz Hotel in East Jerusalem, now closed, and spoke with a group of Palestinian boys. They had heard there was an American staying there and had come, a dozen of them, to talk to me. They had a lot of questions. One of them asked, "What is it like to talk to a girl?" The part of East Jerusalem near the Old City where I lived was close to the National Palace Hotel, where the PLO was founded and had its first meetings; it is also closed now. On the roof of the hotel was a restaurant, with white linen tablecloths. If one wanted a steak in the Old City, that was the place to go. I would sit at a table on the rooftop of the hotel and talk to the waiters. One of them was seventeen and came from Hebron. He had three children, and he wanted to own a hotel one day, he told me.

One summer I went with my friend Asad Masri—a Palestinian doctor from America—to visit his great-aunt in the Old City. We walked along the quiet streets deep into the Arab quarter. We turned through a small stone gate and then walked up some stone steps. It was midday, very hot, and the sun was overhead, beating down. We were both sweating when we arrived at his great-aunt's house. She smiled and hugged him and smiled at me. This was the family home. She sat and talked with her nephew. She asked whether I liked the tea.

Her niece came in from school to talk with us and greeted her uncle: "May Allah bless you, uncle." She was wearing a scarf. Her arms were covered and her dress lapped over her shoes. She wore glasses. Her great aunt bragged about her, calling her an excellent student. My friend the doctor smiled at her, a broad smile. "Aren't you hot in that scarf?" he asked. She shook her head. "Are you sure? It is very hot in here." She looked at him, her mouth set.

"No, uncle," she said. "It is not hot." She eyed him, her mouth
twisted. He talked with his great-aunt for a moment and then
turned back to her. "Are you sure you are not hot?" He had a twin-
kle in his eye. She looked at him sternly. "You know, if you are
hot, you should take off your scarf." She sighed, exasperated, and
this only goaded him. "It looks very hot in this scarf." She shook
her head, taking the bait. "Yes, beloved uncle," she said. "It is very
hot in this scarf. But not as hot as the fires of hell."

OUTSIDE THE DAMASCUS Gate leading into the Old City of
Jerusalem, a long road winds down the hill from the ornate offices
of the Latin Patriarch of Jerusalem, which represents all of the
Roman Catholics in Israel and Palestine. The road is filled with
Palestinian shops, all packed neatly underneath an overhang,
and vendors shout about their wares. The sidewalks are always
crowded, the air is filled with diesel fumes, and at night, summer
or winter, the street's stones are slippery. I buy delicious fresh
olives from a grocery there, whose owners I know well, and eat
them in my room overlooking the Old City.

The street is close to a girl's school. After school, the girls come
down the street to eat their after-school meal at a cheeseburger
joint that is close to my grocery store. The cheeseburger restaurant
also serves french fries; it might be transplanted from any American city. The Palestinian owner once told me he was from Ar-
kansas. "Just like Clinton," he said. "Honest, he is a good friend of
mine." Then he smiled and laughed. "I am lying." One day, while
I was sitting in the restaurant—it was a cold day—I heard music
coming from outside. It was the Bryan Ferry rendition of "Street
Life." At a nearby table, the girls from the school—all wearing
blue smocks, their heads covered by white scarves—ate their food
and giggled and traded stories that all teenage girls have. "Street
Life" was playing in the background. From further away, out over
the Old City, I heard the call to prayer. One of the girls mouthed

the words of the Bryan Ferry song, pretending she was a rock star. They all tapped their feet.

ON JULY 22, 2003, I was gassed and beaten at the Kalandia checkpoint outside Ramallah. The crowd was pushing forward, and everyone was shouting at the Israelis to open the checkpoint. They refused. The men at the front of the crowd were very angry. Suddenly, an Israeli soldier grabbed his rifle, and everyone scattered. As I scrambled with the Palestinian crowd to get away, being pushed by the people behind me, I saw the Israeli soldier throwing a tear gas grenade. He threw it underhand, and it skipped along the street under my feet. The crowd was running. I turned to look at the soldier, while I was still running, and saw him lob another grenade along the ground. It was artfully done. It was a concussion grenade. A dirty trick: We would be gassed and then not able to move. The grenade knocked everyone down. I felt as if my insides had melted. I vomited into the street, holding my stomach, my eyes watering. I gasped for air and thought, don't have a heart attack, not here, not now. I was crawling away because the concussion grenade had turned my legs to jelly. I was helped by a Palestinian doctor who had also been gassed. Between breaths, mucus coming from his nose, he gave me his name. Like me, he was trying to get to Jerusalem. We sat in a nearby field for a moment recovering and watching the Israelis clearing the checkpoint.

A short distance away, two Israeli soldiers took careful aim and killed two Palestinian boys. I remember thinking, why aren't I enraged, or frightened? Why don't I run? The man and I sat there and watched it happen.

After a few minutes the ambulances came. The doctor then told me to follow him and, using a circuitous route, we found ourselves on a West Bank hilltop negotiating with Palestinian drivers who had somehow wrangled some Israeli license plates. The sun was just going down, and the stars were coming out. I could see across the hills of the desert. There were mosques in the distance, their green lights showing. It was very beautiful.

"Don't speak English," the doctor told me as we approached the taxis. "Just keep silent." Men stood in groups smoking. We gave the drivers fifty dollars each in Israeli shekels to drive us to Jerusalem. There were seven people in the car; I sat on the doctor's lap. We made it to Jerusalem by traveling on settler roads.

Once I arrived, even though my sport coat was drenched in gas, I decided I would postpone my shower and grab a beer. I was angry about the day and about being gassed, and I didn't care who smelled me. I walked to the American Colony Hotel, two miles from my hotel. I smelled the gas when I entered the bar, but the smell did not come from me and I looked around. There was the doctor, sitting at the bar. He laughed and waved me over. "You smell like tear gas," I said. "So do you," he responded. I told him I would buy him a drink.

I SAW THE aftermath of a bombing in Israel. The smell was different from that of the teargassing. I heard the explosion from far off and knew what it was. I could feel the shape of it as the vibration passed under my feet. I walked away from the bombing but nevertheless—after a few wrong turns—inadvertently came across its effects. I did not mean to see it. People in the street were bent over, picking up human flesh.

Once, mingling with people shopping on Ben Yehuda Street, I heard their cell phones ring and saw all of them flinch, afraid to answer, fearful of the news. In Israel, during the Second Intifada, all the cell phones rang whenever there was a bombing. Families were calling one another, to see who was still alive. Once, in line waiting for a bus in Jerusalem, eyeing the passengers and wondering, I suddenly thought, there are people who do this here, every day. I am only doing this one time. A circular put out by the militant Palestinian al-Aqsa Martyrs' Brigade appeared during the

Second Intifada warning of a suicide bombing. Distributing such circulars was standard practice by the brigades, to sow fear among the Israeli population. Several days went by without a bombing, however, and the Israeli population began to breathe easier. Then another circular appeared, using the same language and giving the same warning. "Some kind of mix-up," I told an Israeli friend. He shook his head: "No," he said. "It means there are two bombs." There were.

A Palestinian friend of mine, Salah Ta'amri, a famous man in his own society, was once given a special pass to go to Jerusalem and walk the streets near the Knesset. He walked through the cafés and restaurants. He met and talked to people, and he later told me about it in great detail. "I was surprised at how young the Israelis were," he said, "and I thought when I saw them . . . well I wanted to go up to them and say, 'This is not your fault. This is not your fault.'" I and a British colleague once met Salah in the lobby of the Bethlehem Hotel. There had been troubles in Bethlehem, and we were trying to help. Salah walked through the door with some friends, saw us, and stopped: "Oh great," he said. "The great Anglo-American alliance is here to help us. I'm sure everything will be alright now."

Salah once took me to a Palestinian village, deep in the mountains and hills of the West Bank. The villagers were celebrating the opening of a school, and everyone turned out. I was the guest of honor. They brought out a sheep and cut its throat. The sheep sank onto its front knees, and its eyeballs rolled back before it toppled over. Its blood sank into the stones. The villagers cut up the sheep and grilled the meat. I was given the eyeball and the tail. The women asked if I enjoyed the meat, and I assured them I did.

I took my wife Nina to Bethlehem in 1996. She had never been there. "You have to see it," I said. We arrived in midafternoon. After checking into a hotel, we walked up the long hill to Manger Square. I was a good host. I said nothing, did not expound, did not tell her what she should look for or notice or what she would see. I sat and watched her do her own seeing as she looked around the square in the sunlight. The Palestinian tourist police, young boys in blue uniforms, were standing in the square helping tourists. There was a bus of tourists, all cameras and fanny packs, visiting the Church of the Holy Nativity. They came across the square and went into one of the stores. "Welcome, welcome," the storekeeper said. They bought crosses and postcards. They bought wooden camels and pictures of the saints. Some of them bought Muslim prayer beads as a souvenir of their visit. At a table nearby, two middle-aged men, Israeli settlers, were sitting and talking. One of them was wearing a T-shirt that had a picture of a jet with a Star of David on the wings; over the jet were the words: "Don't worry America, we're coming." The waiter brought us coffee and juice. A group of priests from the church walked through the square as a crowd gathered for afternoon prayers. The call to prayer came out from the mosque's loudspeaker. A limousine pulled up to the civil offices, on the other side of the square, carrying the mayor, wearing a black suit. He shook hands with some well-wishers. An old woman came to our table to beg for money. The waiter turned her away. And then a little boy came. The waiter was angry. He told us the boy did not need to beg, because his family had money. Near us a young man laid out his prayer rug and knelt on it. My wife looked at the square and looked at me. "Oh my God," she said.

On December 31, 2003, I took my friends Bobby Muller, Solange McArthur, and John Terzano to see the West Bank and Gaza and Israel and to meet with Israelis and Palestinians. My son Cal, who lived in Bethlehem and was then in his early twenties, came with us. I called ahead to Gaza to see if we could get in and if we could get a meeting with some Palestinian leaders. I was told it was not a good time to come. It was the anniversary of the founding of Fatah, and Gaza was tense, but we went anyway.

We drove across Israel and walked into Gaza through the Erez checkpoint. There were enormous crowds in Gaza and a huge parade with marching units complete with papier-mâché rocket-propelled grenades. The al-Aqsa Martyrs' Brigade units trooped past proudly, their heads masked, their faces hidden. Everyone filed into a concrete stadium. We watched the crowds along the streets and strained to see the people in the stadium, where Yasser Arafat's voice came over the loudspeaker. He was speaking to the members of Fatah from his headquarters in Ramallah. The crowd cheered. Thousands of people chanted slogans.

Outside, a young boy was squatting in the dirt, lifting a poster that had a large photograph of a martyr. Everywhere there were posters of martyrs, for people to carry, and stick-pins and cardboard so people could make their own banners. The boy, barefoot, no more than seven, was trying to pin it to the stucco walls on the side of a house. He was struggling to lift the poster, intent on being a part of the day, on doing what people do in Gaza. My son kneeled to help him; they picked up the poster and centered it on the wall. There were tacks in the wall, left there by the organizers of the event, for just this purpose. The little boy never looked at my son, except out of the corner of his eye. The poster showed the photograph of a young man, dead now. It told about his life, about his sacrifice. My son pinned one corner of the poster. The little boy strained to reach his tack to pin the other. My son helped him, and they both pushed the tack into the wall. The boy looked at it and looked at my son and walked away.

Later we met my good friend Hani al-Hassan, one of the senior leaders of Fatah. I had known him for many years, and now I wanted my friends to meet him. He knew the entire history of Fatah. He had been there from the beginning and had fought all his life. He had organized the celebration and had given the speech after Arafat. He was in charge of Palestinian security that day and had been worried about us. He sent security people to guard us, and when he saw us after the celebration—in a hotel along the Gaza beach—he was relieved. "There was supposed to be trouble," he said, "and so I was worried. Today was not the best day to come here." But I could see something more in his eyes, and so I asked him about it. He nodded. "I gave strict orders that there would be no shooting. Not even one shot. No discharge of guns. None of that. But there was a young man who disobeyed the order. And it was an order. The young man should have known better. The penalty for this was severe, so we enacted the penalty. I gave the order." Hani was silent for a long moment, and then he looked out the window. He shook his head. "He was eighteen."

My friends asked him how he had become a part of the PLO, how he had become a senior official. "One day when I was very young," he said, "my family was very worried. My mother was very worried. And so I was frightened too. And there was shouting in the streets. And then the Haganah came. And they did things with my sister." He looked down at the table. "So that is when I decided and that is how it . . . ," and he bit his lip and looked away, the memory still there. "That is how it happened."

I will never forget the scene of my son helping that little boy, not as long as I live.

In Beirut I sat with my friend Nawaf and smiled as he handed me a cigar. He told me about the 2006 war with Israel. "I lost a lot," he said. "But I did not lose my family." Nawaf has a beautiful family whom I met in a Beirut restaurant. He introduced me proudly to his daughters, one by one, telling me their names. I have traded jokes with the leaders of Hamas, who like my stories about Arafat. Usamah Hamdan smiles and talks about his family and asks about mine. "Please be sure to say hello to your family," he says whenever I leave. "Please be sure to do that." He has a Ph.D. in chemistry. His home is in Gaza, but he does not go back there. He travels back and forth from Beirut to Damascus. When I tell a funny story about Arafat, he laughs and holds out his hand for me to slap. When I spoke with Musa Abu Marzouk, he asked me about Chicago. We had both once lived there. "I miss it," he says. "But I do not miss the cold." I agree. I have been to the home of General Michel Aoun, a dignified and serious man who thinks about every word he says. He lives at the top of a mountain, outside Beirut, inside a gated compound. "I am happy to be back in my home country," he once told me. "I would like it better if it were safe. But safe or unsafe, it is my country. I would not be anywhere else."

One time, at the Amman airport, I was greeted by a driver, a young man dressed in blue. He was an army officer sent by Princess Dina—the first wife of King Hussein—to retrieve me after a long flight from America. He ushered me through customs, waving off the requirement that I pay for a visa. "A guest of Princess Dina," he told the customs officer. He took my bags, placed them on a cart, and then began to wheel it across the terminal to the car. The cart squeaked with every turn of the wheels. Halfway across the terminal he stopped, removed the bags, and carried them back to a second cart. I protested, but he waved me off. He put the bags on the new cart and tested it, rolling it back and forth to make sure the wheels did not make a noise. "In America," he said, "the carts don't squeak."

In Tunis I met Sachar Habash, a member of the Fatah central committee. He collects paintings of the Palestinian revolution, and he writes poetry. We met in his office, on a square in central Tunis, on a hot summer afternoon. There was a crowd of people outside in the square, hundreds of them. I thought it was some kind of political event. "Oh no," he said, "they're opening up a Pizza Hut." He noticed my blank stare, and gave an explanation: "Well, it's the first one in Tunisia."

I spent a pleasant afternoon with two young Israeli couples on the beach at Tel Aviv. They came over and introduced themselves when they saw me sitting alone at a table overlooking the ocean. "Do you mind if we join you?" They found out that I grew up in Wisconsin. "Is it true?" one of them asked. "You know, *That '70s Show*,—is Wisconsin really like that?" They were astounded when I said that I had never seen it. "Oh you've got to watch it," one of them said. "It's awesome." They were not the only ones interested in America. Each Wednesday night, at the height of the Second Intifada, the streets of Bethlehem outside my hotel would empty. I would sit with the owner—a Palestinian originally from Philadelphia—on the veranda at the front of his hotel, drinking Turkish coffee. When the Israeli soldiers came up the streets, we would duck inside. One Wednesday night, I suddenly realized that there was no one on the streets, no confrontations, no distant firing. There wasn't a Palestinian to be seen, anywhere. I asked the hotel owner whether there was a ceasefire. He laughed. "Oh no," he said. "*Murder She Wrote* is on." And he added, "Reruns."

I remember that, during some of the fighting in Bethlehem, groups of Palestinian teenagers would dodge the Israeli patrols to meet at an internet café to play computer war games. There was one boy at each computer, with headphones on, playing war games—squad leader; mech warrior; Napoleon.

I once lectured to a communications class at Bir Zeit University. The professor wanted me to talk about what it was like to write books. I spoke to the students while the professor translated for those few who did not speak English. Then I took questions. One young woman in the class was covered head to foot. This is very unusual in Palestine, where the young women dress like any Western coed: jeans and blouses, lipstick and knapsacks. Chewing gum seemed the rage. My professor spoke to the woman who was covered, though she had not asked a question. He smiled at her, pretending to peek at her through her covering. "I know you have a question," he said to her. "It is alright to ask it. You can ask anything you want." She lowered her head and averted her eyes, and her voice was muffled. I could hardly hear what she asked. The professor translated for me: "Do you think we will ever have a state?"

One day, during the Second Intifada, a friend in Bethlehem told me that someone had posted a sign at an elementary school asking for volunteers for suicide bombings. Dozens of children had signed up. "My God," he said, "we have to stop this." On another day, I waited at the Rachel's Tomb checkpoint outside Bethlehem to pass through the Israeli soldiers, who were checking Palestinian permits, one at a time. An elderly man in front of me was holding his shoe-shine kit. He wanted to go to Jerusalem. An Israeli soldier, who looked very young, motioned to him to come forward, and he walked down under the long awning and handed the Israeli soldier his papers. The Israeli soldier checked them, said something to the man and motioned him down. To shine his shoes. The man went down on his hands and knees and shined the Israeli soldier's boots. One at a time. When I was told to come forward, I ambled forward and gave the Israeli soldier a hard stare. "Is there anything wrong?" he asked. I didn't answer. He made me wait. Finally, without looking at me, he handed me my passport. "You can go," he said. When I passed he spit on the ground.

During my first trip to Gaza, during the First Intifada, I met a young Palestinian boy named Abdullah. He attached himself to me and followed me around all day, from camp to camp and meeting to meeting. I had a little trouble that day. When I was walking through one camp, a little girl ran up and threw a stone at me. She was just a little thing, but she knew how to throw a stone. It hit me in the back, and it hurt like hell. My translator, a friend, wagged his finger at her. "Not Israeli," he said, in Arabic. "A friend." Abdullah looked at me and laughed after the little girl threw the stone. He thought it was very funny. From time to time during the day Abdullah tugged at the back of my shirt to make sure I knew he was still there. I gave him a baseball cap, and he wore it proudly. None of his other friends, watching from a distance, had one. He would look at them from time to time, with a big grin on his face, and wave the hat at them.

At the end of the day, as I was about to leave, Abdullah asked my translator if I would answer his questions. My translator said that I should not be bothered. But he insisted and, of course, I agreed. He put the questions carefully, looking at me intently. "Why are you here?" he asked. And then: "Where is your family?" And finally: "Do you believe in God?" The three most important questions, it seems, in any language. My translator, a Palestinian friend and now a respected scholar, listened as I answered. "I have friends here, and I came to visit them," I said, and then: "I had to leave my family at home, but they do not mind." But on the third question, I hesitated. Do I believe in God? When my translator saw this he interrupted my thinking. "This is not the place for that kind of reflection," he said. "Here the answer is always yes."

WINNING

"We have to face it."

—Jeff Aronson

THIS IS THE doctrine of Osama bin Laden's revolutionaries: that in refusing to differentiate between al Qaeda and more moderate groups, in refusing to empower those groups in their own societies, and in denying the peoples of the region the tools of democracy and self-government that the West extols, the United States and its allies have helped spread the jihad.

That message is not incoherent. It has appeal. Bin Laden and his followers view the West as promoting purposeless lives based on a meaningless consumerism and political fragmentation. They see Western commercial interests as dehumanizing and exploitative and the Western financial structure as skewed toward large corporations at the expense of the individual and community enterprise. Finally, they believe that the United States and its allies are incapable of differentiating between moderate revivalist Islam and militant revolutionary Islam—that we are incapable of differentiating between Hamas, Hezbollah, the Muslim Brotherhood, and other Islamist political movements that believe in participatory democracy.

These groups do not want to burn down their societies; rather, they want to change them. They do not want to return the world to the dark ages; they do not hate our freedoms; they do not reject modernity; they are not in love with death. In the wake of 9/11, Osama bin Laden hoped that we would abandon the moderate groups, that we would marginalize them and isolate them. He believed that Western leaders would fail to differentiate the "revolutionaries" from the "revivalists."

The invasion of Iraq provided Osama bin Laden with the circumstances in which to build a genuine takfiri revolutionary movement by capitalizing on the West's missteps. One misstep was the invasion of Iraq. Israel's war on Hezbollah and Hamas was another misstep. These actions confirmed bin Laden's beliefs about who we are and what we want. As Muslims watched, we fulfilled his expectations. We, and not bin Laden, unveiled the hypocrisy in Western intentions. Bin Laden's aim was and is to create a revolutionary climate that will radicalize the Islamic world and lead to the fall of the Arab "colonial" regimes, that will defeat the "Western crusaders and their Zionist friends." This methodology is neither medieval nor regressive but global, modern, and without borders. Its methods are sophisticated, psychological, nuanced, and carefully planned.

Following 9/11, bin Laden's jihadist movement diligently worked to broaden its appeal by talking to its coreligionists with words that reflect the language of the oppressed. He has responded to our military strategy by speaking not of victory but of respect and dignity. "Violence, though definitive of the jihad today, is probably the least important of these responses, and likely the most short-lived compared to the other transformations that al-Qaeda has wrought," Faisal Devji wrote. "Indeed, such violence might well represent the final agony of an old-fashioned politics centered on a specific geography and based on a history of common needs, interest or ideas. Rather than marking the emergence of a new kind of Muslim politics, in other words, al-Qaeda's jihad may signal the end of such politics." We never understood this salient truth—that what bin Laden had to say was not "rigmarole," but that what we said was. We talked of "getting our message across," of "communicating directly to Muslims." We are only now beginning to realize that the reason we have failed to communicate our message is that we don't have one.

The foundational belief of the war on terror is that we are fighting not a credible movement with a set of core beliefs but "evildoers"—people who have nothing to say, who are without values, who hate our freedoms, and who want to return their societies to the seventh century. We believe and act as if militant Islam is much like worldwide communism, an empty shell that, if confronted with overwhelming power, will crumble. It will not—it has not. That it hasn't has fueled our frustration. We have the strange feeling that we have somehow gotten the war on terror wrong, that not only are we not winning this conflict but, if we follow our current policies, we cannot win it. We have a growing sense that the enemy we are fighting cannot be contained, limited, or quarantined, that its foot soldiers are not easily identified, and that its ideology is ever changing. We fear that what we face is not terrorism at all, but a coalescing transnational uprising that does not so much oppose our beliefs as demand that we live up to them—and that gains strength with every aircraft carrier we deploy.

Jeff Aronson—who was a part of the exchanges in 2005—put it this way: "We have to come to terms with a disturbing and blunt truth and finally face it—that after 9/11 a segment of our planet celebrated. We cannot simply pass it off; we cannot ignore it. We have to face it." We cannot simply condemn that celebration as the work of people who "do not share our values." We must find out why they celebrated.

Here is what we face: We do not understand the enemy we are fighting. We have not listened to the diverse voices of Islam. Despite all our talk, we have not recruited Muslims to our side. It is true that Hosni Mubarak is with us, Benjamin Netanyahu supports us, and Saad Hariri is our friend, but that does not matter. They cannot help us. They parrot our language; they repeat our words. They know less about political Islam than we do—and they *live* there.

We have drowned out the diverse voices of Islam. We say we support democracy, but our initiatives purposely undermine it. We say that the difference between "us" and "them" is that they purposely target innocents, whereas we don't—as if we can continue to speak of our intentions, instead of recognizing the dead. When a Palestinian is killed by an Israeli, we call it an act of self-defense. When a Palestinian kills an Israeli, we call it a terrorist attack. When an innocent American is killed, we say it is because "they don't have our values." When an innocent Iraqi dies, we label it "collateral damage."

We might list solutions to all this: resolving the Israeli-Palestinian conflict, spurring economic development in the Muslim world, ending support for extremist Muslim teachings, reforming the Arab educational system. They are all bunk, unless we change our language and recast the way we think about the Muslim world. It is not just our policies that stand in the way; it is the language that has led us to adopt those policies. We must change that language—or we will lose.

Bin Laden and his takfiri allies believe that their actions are not subject to Islamic legal restraints, especially those prohibiting the killing of noncombatants. His explanation is that Islam is fighting an existential battle against an intransigent enemy and that differentiating between innocent and guilty is a useless enterprise, since the guilty and the innocent are "all the same." We westerners believe the same thing about Islam. Benjamin Netanyahu talks of moral equivalence precisely because he knows that the IDF is not "the most moral army in the world" (as Ehud Barack described it)—by the admission of Israel's own soldiers, Palestinian women and children were shot down in cold blood. So too, the abuses at Abu Ghraib did not happen because we were fighting the war on terror; they happened because American military men and women did not respect their captives. They treated them like animals because they believed they were animals.

Bin Laden would undoubtedly argue that any exercise that fails to recognize the fact of Western oppression—that fails to see the difference between the lives of innocent Muslims living in oppressed societies and those of westerners living in the oppressor nations—is guilty of moral relativism. He enumerates our failures: "The West" refuses to differentiate among its enemies, dividing the world only into "us" and "them." When he and his coreligionists, he says, talk about building a just world, they are telling the truth; when we, "the Zionists and colonialists" talk about it, we're lying. He and his coreligionists are not the takfiris, he says, we westerners are. He and his want to spread freedom, we want to build a "crusader and Zionist" caliphate.

Many years ago, French philosopher Maurice Merleau-Ponty wrote a book called *Humanism and Terror*. It's a brilliant exposition of the plight in which we find ourselves. He wrote that we, in the West, "understand that one does not become a revolutionary through science," as Marxists believe, but out of indignation. He said that we understand that there are grievances, but we must also understand that some of them are just. If we cause the deaths of innocents, the fact that we did not intend to do so does not excuse the crime. But, Merleau-Ponty says, it is not necessary for us to disassociate ourselves from our own history simply "because it is sometimes shameful." That we engaged in an inquisition does not make our condemnation of any future inquisition moot; our support for Saddam Hussein against a revolutionary Iran does not justify his gassing of the people of Halabja; 9/11 does not justify the fact that American soldiers murdered innocent Iraqis at Haditha. We are not naive. We know, to use Merleau-Ponty's formulation, that "there is no line between good people and the rest and that, in war, the most honorable causes prove themselves by means that are not honorable. That the bully does not know what he is doing does not excuse the bully."

I noted the lessons of Merleau-Ponty, and quoted him liberally, in a series of articles on the talks with political Islamists in the pages of *Asia Times* in 2006.

> We have talked with those political Islamists whom we define as "revivalists" because they derive their beliefs from a set of principles that hold that human actions must be moral and just. They believe that there is an indisputable system of values, articulated in the foundations of their religion, that provide a guide for all actions: not simply that policies must be grounded in principles, but that the ends can never justify the means. These "revivalists" are committed to the proposition that as God has given humans the right to choose their beliefs, so too God has given individuals the right to choose their leaders. The takfiris on both sides reject these principles, holding that some lives are inherently more valued than others, that "there must be a balance of terror," that "pity is treason," that the innocent may be made to pay for the crimes of the guilty, that "power is virtue," that all compromise is perfidy, that the ends justify the means.

Islam's revivalists believe that there is justice in the universe, that it must be pursued, and that it can be implemented. They know, as do we, that not all people pay for their crimes and that some are even rewarded. They are adults, not children. They know we are angry; so too are they. They expect that we will continue to defend ourselves against takfiris, but they fervently believe that takfiris are present everywhere, not just in the Middle East. So too, we in the West need to understand that our search for justice is not dependent on its perfection and that pointing this out is not an exercise in "moral equivalence." The fact that Israelis kill innocent Palestinians does not justify café bombings; it simply makes killing innocent Palestinians wrong—and humans must pursue justice, despite their imperfections. The people who fell to their deaths through the air of lower Manhattan did not bear the guilt of a generation of leaders; they were not a fit sacrifice for our mistakes. Not all Sunnis are responsible for the gassings at Karbala, nor all Jews for Israel's occupation of the West Bank, nor all Christians for Auschwitz, nor all Shias for Iraq's death squads. *Persons* are responsible for their actions and must be held to account. I noted this in an *Asia Times* articles of 2006:

> We do not condemn Osama bin Laden or Islamic revolutionaries because we deny our own hypocrisy, but because we believe that the only answer to hypocrisy is justice. To believe otherwise, to claim that our children must pay for our sins—that the victims of 9/11 are somehow responsible for their own murder—is not simply to rob language of its content, but to rob morality of its meaning. The leaders of political Islam with whom we spoke, and will continue to speak, agree with this. Osama bin Laden does not.

Thousands of Americans died on 9/11. Hundreds of people died in Europe in the London subway bombings of 7/7. That they died is not our fault. We did not kill them. Their deaths are not defensible. But they were not killed by "militant Islam"; they were killed by Osama bin Laden. Men are tortured to death in Egyptian prisons, but they do not torture themselves—it's their government's fault. We are not responsible for the attack in Mumbai or for the bombings in Pakistan or Bali. The women and children of

Ben Yahuda Street who died in cafés did not wish their own death. Israelis did not plant those bombs. So too, the more than 2,000 Palestinians who died in Gaza and the more than 1,000 who died in Lebanon were not killed by Palestinians or by Hezbollah or by "the Jews." They did not want to die. They did not hate life or our freedoms or modernity or our values. They were killed by Israelis. The blood of tens of thousands who died in Iraq as the result of the U.S. invasion and occupation were not killed by their fellow countrymen. They were killed by us. Their blood is on our hands. The inmates at Guantánamo did not torture themselves. We tortured them.

America and its allies did not intend to kill thousands of Iraqi men, women, and children. But then, as Merleau-Ponty reminds us, Oedipus did not mean to kill his father and marry his mother. "But he did it, and it's a crime." The men and women and children who have died in the wars of the Middle East, European, Israeli, Iraqi, or Palestinian, the Americans who fell through the sky on a clear September day in Manhattan—all of them had one thing in common, no matter who killed them.

They were innocent.

NOTES

PROLOGUE

1   **a series of articles began to appear in *Asia Times*:** The five articles appeared in *Asia Times* beginning in March 2006. The articles were bylined by Mark Perry and Alastair Crooke. The second half of this book is based on those articles, but material has been added to reflect subsequent events. The details of the Beirut dialogues are the subject of the second part of this book, which includes the names of some of the participants and shows how the meetings were organized.

1   **political Islam:** "Political Islam" is a recognizably ambiguous term, meaning different things to different people. It is used here to describe those political organizations that believe that Islam provides the basis for a just society. The political Islamist organizations described in this book, and with whom we met in Beirut, do not find Islam incompatible with democracy. Their enemies in the region, the al Qaeda network and associated jihadist organizations, do.

2   **Prime Minister Clement Attlee normalized relations with China:** Mark Perry, "The China Syndrome," *Bitterlemons-international.org* 7, edition 11 (March 19, 2009), http://www.bitterlemons-international.org/previous.php ?opt=1&id=265.

2   **"We can't be frustrated":** Interview with Michael Ancram, March 2009. Ancram was in Washington to discuss his meetings in Beirut with American officials.

2   ***Talking to Terrorists*:** Interviews with participants in the Beirut meetings were conducted by the author independently of the seminars themselves or appeared in a subsequent article on the Beirut meetings titled "How to Lose the War on Terror," published in *Asia Times*. See http://www.atimes.com/ atimes/others/howtolose.html.

4   **"You're the sheikh":** I met with Talal al-Gaood in August 2005.

5 **in World War II Americans and Brits shed our blood together:** I wrote about the nature of this World War II alliance and its political difficulties in *Partners in Command* (Viking, 2007).

CHAPTER ONE

7 **"criminal elements":** "Operation Scorpion Sting," *Global Security.org*, http://www.globalsecurity.org/military/ops/scorpion-sting.htm.

8 **Eighty-four Iraqis died:** U.N. High Commissioner for Refugees, "Chronology of Events in Iraq," New York, February and March 2004.

8 **In public Rumsfeld pointedly accused the press:** Dana Milbank, "Rumsfeld's War on 'Insurgents,'" *Washington Post*, November 30, 2005, http://www.washingtonpost.com/wp-dyn/content/article/2005/11/29/AR2005112901405.html.

9 **Later, speaking privately:** Senior defense official, interview by author.

9 **"He kept asking":** Senior Pentagon official, interview by author.

9 **Their report was blunt:** The assessment team report was finalized and submitted to Rumsfeld in January 2004. It remains classified.

9 **By October, Rumsfeld was receiving regular memos:** Senior U.S. Pentagon official, interview by author.

10 **One of the most prophetic memos Rumsfeld received:** The memo was shown to the author by a Pentagon official.

11 **"All of these reports were coming across his desk":** Senior U.S. Pentagon official, interview by author.

11 **"No one checked to see if it was true":** Senior U.S. Pentagon official, interview by author.

11 **Chalabi reinforced his views:** Ahmed Chalabi, "Iraq for the Iraqis," *Wall Street Journal*, February 19, 2003.

11 **"Just as in our occupation of Germany":** L. Paul Bremer, interview on "The Lost Year in Iraq," *PBS Frontline*; see http://www.pbs.org/wgbh/pages/frontline/yeariniraq/analysis/fuel.html.

12 **"If you had taken a poll":** This aide had access to the Burgess paper and was one of the senior officers who helped draft it.

12 **"we can't paint everyone":** Lieutenant Colonel Roy D. "Dave" Harlan (USMC, retired), interview by author.

12 **On December 19, he wrote:** Copies of the memorandum were provided to General Richard Myers, the chairman of the Joint Chiefs of Staff, and Paul Wolfowitz, the deputy secretary of defense.

12 **led by his own Jibouri tribe:** The Jibouri tribe is one of the two prominent tribes of Diyala Province.

13 **self-promoting," they reported:** A senior JCS officer showed a copy of the DIA memorandum to the author, December 2008.

13 **"Wolfowitz was almost unbalanced":** Senior civilian defense official, interview by author.

13   **"He just let the initiative die":** Senior Pentagon official, interview by author.

13   **"It shows you":** Ibid.

14   **"The Sunni Heartland":** The paper, dated April 12, 2004, ended up in Rumsfeld's hands after the defense secretary had penned his April 12 memo.

14   **word he used.":** Author interview with senior JCS officer, December 2008.

15   **under Conway's leadership:** U.S. Department of Defense News Transcript, May 30, 2003, http://www.defenselink.mil/transcripts/transcript.aspx? transcriptid=2681.

16   **"What the hell are they thinking?":** The quote is reported by an officer who served on Conway's staff.

16   **his commander "threw his cover":** Major Patrick Maloy (USMC, retired), interview by author, December 23, 2008.

16   **"Conway went to the top with this":** Retired member of General James Conway's senior military staff, interview by author, November 22, 2008.

17   **"They want us to fight, we fight":** Retired member of General James Conway's senior military staff, interview by author, November 22, 2008.

17   **'No,'" a subordinate said.:** Author interview with a senior officer of General Conway's staff, April 2009.

17   **"When we were told to attack Fallujah":** Rajiv Chandrasekaran, "Key General Criticizes April Attack in Fallujah," *Washington Post*, September 3, 2004.

17   **told one of his staff assistants:** Former member of General James Conway's senior staff, interview by author, November 16, 2008.

18   **"a part of the insurgency":** Major Pat Maloy, interview by author, November 16, 2008.

18   **Orders or no orders, he thought it was a bad idea:** On Conway's reaction to the fighting, see Mark Perry, "U.S. Military Breaks Ranks, Part 1: A Salvo at the White House," *Asia Times*, January 23, 2008, http://www.atimes.com/ atimes/Middle_East/JA23Ak02.html.

18   **barely penetrated the insurgency's defenses:** "US Strikes at Iraqi Resistance," *BBC News*, http://news.bbc.co.uk/2/hi/middle_east/3030494.stm.

18   **ordered to end the offensive:** Rory McCarthy, "Uneasy Truce in a City of Ghosts," *Guardian*, April 24, 2004.

19   **In the ensuing weeks:** The commander of the city's Fallujah Brigade told reporter Nir Rosen that as a part of the agreement the brigade had to promise to take on the Islamists—what he described as "the al Qaeda cells" in the city—after the marines withdrew. "We had no problem with that as a part of the agreement," he told this reporter, "as that is what we planned to do anyway." Nir Rosen, "Fallujah, Inside the Iraqi Resistance," *Asia Times*, July 19, 2004.

19   **"We felt like we had a method":** Conway, quoted in Perry, "U.S. Military Breaks Ranks, Part 1."

19   **"do things a little differently in Anbar":** Colonel Mike Walker (USMC, retired), interview by author, September 19, 2008.

19   **"This wasn't just about business":** Ibid.

19   "He gave the best briefing": Ibid.

20   "It was a good conference": Ibid.

20   "You know, you can hold all kinds of conferences": Ibid.

21   "He wanted to find a way to unlock the province": Major Patrick Maloy, interview by author, December 16, 2008.

21   "In addition, we would like to have school supplies": "History of District 5340's Support of Our Deployed Marines and Sailors During Operation Iraqi Freedom (OIF)," http://www0.rotary5340.org/notes/pdf/military1.pdf.

21   a Texas businessman named Ken Wischkaemper: I introduced *Vanity Fair* reporter David Rose to Wischkaemper in October 2008. The resulting article, "Heads in the Sand," appeared in the June 2009 edition of *Vanity Fair*'s online edition, http://www.vanityfair.com/politics/features/2009/05/iraqi-insurgents 200905.

21   the most important industry in Shamrock, Texas: ADI is registered in Washington, D.C., and its Web site, http://www.agdevi.com/, says its corporate headquarters is located in Amarillo, Texas.

21   "You can't believe how complicated": Kenneth Wischkaemper, interview by author, April 16, 2008.

22   ADI had built a solid reputation: Agriculture Development International Web site, at http://www.agdevi.com/.

22   "I was in Russia in late 2003": Wischkaemper interview.

22   "Talal was a very serious man": Ibid.

23   "We went up to his home in Amman": Ibid.

24   "I sat down and I thought about it": Ibid.

24   "Larry just dismissed Meyers": Senior Pentagon official, interview by author, August 16, 2008.

24   "was purposely putting obstacles in our way": Wischkaemper interview.

24   "The contact went absolutely nowhere": Ibid.

24   "We briefed Marty on Ken's trip to Amman": Larry Meyers, interview by author, April 14, 2008.

25   "In West Texas you do business with a handshake": Jerry Jones, interview by author, November 22, 2008.

26   "If anyone had found out": Meyers interview.

26   "Please know that there is a deep, deep divide at the Pentagon": Kenneth Wischkaemper to Talal Al-Gaood, e-mail message, May 8, 2004. The e-mail from Wischkaemper to al-Gaood was placed on the stationary of the Elm Valley Agricultural Group, Shamrock, Texas. In the author's possession.

27   "It is of extreme importance": Ibid.

27   "There were about ten of us": Noel Koch, interview by author, November 16, 2008.

27   In addition to his duties: Ibid.

28   "laid the tape for June 23, 1971, on the table in front of me": Jerry Jones, interview by author, November 22, 2008.

28 **The June 23 tape was the smoking gun:** The transcript of the meeting between President Richard M. Nixon and H. R. Haldeman on June 23, 1972, is available on the Web site Watergate.info at http://www.watergate.info/tapes/72-06-23_smoking-gun.shtml.

29 **"We're not only losing":** Related to the author by senior Pentagon official, December 13, 2006.

29 **"Talal wanted to make the conference in Baghdad":** Meyers interview.

29 **"very selective and very small":** Talal al-Gaood to Ken Wischkaemper, e-mail message, April 15, 2004. A number of e-mail exchanges between al-Gaood and Wischkaemper are in the author's possession.

29 **"The governing council and its appointed Ministers":** Jones interview.

29 **and U.S. Marine Colonel Mike Walker:** Colonel Mike Walker, e-mail message to author, July 23, 2004.

30 **"We DoD types":** Jerry Jones, "Dear Ambassador Jeffrey," note (signed "Jerry H. Jones"), July 12, 2004. In the author's possession.

30 **"I had never met Talal":** Jones, interview, November 16, 2008.

CHAPTER TWO

33 **he was sending e-mails:** Talal al-Gaood to Colonel Michael Walker, copy to Claude M. "Mick" Kicklighter, "Tabouk Commercial Agencies Co.," e-mail message, June 21, 2004.

34 **"with orders to hold a 130-mile swath":** David Rose, "Heads in the Sand," *Vanity Fair*, June 2009, online edition, http://www.vanityfair.com/politics/features/2009/05/iraqi-insurgents200905.

34 **al-Hamdani survived two separate assassination attempts:** Nawar Obaid, "Meeting the Challenge of a Fragmented Iraq," paper prepared for the Center for Strategic and International Studies, Washington, D.C., April 6, 2006.

35 **he began work on a presentation:** Lieutenant General Ra'ad Hamdani (retired), head of Military Department, Iraq House for Future Studies (Tabouk Holding Group), "Iraqi Perspective of US Military Strategy in Iraq," PowerPoint presentation, undated.

35 **"I was surprised and pleased":** Jaber Awad, interview by author, November 2008.

35 **Garner's staff had three objectives:** Ibid.

36 **"We knew we had to pay the civil servants":** Lieutenant General Jay Garner (retired), interview on "The Lost Year in Iraq," *PBS Frontline*; see http://www.pbs.org/wgbh/pages/frontline/yeariniraq/interviews/garner.html.

36 **"We have to do this fast and do this well":** Awad interview.

36 **"Hey, I'm calling just to tell you":** Ibid.

37 **Bremer arrived in Baghdad on May 13:** Patrick E. Tyler, "New Overseer Arrives in Iraq in U.S. Shuffle," *New York Times*, May 13, 2004.

37 **"Bremer changed everything":** Awad interview.

37   Awad asked for a private meeting with Bremer: Ibid.

37   "organize with the good people on the American side": Ibid.

37   "It was really quite a poignant scene": Senior Pentagon official, interview by author, July 13, 2006.

38   "The idea was to keep them on our side": Colonel Paul Hughes (retired), interview by author, August 22, 2007.

39   "This was a small economic thing": Colonel Mike Walker (USMC, retired), interview by author, December 3, 2008.

39   "you know, just milled about": James Clad, interview by author, December 2008.

39   "I was really taken aback": Jerry Jones, interview by author, November 22, 2008.

39   "Well, this is not exactly what I had in mind": Walker interview.

40   "Dear friends and guests": "Remarks of Talal al-Gaood," undated. Document is in the author's possession.

40   "I have never heard such denunciations": Clad interview.

40   "Talal was masterful": Jerry Jones, interview by author, November 22, 2008.

40   "People were just ranting": Clad interview.

40   "You could never say that Saddam was good for Iraq": Colonel Mike Walker, interview by author, December 3, 2008.

41   "Tadashi was a very courtly man": Tadashi's comments were reported by James Clad and confirmed by Mike Walker and Jerry Jones.

41   "I told them that I understood a lot of their complaints": Walker interview.

42   "He was angry, very angry": General al-Hamdani's comments were reported by Jerry Jones and confirmed by James Clad.

42   "What we did was shameful": Clad interview.

42   "Word got around": Jerry Jones, interview by author, March 2009.

43   "This group, numbering twenty-three": Colonel Mike Walker to "Dept of Defense WH Liais," "The Surprise," e-mail message, August 2, 2004." In the author's possession.

43   "a messenger from the insurgents": Jones interview.

43   Jerry [Jones] came to meet at the end of the day": Walker interview.

43   Walker and Jones were on one side of the table: Quotations from and information about the meeting are from interviews with Colonel Mike Walker and Jerry Jones.

44   Dr. Ismail was blunt: "The doctor's" conversation here has been related by Jerry Jones, Mike Walker, and Dave Harlan.

46   The next morning, a delegation of Americans: The participants in this meeting give different dates for its occurrence. I have used the date given to me by Mike Walker.

46   an e-mail message to Colonel John Coleman: Colonel Michael M. Walker to Colonel John Coleman, "Subject: Amman Wrap-Up," e-mail message, July 23, 2004 (copy of e-mail of July 20); and Walker interview. E-mail message in the author's possession.

46   **"My perspective about the skeptical treatment":** Colonel Mike Walker, e-mail message to author, December 3, 2008.

47   **"Our negotiating position was hopeless":** Colonel Mike Walker, e-mail message to author, December 3, 2008.

47   **"We had no illusions":** Walker interview.

47   **As the Fallujah Brigade marched into the city:** John Kifner, "The Struggle for Iraq: Security," *New York Times*, May 2, 2004, online edition, http://www.nytimes.com/2004/05/02/world/struggle-for-iraq-security-new-iraqi-force-goes-work-falluja-questions-arise.html.

48   **The press picked up the story:** Colin Freeman, "Marines Turn Over Control of Fallujah to Iraqi General Once Loyal to Hussein," *San Francisco Chronicle*, May 2, 2004; Kifner, "The Struggle for Iraq."

48   **"The Iraqi armies do not fuck about":** Freeman, "Marines Turn Over Control of Fallujah."

48   **al-Gaood had pleaded with Wischkaemper:** Tabouk Commercial Agencies Co. to Kenneth Wischkaemper, e-mail message, June 20, 2004.

48   **The IMEF commander was still seething:** Senior marine commander on General James Conway's staff, interview by author, December 19, 2008.

49   **"This is a simple dimple story":** Ibid.

49   **"Conway just looked at him":** Ibid.

49   **"That's when we began to take casualties in Fallujah":** Walker interview.

50   **no one coordinated the decision with the Coalition Provisional Authority:** Ibid.

50   **Bremer was furious:** David Isenberg, "Fallujah: The First Iraqi Intifada," *Asia Times*, January 8, 2008, http://wikileaks.org/wiki/Fallujah:_The_first_Iraqi_intifada.

50   **"Bremer disbanded the Iraqi army":** Senior officer of General James Conway's staff, interview by author.

50   **"The people in the Green Zone were living in an aquarium":** Ibid.

51   **"The people in the aquarium were giving us reports":** Ibid.

52   **"The main highlights of the agreement to be finalized":** Michael M. Walker to John C. Coleman, e-mail message, July 20, 2004. In the author's possession.

53   **"When Coleman received the e-mail":** Walker interview, December 3, 2008.

53   **a disturbing meeting in Talal al-Gaood's suite:** Walker interview.

54   **Barjas's three sons were kidnapped:** The kidnapping of the governor's sons was attributed to Abu Musab al-Zarqawi's group, Al Qaeda in Iraq, which was affiliated with and allied to Osama bin Laden.

54   **"I am Abd al-Karim Barjas":** "Fierce Fighting Escalates in Iraq," *Global Security.org*, August 6, 2004, http://www.globalsecurity.org/military/library/news/2004/08/mil-040806-rferl01.htm. After the tearful repentance, Barjas's sons were released and the former Anbar governor retired from public service.

54   **Walker took the measure of al-Gaood:** Walker interview.

55   **"The papers were presented by each committee leader":** Jones interview.

55   **The resulting findings were summarized:** "What We Heard," draft copy
      from Meyers & Associates (the Washington, D.C.–based law firm of Larry
      D. Meyers, the associate of Kenneth Wischkaemper), 2nd day, July 20,
      2004. In the author's possession.

56   **"I think it was probably the most important document":** Jones interview.

57   **"this was never Saddam's army":** Related to the author by Jerry Jones, De-
      cember 2008.

57   **"gradual [five year] withdrawal":** al-Hamdani, "Iraqi Perspective of US
      Military Strategy in Iraq."

57   **"It made perfect sense":** Kenneth Wischkaemper, interview by author,
      April 16, 2008.

57   **General al-Hamdani said that he would start:** Tabouk Commercial Agen-
      cies to Ken Wischkaemper, e-mail message, July 26, 2004, confirming con-
      versation on the second day of the conference. In the author's possession.

57   **al-Gaood approached Walker:** Walker interview.

58   **"I am bewildered and touched":** Colonel Mike Walker, e-mail message to
      author, December 8, 2008.

CHAPTER THREE

59   **Reversing a wishful policy:** Barbara Tuchman, *Stilwell and the American
      Experience in China* (New York: Macmillan, 1970), 354.

59   **"We don't talk to terrorists":** White House official, interview by author,
      April 2005.

61   **in the wake of his report on the Amman conference:** Jones had put to-
      gether an exhaustive account of the Amman conference—enclosed in a
      large folder that he dubbed "the book"—and submitted it to Rumsfeld.

61   **Wolfowitz raised his voice:** Jerry Jones, interview by author, December 2008.

62   **"I was told to report to Jim Jeffrey":** Colonel Mike Walker, interview by
      author, December 28, 2008.

62   **"Since we parted on 21 July":** James Clad to Jerry Jones, e-mail message,
      25 July 2004. In the author's possession.

63   **Clad also suggested:** James Clad, interview by author, December 2008.

63   **Walker briefed IMEF commander James Conway and his chief of staff,
      John Coleman:** Walker interview, December 3, 2008.

63   **"It just didn't work out":** Ibid.

64   **"Our chain of command is in the support camp":** Tabouk Commercial
      Agencies Co. to Ken Wischkaemper, e-mail message, August 3, 2004, first
      message. In the author's possession.

64   **"Today Ramadi under siege":** Tabouk Commercial Agencies Co. to Ken
      Wischkaemper, e-mail message, August 3, 2004, second message. In the au-
      thor's possession.

64   **"The commanders in Fallujah":** Tabouk Commercial Agencies Co. to Ken
      Wischkaemper, e-mail message, August 3, 2008, third message. In the au-
      thor's possession.

64   **the "atmosphere in Washington is highly politically charged":** Ken Wisch-
      kaemper to Talal al-Gaood, e-mail message, August 3, 2004.

64   **"There were three problems":** Patrick Maloy, interview by author, De-
      cember 23, 2008.

65   **In mid-August General al-Hamdani finished his plan for a Desert Pro-
      tection Force:** General Ra'ad al-Hamdani, "Al Anbar Security Proposal,"
      August 17, 2004. Document in the author's possession.

65   **"The proposal presented":** Ken Wischkaemper to Talal al-Gaood, e-mail
      message, August 14, 2004. In the author's possession.

66   **began to feel pressure from Muqtada al-Sadr's Mahdi Army:** Scott Bal-
      dauf, "The Battle for Najaf," *Christian Science Monitor*, August 9, 2004.

66   **The Battle of Najaf began on August 5:** Alex Berensen and John F. Burns,
      "The Conflict in Iraq: Looking Back," *New York Times*, August 18, 2004.

66   **Progress was being made, he argued:** Claims made by al-Gaood were re-
      ferred to in an e-mail from Captain Rodrick H. McHaty to Colonel Dave
      Harlan, August 12, 2004. In the author's possession.

67   **every day American soldiers found Iraqi corpses:** Bing West, *The
      Strongest Tribe* (New York: Random House, 2008), 48.

67   **torture and "execution" of Lieutenant Colonel Suleiman Hamad al-
      Mawawi:** The marines determined that Suleiman's murder had been car-
      ried out by Abdullah Janabi, a member of the far-flung Janabi tribe, a very
      prominent one in Iraq.

67   **"He was murdered because":** McHaty to Harlan, e-mail, August 12, 2004.

67   **"Lieutenant Colonel Suleiman had entered Fallujah":** Walker interview,
      December 3, 2008.

68   **"We had to prove":** Former staff member of the Iraq Futures Foundation,
      interview by author, December 28, 2008.

68   **"Every time the Americans launched a raid":** West, *The Strongest Tribe*, 49.

68   **General George Casey sympathized with Conway:** Bradley Graham,
      "New Job in Iraq Will Be as Top U.S. Military Leader," *Washington Post*,
      June 25, 2004.

69   **The new commander told his senior combat commanders:** Thomas E.
      Ricks, *Fiasco* (New York: Penguin Press, 2006), 392–393.

69   **During one mid-August 2004 video conference:** Senior defense official
      privy to the Casey meeting, interview by author, October, 19, 2008.

70   **"They're kids," he screamed:** West, *The Strongest Tribe*, 49.

70   **"an interim auxiliary security force":** [Ra'ad al-Hamdani], "Al Anbar Se-
      curity Proposal" (unsigned), August 17, 2004. In the author's possession.

71   **The message was communicated from the delegation to Amman:** Tabouk
      Commercial Agencies to Dave Harlan, e-mail message, August 19, 2004. In
      the author's possession.

71   **he had died of a heart attack under interrogation:** As one marine later noted in an interview with the author (December 2008), "Possibly true, as we later obtained indisputable evidence of Lieutenant Colonel Suleiman having his throat slit during a torture session. Suppose it is possible to have a heart attack under such circumstances."

72   **After this short discussion:** The details of the meeting were gathered from one of the participants, who declined to be named, and a senior marine commander who spoke with members of the delegation upon their return to Fallujah.

72   **As commander of the II Republican Guard Corps:** See Michael R. Gordon and General Bernard E. Trainor, *Cobra II: The Inside Story of the Invasion and Occupation of Iraq* (New York: Pantheon, 2006), 60–61.

73   **al-Hamdani ordered his aides to prepare a briefing:** Aides to General Ra'ad al-Hamdani and officials of the Iraq Futures Foundation, interviews by author, August 26, 2005.

73   **Al-Hamdani remembered the lesson of Remagen:** Lieutenant General Ra'ad Al-Hamdani, interview on "The Invasion of Iraq," *PBS Frontline*; see http://www.pbs.org/wgbh/pages/frontline/shows/invasion/interviews/raad.html.

74   **"The minister of defense conveyed a message":** Ibid.

74   **"We all make mistakes":** Ibid.

75   **"The general idea is to separate":** General Ra'ad Al-Hamdani, "An Iraqi Plan to Achieve Legitimacy for the Transitional Government," July 27, 2004. In the author's possession.

76   **"Ok, I need an e-mail":** Colonel John Coleman to Mike Walker, e-mail message, August 22, 2004. In the author's possession.

76   **"The last thing we needed":** Colonel John Coleman (USMC, retired), interview by author, November 13, 2008.

76   **"This is progress":** Colonel Mike Walker to Colonel John Coleman, e-mail message, August 22, 2004. In the author's possession.

76   **al-Gaood had passed a message to him:** Lieutenant Colonel Roy D. Harlan to Colonel Mike Walker, e-mail message, August 21, 2004. In the author's possession.

77   **"can roughly be likened":** Colonel Michael M. Walker to Lieutenant General James T. Conway, e-mail message, August 24, 2004. In the author's possession.

77   **"My attendance could be seen":** Jerry Jones to Talal al-Gaood, e-mail message, August 23, 2004. In the author's possession.

77   **Al-Gaood noted that the proposed conference:** Tabouk Commercial Agencies Co. to R. A. Manning (copy to Kenneth Wischkaemper), e-mail message, August 25, 2004. In the author's possession.

77   **"This is the dark side":** Senior Marine Corps officer on General Conway's staff, interview by author, December 2008.

77   **"Conway had me going to D.C. as his rep":** Colonel John Coleman, interview by author, December 28, 2008.

78   **"I was very nervous about the dinner":** Ibid.
78   **"There were twenty-four chairs around the table":** Coleman interview, November 13, 2008.
79   **"The proposal called for the creation of an Anbar military force":** Ibid.
79   **"General Ra'ad was at his best":** Walker interview, December 28, 2008.
80   **"There were three guys there":** Ibid.
80   **"I just sat there and let John do his thing":** Ibid.
80   **Coleman turned to the chargé d'affaires:** Ibid.
80   **"I kept waiting for John to talk about the insurgency":** Ibid.
80   **"I told them what they needed to know":** Coleman interview, December 28, 2008.
81   **"The DHI was all over this":** Walker interview, December 28, 2008.
81   **A secretary escorted him to a private office and handed him a telephone:** Coleman interview.
82   **"strong believer in Phase IV operations":** Lieutenant Colonel Roy D. Harlan (USMC, retired), interview by author, December 12, 2008.
82   **"I am a big fan of the marines doing windows":** Ibid.
82   **"The whole room was just filled with tension":** Lieutenant Colonel David Harlan, interview by author, March 22, 2009.
82   **"you are to proceed to King Hussein International Airport":** Ibid.
83   **"I could hardly look at him":** Ibid.
83   **"By the Jordanians?":** Ibid.

CHAPTER FOUR

85   **"It was long ago":** Colonel John Coleman (USMC, retired), interview by author, November 13, 2008.
85   **so long as Harlan didn't let him out of his sight:** Lieutenant Colonel Roy D. Harlan (USMC, retired), interview by author, December 12, 2008.
86   **"That's not what happened":** Ibid.
86   **After Harlan confronted Coleman:** Harlan interview, December 12, 2008.
86   **"Go up there and see":** Ibid.
86   **"I keep my hand in":** Major Patrick Maloy (USMC, retired), interview by author, December 23, 2008.
87   **"Maloy is something, isn't he?":** Jerry Jones, interview by author, December 2008.
87   **"I haven't thought about this in a long time":** Walker interview, November 13, 2008.
87   **A week later he wrote, "It's all coming back":** Colonel Mike Walker, e-mail message to author, November 16, 2008.
87   **"This is keeping me awake at night":** Ibid.
87   **"No one likes it":** Maloy interview, December 23, 2008.
87   **"I wonder, really, what would have happened":** Harlan interview, December 12, 2008.

87   **"I was a marine officer":** Author interview with Colonel John Coleman,
      May 16, 2009.

88   **"Our country got a lot wrong in Iraq":** Walker interview.

88   **"working political issues outside Iraq":** Henry W. Stratman to George
      Casey, e-mail message, Sunday August 29. In the author's possession.

88   **"Casey was in their crosshairs":** Senior army officer of MNF-I, interview
      by author, December 16, 2008.

89   **"Allawi was in a real lather about this":** Senior Defense Department offi-
      cial, interview by author, December 16, 2008.

89   **Metz provided that guidance to Conway in a brusque e-mail:** Thomas F.
      Metz to Lieutenant General James T. Conway, e-mail message, August 30,
      2004. In author's possession.

89   **"The MEF has no authority in Jordan and should plan no action there":**
      George Casey to General Henry W. Stratman (with copy to Thomas F.
      Metz), e-mail message, August 30, 2004. The e-mail was forwarded from
      Metz to Conway. In the author's possession.

90   **"He stewed about it for about two hours":** Senior Marine Corps officer,
      interview by author, December 16, 2008.

90   **"General Conway did not like being laughed at":** Ibid.

90   **"We are not working what I would call [a] political agenda":** Lieutenant
      General James T. Conway to Lieutenant General Thomas Metz (with a copy
      to George Casey), e-mail message, August 30, 2004. In the author's possession.

91   **"My first impression of LtGen Ra'ad al Hamdani":** Captain Rodrick
      McHaty, "Jordan Meetings Roundup," memo (I MEF G-3, FAO), undated.
      In the author's possession.

92   **"Get the hell out of Jordan and stay out."** Coleman interview, November
      13, 2008.

92   **"When it came down to backing either Allawi or the U.S. Marines":**
      Major Patrick Maloy, interview by author, March 2009.

92   **"Many people in our system knew":** Quoted in David Rose, "Heads in the
      Sand," *Vanity Fair*, June 2009, http://www.vanityfair.com/politics/features/
      2009/05/iraqi-insurgents200905.

92   **"For State, it became a turf war":** Quoted in ibid.

92   **"a little more forthcoming":** Senior Pentagon official, interview by author,
      December 2008.

93   **"Anyone in government":** Quoted in ibid.

93   **"I was sending Rumsfeld a memo based on Talal's information":** Quoted
      in ibid.

94   **"We were simply trying to get people to pay attention":** James Clad, in-
      terview by author, December 2008.

94   **"it really went nowhere":** Talal al-Gaood, interview by author, July 2005.

95   **"those angry young men":** Ibid.

95   **"The city was turning into an Islamist state":** Senior marine officer, inter-
      view by author, December 2008.

95   **A post-Amman memo to Conway:** Colonel Mike Walker, briefing memo, undated. In the author's possession.

95   **"Dr. al-Hamadani provided a vivid, if horrific, insight":** Mike Walker, e-mail message to the author, November 5, 2008.

96   **"I felt the die was cast at that point":** Ibid.

96   **"One of the untold stories of Fallujah":** Senior Pentagon official, interview by author, December 8, 2008.

97   **"There was a lot of close-in combat":** Marine veteran officer who fought in Fallujah, interview by author, November 2008.

98   **"In individual and group consciousness and unconsciousness":** Lieutenant General Ra'ad al-Hamdani, "Evaluation of the Latest American Military Operations in Fallujah," November 24, 2004. In the author's possession.

98   **The United States should "acknowledge the national resistance":** Ibid.

99   **After Phantom Fury:** Ibid.

99   **He then added some points:** Al-Hamdani, "Evaluation of the Latest American Military Operations in Fallujah."

99   **Even the marines, with all their firepower:** The marines reported positively identifying fighters from Chechnya, the Philippines, Iran, Italy, and Syria, as well as indigenous Iraqis.

100 **The eleven-day operation netted 125 insurgents killed:** "U.S. Calls Iraq Border Operation a Success," *USA Today* (AP), May 14, 2005.

100 **"The tribes only saw us":** Bing West, *The Strongest Tribe* (New York: Random House, 2008), 49.

100 **"We needed the real enemy to make mistakes":** Ibid., 67.

101 **At just after noon on July 23, 2005, Wischkaemper received a telephone call:** The story of al-Qaim narrated here is from Jerry Jones, Ken Wischkaemper, and John Coleman.

101 **"I could tell from the way that Talal spoke":** Quoted in Rose, "Heads in the Sand." Direct quotations in this section are also taken from interviews conducted by the author with Kenneth Wischkaemper, Jerry Jones, and John Coleman.

101 **"It did seem somewhat of an irony":** Jones interviews, December 2008 and April 2009.

102 **"It was a turning point":** Coleman interview, November 13, 2008.

103 **"Just imagine":** Jones interviews, December 2008 and April 2009.

103 **"stabilization of Iraq through political and economic initiatives":** Iraq Initiative for Unity and Development to Ambassador Select Dr. Zalmay Khalilzad, May 25, 2005. In the author's possession.

103 **a new plan for al-Anbar:** "Winning Iraq One City at a Time," briefing for USMC MEFII, May 2005. In the author's possession.

103 **U.S. Army commanders held a "breakthrough" meeting with Sunni sheikhs:** Todd Pitman, "Sunni Sheiks Join Fight Vs. Insurgency," *Washington Post*, March 25, 2007.

104 **They were deeply mistrustful of the Americans:** Jim Michaels, "An Army Colonel's Gamble Pays Off in Iraq," *USA Today*, May 1, 2007.

104 **"It's hard to blame them":** James Clad, interview by author, December 2008.

104 **"We get there in late May and early June 2006":** Quoted in Michaels, "An Army Colonel's Gamble Pays Off in Iraq."

104 **"The way we went about it helped to prove that we were reliable partners":** Major Niel Smith (U.S. Army) and Colonel Sean MacFarland (U.S. Army), "Anbar Awakens: The Tipping Point," *Military Review*, March–April 2008.

105 **"at which he declared 'the Anbar Awakening' officially underway":** Ibid.

105 **One of them asked Sattar what he had said to Bush:** Senior official of the Anbar Awakening Council, Amman, Jordan, telephone interview by author, April 2009.

105 **"What Sean MacFarland did in Ramadi":** Jones interview.

105 **"We operated aggressively across all lines of operation":** Smith and Mac-Farland, "Anbar Awakens."

106 **Jerry Jones argued with the State Department:** Jones interview, December 2008.

106 **"I told him, 'Dave, you have to be there'":** Ibid.

106 **On March 23, 2008:** Senior Pentagon official, interview by the author, March 2009.

107 **"He spoke in Arabic":** Quoted from Rose, "Heads in the Sand."

108 **a newly minted COIN (counterinsurgency) clique:** Celeste Ward, "Countering the Military's Latest Fad," *Washington Post*, May 17, 2009.

109 **"Al-Anbar was not transformed; we were":** James Clad, interview by author, December 2008.

CHAPTER FIVE

111 **Yasser Arafat arrived in Gaza:** An account of the negotiations leading up to the signing of the Declaration of Principles between the Israeli government and the PLO can be found in Jane Corbin, *Jericho First* (London: Bloomsbury, 1994), and in Mark Perry, *A Fire in Zion* (New York: William Morrow, 1994).

111 **Arafat and Israeli prime minister Yitzhak Rabin had met in Washington, D.C.:** "Mideast Accord: Chronology; The Final Steps Toward Self-Rule," *New York Times*, May 5, 1994, http://query.nytimes.com/gst/fullpage.html?res=9E01E5D81F30F936A35756C0A962958260.

112 **Arafat and Rabin began the long and difficult process of rebuilding Israeli-Palestinian relations:** Alison Mitchell, "Mideast Accord: The Overview; Arafat and Rabin Sign Pact to Expand Arab Self-Rule, *New York Times*, September 29, 1995, http://query.nytimes.com/gst/fullpage.html?res=990CE1D7103EF93AA1575AC0A963958260.

113 **"We're sorry to keep you waiting, Dr. Rantisi":** Nabil Abu Rudineh, a key Arafat personal assistant, interview by author, conducted at the time of the meeting between Arafat and Rantisi.

114 **Rantisi began to shout:** Aide to Yasser Arafat, interview by author, conducted at the time of the meeting between Arafat and Rantisi.

114 **Rantisi thought for only a moment:** Rantisi was killed on April 17, 2004, when an Israeli Apache helicopter fired a missile at his car.

115 **"Salafists" and "takfiris":** Salafists want Islam to return to its roots. *Salaf* denotes the first generation of Muslims, the authoritative source of Islam. Salafists consider any practices put into society after the original generations to be unwarranted innovations. The word "takfiri" comes from the word *kafir*, "impiety." Those Muslims accused of impiety face the ultimate penalty. The takfiris hold that *kafirs*, Muslims who are impious, should be executed.

115 **"By establishing a frontier:** S. Sayyid, *A Fundamental Fear: Eurocentrism and the Emergence of Islamism* (London: Zed Books, 2003), xi.

115 **"The articulation of an 'international community' in opposition to (Islamist) terrorism":** Ibid., 23–26.

116 **"But [what] I would like to say":** Joint press conference with President George W. Bush at http://yonanu.blogspot.com/2006/04/talking-with -terrorists.html.

117 **"But the commonly accepted international principle of fighting terror":** Statement of President Vladimir Putin, September 2, 2004, at http://www .ln.mid.ru/bl.nsf/062c2f5f5fa065d4c3256def0051fa1e/cdad3a4346c78f 4ec3256e350033758d?OpenDocument.

117 **"Terror must be stopped":** Quoted in Michael Moran, "Terrorist Groups and Political Legitimacy," prepared for the Council on Foreign Relations, March 16, 2006. See http://www.cfr.org/publication/10159/.

117 **"As Nazi tanks crossed into Poland in 1939":** CNNPolitics.com, May 15, 2008, http://www.cnn.com/2008/POLITICS/05/15/bush.mideast/index.html.

117 **"clear pitfalls to negotiation":** John Bew and Martyn Frampton, "Talking to Terrorists: The Myths, Misconceptions and Misapplication of the Northern Ireland Peace Process," paper prepared for the Jerusalem Center for Public Affairs, no. 566 (August–September 2008), http://www.jcpa.org/ JCPA/Templates/ShowPage.asp?DBID=1&LNGID=1&TMID=111&FID =443&PID=0&IID=2336.

118 **an exhaustive analysis of the reasons:** Stacey Pettyjohn, "Talking with Terrorists: American Engagement of the ANC, PLO and Sinn Fein," paper presented at the annual meeting of the Political Science Association, University of Virginia, August 30, 2007. See http://www.allacademic.com/ meta/p210690_index.html.

118 **"Those negotiations failed":** George J. Mitchell, *Making Peace* (Berkeley and Los Angeles: University of California Press, 1999), 19.

119   **legitimacy is not conferred, but earned:** Robert Nozick, *Anarchy, State and Utopia* (New York: Basic Books, 1975).

119   **"is not a clash between civilizations":** Tony Blair, "A Battle for Global Values," *Foreign Affairs*, January–February 2007.

120   **"This just wasn't the elimination of a threat to Iraq":** Quoted in Peter S. Canellos, "McCain's 'Judeo-Christian Values' Reference Puzzles," *Boston Globe*, August 19, 2008.

120   **"to end violence":** Comments made by State Department official during dinner hosted by the Carnegie Endowment for International Peace.

120   **"Therefore if I know not the meaning of the voice":** 1 Cor. 14:11.

121   **"It's the same old jihadist rigmarole":** Quoted in Faisal Devji, *Landscapes of the Jihad* (Ithaca, NY: Cornell University Press, 2005, p. 125).

121   **a delegation of Americans and Europeans traveled to Beirut:** The subsequent meetings in Beirut included the leaders of Pakistan's Jamat i-Islami and Lebanon's Muslim Brotherhood.

124   **Instead, the leaders of the movements:** The quotes in this chapter are from interviews of the participants conducted by the author independently of the seminar or appeared in a subsequent article on the Beirut meetings titled "How to Lose the War on Terror," published in *Asia Times*. See http://www.atimes.com/atimes/others/howtolose.html.

124   **"feel heard":** Quoted from David Steele, "Reconciliation Strategies in Iraq," report prepared for United States Institute of Peace (Washington, D.C.), Special Report 213, October 2008, 3.

125   **The Muslim Brotherhood, founded in 1928 by Hassan al-Banna:** Robert S. Leiken and Steven Brooke, "The Moderate Muslim Brotherhood," *Foreign Affairs*, March–April 2007.

125   **"luring thousands of young Muslim men":** Quoted in Leiken and Brooke, "The Moderate Muslim Brotherhood," 72.

126   **Egypt's Islam Jihad:** The organization was responsible, in 1981, for the assassination of Egyptian president Anwar Sadat.

126   **"afflicted by an overwhelming assault":** "Our Testimony, Issued in 1994," http://www.ikhwanweb.com/Article.asp?ID=4185&SectionID=83.

126   **Douglas Farah dismisses the brotherhood's claim:** Douglas Farah, "The Amazing Deception in the Muslim Brotherhood's Charm Offensive," May 7, 2007, http://www.douglasfarah.com/article/197/the-amazing-deception-in-the-muslim-brotherhoods-charm-offensive.com.

127   **"a group that worries us not because it deals with philosophical or ideological:** Quoted in "A New Low," June 17, 2009, http://ibloga.blogspot.com/2009/06/new-low-obama-now-wants-dialog-with.html.

127   **the movement is rooted in its commitment to constituent services:** Mark Perry, "Hamas as a Revolutionary Movement," *Palestine Internationalist* 2, no. 3 (March 2007), http://www.palint.org/article.php?articleid=28.

127   **The Muslim Brothers of today:** Dr. Azzam Tamimi, Institute of Islamic Political Thought, interview by Daniel Pipes, *BBC News 24: HardTalk*, No-

vember 2, 2004, http://www.danielpipes.org/2813/interview-with-dr-azzam
-al-tamimi-institute-of-islamic.

127 **The Islamic Resistance Movement was created in 1987:** This information appeared, in part, in Perry, "Hamas as a Revolutionary Movement."

127 **"The Brothers are always the first on the streets after any disaster":** Senior Egyptian political leader of the ruling National Democratic Party, interview by author, March 2006.

128 **Hamas derived at least a part of early senior leadership cadre:** Con-
versely, PLO leader Abu Jihad [Khilil al-Wazir] was, in fact, once a member
of the Muslim Brotherhood.

128 **The best-known members of its political committee are well educated
and politically sophisticated:** Azzam Tamimi, *Hamas: Unwritten Chapters*
(London: Hurst and Co. Publishers, 2006).

128 **The initial cluster of Muslim Brotherhood activists:** Ibid.

129 **The three began their presentation:** All quotations from Musa Abu Marzouk, Sami Khatar, and Usamah Hamdan in the sections that follow are
from the March or July 2005 meetings in Beirut unless otherwise indicated.

129 **"We are willing to resolve the differences we have with Israel that are
the easiest to resolve":** Although Hamdan's statement appeared prior to
the fighting between Fatah and Hamas in Gaza in June 2007 and before the
Israeli assault on Gaza in 2008–2009, he has maintained these positions.

130 **"Sheik Yassin [would] announce the *hudna*":** Sheikh Ahmad Yassin, with
Rantisi, was the founder of the Islamic Resistance Movement. He was assassinated by the Israelis in an attack by a helicopter gunship in 2004.

132 **"after the Hebron Mosque massacre [perpetrated by Israeli settler
Baruch Goldstein]":** On February 25, 1994, settler Baruch Goldstein entered the Cave of the Patriarchs in Hebron and opened fire on Muslim worshippers, twenty-nine of whom were killed.

133 **If our tactics work:** Despite the Israeli attack on Gaza, and Hamas, in December 2008—and despite threats from Hamas officials to begin their program of suicide bombing—the pledge that they gave in 2004 and reiterated
during their meetings in 2005 remains in place.

134 **"represent all factions of the Palestinian people":** Statement of Usamah
Hamdan, Beirut, March 2005.

135 **Hamas and Fatah leaders agreed to govern together:** Hussein Agha and
Robert Malley, "The Road from Mecca," *New York Review of Books*, May 10,
2007.

135 **President Bush signed a "finding":** Mark Perry and Paul Woodward, "Document Details US Plan to Sink Hamas," *Asia Times*, March 16, 2007, http://
www.atimes.com/atimes/Middle_East/IE16Ak04.html. The reporting in *Asia
Times* was followed by a number of articles, in prominent publications, on
the U.S. plan and how it failed. See David Rose, "The Gaza Bombshell,"
Vanity Fair, June 2009, http://www.vanityfair.com/politics/features/2008/
04/gaza200804.

135 **"This was a CIA operation":** CENTCOM senior officer, interview by author, June 2009.

135 **"We told the CIA that this wouldn't work":** Israeli cabinet member, interview by author, May 2008.

136 **"We knew we were going to be put on the list":** Usamah Hamdan, interview by author, March 2005.

CHAPTER SIX

137 **In a dramatic scene from the 2005 movie** *Syriana:* Stephan Gaghan, *Syriana*, screenplay, http://wbads-01.vo.llnwd.net/e1/wbmovies/syriana/site/med/Syriana-Screenplay.pdf.

138 **was once (and others claim is still) the spiritual leader of Hezbollah:** Fadlallah is influential in Lebanon but is politically independent of Hezbollah.

138 **"Most liberalism is angst- and guilt-ridden":** Charles Krauthammer, "Oscars for Osama," *Washington Post*, March 3, 2006.

139 **"Why would I talk to them":** Washington, D.C.–based senior think-tank official, interview by author.

139 **"I don't like Arabs":** Washington, D.C.–based senior policymaker and analyst, interview by author.

139 **"You know, I'm actually a little afraid of doing this":** American Enterprise Institute (AEI) official, interview by author.

140 **"the A-team of terrorism":** Quoted in Walter Reich, "The Terrorism of Hizbollah: Ideology, Scope, Threat," report prepared for the Woodrow Wilson International Center for Scholars, January 16, 2003, http://www.wilsoncenter.org/index.cfm?fuseaction=events.event_summary&event_id=16184.

140 **"to attack almost worldwide with little warning":** Quoted in Sara A. Carter, "Federal Bulletins Warn of Hezbollah Retaliation," *Washington Times*, February 28, 2008, http://goliath.ecnext.com/coms2/gi_0199-7562897/Federal-bulletins-warn-of-Hezbollah.html.

141 **the nation's confessionally based democratic system:** Officially, Lebanon is a parliamentary democratic republic, but under its system the major offices of the republic are divided among the nation's major religious groupings. The office of the president is reserved for a Maronite Christian, the prime minister's office is reserved for a Sunni, and the position of speaker of the house—Lebanon has a unicameral legislature—is reserved for a Shia.

141 **"a round and rather jovial individual":** Judith Palmer Harick, *Hezbollah: The Changing Face of Terrorism* (London: L. B. Tauris, 2005), 59.

141 **"Well, maybe that's what we should do":** State Department official, interview by author, August 2006.

142 **As a result of the assassination of former Lebanese prime minister Rafiq Hariri:** Hariri was assassinated on February 14, 2005.

142 **Huge anti-Syrian demonstrations:** The anti-Syrian rallies took on the name Cedar Revolution.

142 **"Hezbollah clearly understood the delicacy of its political situation":** Report on the meetings in Beirut to a government agency by one of the participants. Document in the author's possession.

143 **a defender of a minority population:** The Shias probably make up more than one-third of the population of Lebanon, but a census of the country has not been conducted since the 1930s; doing so is proving too controversial.

144 **without any intention of overthrowing the government:** A Qatari-led agreement reinstated the security chief and allowed Hezbollah to retain its telecommunications capability. The author spoke at length to Hezbollah officials on their political intentions during the May 2008 events.

144 **"Everyone talks of Iranian interference in Lebanon through Hezbollah":** The Hezbollah partisan quoted here works as a lawyer in Beirut and moves easily among the communities.

144 **"We are prepared to work hard to maintain Muslim unity":** Senior Hezbollah leader, interview by author, March 2005.

145 **"memorandum of understanding":** An English text of the agreement between Aoun and Hezbollah, translated by Joseph Hitti, appears at http://yalibnan.com/site/archives/2006/02/full_english_te.php.

145 **"They are a trustworthy partner":** General Michel Aoun, interview by author, May 17, 2009. I interviewed Aoun several times for this book.

146 **those who set off the bomb may have, in fact, been trained by the CIA:** "Terrorist Attacks on Americans, 1979–1988: The Attacks, the Groups, and the U.S. Responses," *Target America, PBS Frontline,* http://www.pbs.org/wgbh/pages/frontline/shows/target/etc/cron.html.

146 **"The bombing was timed to coincide with Friday prayers":** Bob Woodward, *Veil: The Secret Wars of the CIA, 1981–1987* (New York: Simon and Schuster, 1987), 286–287.

147 **the head of Hezbollah's department of external relations:** Moussaoui has since left the Department of External Relations. He is currently serving in the Lebanese parliament.

147 **"He knows more about neoconservatism":** American official who met with the Hezbollah official in Beirut in March of 2005.

148 **"He is one of the brightest and most careful speakers I have ever met":** Michael Ancram, interview by author, January 2009.

148 **"Mr. Moussaoui, I am convinced, understands English perfectly well":** This senior official participated in the dialogue with Hezbollah in March and July 2005.

148 **"by Hezbollah radicals":** Robin L. Higgins, "POW or Hostage?" http://www.ojc.org/higgins/.

148 **The delegation of Americans:** The quotes in this chapter are from interviews of the participants conducted by the author independently of the seminar or appeared in a subsequent article on the Beirut meetings titled "How to Lose the War on Terror," published in *Asia Times.* See http://www.atimes.com/atimes/others/howtolose.html.

149   **the subsequent murder of Robert Stethem:** A discussion of responsibility
       for this assassination can be found in Mohammad Bazzi, "Who Killed Imad
       Mugniyah?" interview by Bernard Gwetzman, February 14, 2008, at Coun-
       cil on Foreign Relations, http://www.cfr.org/publication/15507/bazzi.html.

150   **"Following 9/11 we condemned an act of terrorism":** Hassan Nasrallah
       repeatedly condemned suicide bombing in Iraq, counseling his movement's
       followers to also condemn the attacks and to refuse to participate in them.

151   **"we even stopped operations":** Hezbollah officials cite the example of a
       bomb placed under the car of an Israeli officer, with a "man-in-the-loop"
       trigger (that is, a trigger that requires a person to actually activate the bomb,
       instead of having it go off by itself) that could activate the bomb from a dis-
       tance. When the officer's wife emerged from his headquarters, the bombing
       was postponed until the officer could be targeted directly.

152   **"as our technology would have not made that possible":** Moussaoui's
       claim seems to be true, judging by the casualty figures from the war. The toll
       from the 2006 Lebanon War is officially set at 44 Israeli civilians dead, 33
       seriously injured, 68 moderately injured, and 1,388 lightly wounded. Leba-
       non suffered 1,191 dead and 4,409 injured.

152   **And ask them about Operation Grapes of Wrath:** Operation Grapes of
       Wrath was an April 1996 operation in which Israel targeted Hezbollah in
       southern Lebanon. Israel launched more than 1,100 air raids into southern
       Lebanon and nearly emptied the southern quarter of the country. Upward
       of 170 Lebanese civilians were killed in the operation.

152   **"We were fighting a war, and so we fired missiles at Israel":** Nawaf
       al-Moussaoui, interview by author, March 2005.

153   **"The movement seemed keenly interested in establishing a key dialogue
       with the West":** Quoted from an undated memorandum on the meeting
       provided by Milt Bearden. Bearden was a lifelong employee of the CIA.

154   **"controversial and mistaken acts":** Milt Bearden, untitled and undated
       document in the author's possession.

154   **Geagea's Phalange militia is held responsible for the murder:** "Flashback:
       Sabra and Shatila Massacres," *BBC News World Edition*, January 24, 2002,
       http://news.bbc.co.uk/2/hi/middle_east/1779713.stm. The final count of
       the dead is unknown. The BBC puts the number at eight hundred civilians.
       The camps had been placed under siege by the Israeli Defense Forces (IDF).
       IDF officers outside the camps knew the Phalange was murdering the Pales-
       tinians but refused to intervene.

155   **Geagea was punished for his crimes:** "Amnesty for Lebanese Ex-Warlord,"
       BBC News, July 18, 2005, http://news.bbc.co.uk/2/hi/middle_east/4693091
       .stm.

155   **"The man is a convicted murderer":** Senior official of the Free Patriotic
       Movement, interview by author, May 17, 2009.

156   **"The Protocols of the Elders of Zion":** The tract is a notorious and viru-
       lent anti-Semitic forgery.

157   Hezbollah "is, at its core, a jihadist organization": Jeffrey Goldberg, "In the Party of God," *New Yorker*, October 14, 2002, http://www.newyorker.com/archive/2002/10/14/021014fa_fact4.

157   "The bin Ladens and Zarqawi's of the region": Senior Hezbollah leader, interview by author, July 2005.

158   "embedded in the core of Hezbollah ideology": "Anderson Cooper 360 Degrees," transcript, CNN, August 1, 2006, http://www.studentnews.cnn.com/TRANSCRIPTS/0608/01/acd.02.html.

158   has written a book on Hezbollah and Sheikh Fadlallah: Kramer's book on Fadlallah, *Fadlallah, the Compass of Hezbollah* (Tel Aviv: Universitat Tel Aviv, 1998), incorrectly states that Sheikh Fadlallah is "the spiritual leader of Hezbollah." I met with Sheikh Fadlallah and interviewed him in 2007.

158   "These are religious people": Quoted in Goldberg, "In the Party of God."

159   Silverstein journeyed to Beirut in 2006 to meet with Hezbollah leaders: I met Silverstein during this trip and sat with him during his interviews with Moussaoui.

159   "The primary problem, it soon became clear": Ken Silverstein, "Parties of God: The Bush Doctrine and the Rise of Islamic Democracy," *Harper's*, June 2006, http://www.harpers.org/archive/2007/03/0081425.

160   "reached the point of the absurd": Ken Silverstein, interview by author, April 2007.

161   "Hezbollah had a history of inviting reporters": Ibid.

161   "We are not denying that European racists persecuted an entire people": Quoted in Silverstein, "Parties of God."

CHAPTER SEVEN

165   "I am both," he said: The remarks were made to the author during a private visit to Israel in the summer of 2007.

166   "It is very easy to sit in America": Quoted in Mark Perry, *A Fire in Zion* (New York: William Morrow, 1994).

166   poll published by the Israeli Democracy Institute in May 2008: Kobi Nahshoni, "Poll: Most Israelis See Themselves as Jewish First, Israeli Second," YNET, May 8, 2008, http://www.ynet.co.il/english/articles/0,7340,L-3540049,00.html.

167   The pollsters were then told by 51 percent: "Poll: 51% of Israelis Want Separate Secular, Religious Neighborhoods," YNET, March 6, 2008, http://www.ynet.co.il/english/articles/0,7340,L-3515628,00.html.

167   "Jews, Hezbollah Vow Wider War": The actual headline reads, "Israel, Hezbollah Vow Wider War," *Washington Post*, July 14, 2006.

168   When John Mearsheimer and Stephen Walt's book: John J. Mearsheimer and Stephen M. Walt, *The Israel Lobby and U.S. Foreign Policy* (New York: Farrar, Straus, Giroux, 2007), 191–195.

168   "The charge of anti-Semitism": Ibid., 191.

168   **"a classical conspiratorial anti-Semitic analysis":** "Mearsheimer and Walt's Anti-Jewish Screed: A Relentless Assault in Scholarly Guise," March 24, 2006, http://www.adl.org/Israel/mearsheimer_walt.asp. The ADL critique was issued in response to Mearsheimer and Walt's article on the Israel lobby that first appeared in the *London Review of Books*.

168   **"The accusation is likely to resonate among American Jews":** Mearsheimer and Walt, *The Israel Lobby*, 191.

169   **The *New York Review of Books*, the *Financial Times*, and the *Chicago Tribune*:** Ibid., xi.

169   **a loose coalition of American Jews banded together to establish J Street:** J Street, About Us page, http://www.jstreet.org/about/about-us.

170   **recasting the American-Israeli relationship:** Mearsheimer and Walt, *The Israel Lobby*, 349–355.

170   **"was not the only factor behind the Bush administration's decision":** Ibid., 230–231.

170   **"abundant evidence that Israel and the lobby played crucial roles":** Ibid., 233.

171   **a team of senior Israeli intelligence officials came to Washington:** The Mossad is the Institute for Intelligence and Special Tasks—the ha-Mossad le-Modiin ule-Tafkidim Meyuhadim. It is the premier Israeli overseas intelligence organization.

171   **"I knew when I came to Washington":** Former senior Israeli intelligence official, interview by author, July 2005.

172   **"One Israeli source said [US President George] Bush's interest":** Tom Regan, "US Neocons Hoped Israel Would Attack Syria," *Christian Science Monitor*, August 9, 2006; also at http://www.csmonitor.com/2006/0809/daily Update.html.

173   **"American Jews sometimes think":** Quoted in Perry, *A Fire in Zion*, 163–164. I had extensive communications and several interviews with Prime Minister Rabin during this period.

173   **"You've aroused too much antagonism":** Quoted in ibid., 164.

174   **"He told us that the government of Israel resides in Jerusalem":** Quoted in ibid.

174   **"He told us that he did not need our permission to act as prime minister":** Quoted in ibid., 165.

174   **"more harmful to Israel than the PLO":** Matti Golan, *With Friends Like You* (New York: Free Press, 1992), 12–13.

174   **"What you feel for me is a special connection":** Ibid., 23.

175   **"I remember dropping everything":** Ibid., 23–24. A review of Golan's book appeared in the *New York Times*: Clyde Haberman, "My Enemy Brother," *New York Times*, November 29, 1992, http://www.nytimes.com/1992/11/29/books/my-enemy-brother.html.

175   **"To secure its borders":** Max Boot, "It's Time to Let the Israelis Take Off the Gloves," *Los Angeles Times*, July 19, 2006.

176 **"Our focus should be less on Hamas and Hezbollah":** Quoted in *The Progressive*, September 2006.

176 **"Who's *our*? Who's *we*?":** Senior Jewish American policymaker based in Washington, D.C., comment to the author, August 2006.

177 **Of the 7.3 million people of Israel:** See "A Country Study: Israel," Country Studies, http://lcweb2.loc.gov/frd/cs/iltoc.html. In fact, the numbers given here are quite conservative. The CIA Fact Book for Israel for 2007 puts Israel's non-Jewish population at close to 25 percent: "Jewish 76.4% (of which Israel-born 67.1%, Europe/America-born 22.6%, Africa-born 5.9%, Asia-born 4.2%), non-Jewish 23.6% (mostly Arab).

177 **2.5 million Muslims, Christians, Druze, and Samaritans:** The Muslims, Christians, Druze, and Samaritans of Israel are overwhelmingly Arab.

177 **according to this figure:** http://www.jewishvirtuallibrary.org/jsource/Society _&_Culture/newpop.html.

178 **what Israeli historian Walter Laqueur calls "the new Jew":** Walter Laqueur, *A History of Zionism* (New York: Holt, Reinhart and Winston, 1972), 598–599. Laqueur sets out the best definition (or definitions) of Israeli identities to be found—they retain their power and insight.

178 **"While esteem for Jewish determination and prowess":** Ibid., 599.

178 **"spiritual lodestone, a redemptive model":** Ibid., 601.

179 **"I am aware of the special, often confusing, problem we face":** Yossi Melman, *The New Israelis* (New York: Birch Lane Press, 1992), 4.

180 **"Our argument is with Israel":** Nawaf Moussaoui, interview by author, March 2005.

180 **"We are facing an Israeli occupation":** Usamah Hamdan, interview by author, March 2005.

181 **Until then (in our "unredeemed time"):** Senior Hamas official, interview by author, May 2009.

181 **"This is an argument among men":** Senior Hamas official, interview by author, May 2009.

181 **On December 27, 2008, Israel launched an air assault on Gaza:** Nidal al-Mughrabi, "Israel Kills Scores in Gaza Airstrike," *Reuters*, December 27, 2008.

181 **Israeli officials said that 227 Hamas fighters had been killed and over 700 had been wounded:** Ibid.

181 **"Israel's air offensive against the Gaza Strip yesterday":** "Israel Strikes," *Washington Post*, December 28, 2008.

182 **a mounting escalation that had begun:** Sheera Frankel, "Gaza Ceasefire Breaking Down as Violations by Israel and Hamas Continue," *Times* (London), July 5, 2008.

182 **"Here you have a terrorist organization and a member-state":** Quoted in David Gollust, "Rice Defends US Abstention on Gaza Cease-Fire Resolution," VOANews.com, January 9, 2009, http://www.voanews.com/english/ archive/2009-01/2009-01-09-voa75.cfm?CFID=282397297&CFTOKEN =64657764&jsessionid=de30cdfa438d34a0e5d01a634d6c614d6b4f.

182   **"When we saw that the secretary of state":** Quoted in "Olmert Calls Bush
      to Force Change in U.N. Vote" (Reuters), Javno, January 13, 2009, http://
      www.javno.com/en-world/olmert-calls-bush-to-force-change-in-un-vote
      _223617.

183   **"The situation now taking place in Gaza":** Quoted in Robert Burns,
      "Bush on Gaza Fighting: Israel Has the Right to Protect Itself," January 5,
      2009, *Huffington Post*, http://www.huffingtonpost.com/2009/01/05/bush-on
      -gaza-fighting-isr_n_155282.html.

183   **"We told the Israelis in Cairo":** Usamah Hamdan, interview by author,
      January 28, 2009.

183   **"The inherent desire for retribution":** "Define the Objective in Gaza,"
      Haaretz, December 28, 2008.

184   **Senior correspondents for *Haaretz* were even more outspoken:** Quoted
      in Greg Mitchell, "Attack on Gaza," *Huffington Post*, December 28, 2008,
      http://www.huffingtonpost.com/greg-mitchell/attack-on-gaza-as-usual
      -u_b_153757.html.

185   **"a military base for Iran":** Robert J. Lieber, "Hard Truths About the Con-
      flict," *Washington Post*, January 1, 2009.

186   **"We will have peace with the Arabs":** Quoted in a leaflet; see http://www
      .davka.org/where/israel/explained/lovetheirchildren.pdf.

186   **Krauthammer repeated this perverse mantra:** Charles Krauthammer,
      "Moral Clarity in Gaza," *Washington Post*, January 2, 2009.

187   **"There is no question":** Michael Gerson, "Defining Victory for Israel,"
      Washington Post, January 2, 2009.

188   **That is hardly comparable to the London Blitz:** The actual number of
      dead from the Blitz (September 7, 1940, to May 10, 1941) was in excess of
      43,000. See Alfred Price, *Blitz on Britain, 1939–1945* (London: Sutton,
      2000), 101–103.

188   **If Israelis were fighting in their own streets:** On the Gaza assault, see
      Mark Perry, "Questions for Barack Obama," *Bitterlemons-international.org* 7,
      edition 2 (January 15, 2009), http://www.bitterlemons-international.org/
      previous.php?opt=1&id=256#1048.

189   **"If somebody was sending rockets into my house":** Quoted in Ewen
      MacAskill, "Obama Adviser Aligns with White House in Criticism of
      Rocket Attacks on Israel," *Guardian*, December 29, 2008, http://www
      .guardian.co.uk/world/2008/dec/29/barack-obama-israel-gaza.

CHAPTER EIGHT

191   **On my first flight to the Middle East:** I began traveling to the Middle East
      in May 1990, when I visited the West Bank and Gaza to report on the first
      Palestinian Intifada.

192   **"The man smiled and told me, 'My name is Lawrence'":** T. E. Lawrence is a
      beloved figure in the West, though his reputation has been enhanced by the

movie *Lawrence of Arabia*. He is not so highly regarded in the Arab world, where the adoption of the Sykes-Picot Treaty in his wake stained his legacy. The treaty divided the region into spheres of influence, between England and France, placing it once again under foreign colonial administration. The Arabs have a complex relationship with the man and often accuse Westerners heavily engaged in the region of attempting to re-create his experiences.

193 **The hotel was virtually empty:** During the Israeli war with Hezbollah in 2006, the hotel was packed. "In that case," one of the owners told me, "a war was actually good for us." Israel transported thousands of their Israeli-Arab citizens further south. A large number of them stayed at the hotel for many weeks.

194 **The casino was closed during the Second Intifada:** The casino remains inactive. Palestinians, with the exceptions of those who worked at the casino, were not allowed to go there.

194 **In 1993 I was privileged to introduce Yitzhak Rabin to a group of Arab American reporters:** Rabin came to Washington prior to the signing of the Oslo Accords. He spoke, on this occasion, at a seminar organized by a Middle East magazine I then edited.

195 **I had asked Rabin whether he would ever negotiate with Arafat:** My interview with Rabin took place before the public (or I) knew that the Israelis and the Palestinians were negotiating in Oslo and in Stockholm. But Rabin knew.

195 **"the face of terror":** See also John Cooley, "The Face of Terrorism, Then and Now," *New Perspectives Quarterly*, September 1996, http://www.digital-npq.org/archive/1996_fall/face.html.

196 **a legendary moment in Palestinian history:** See "Pirates in the Sky," *Time*, September 21, 1970.

196 **"Did you pass on the message?":** I asked for an interview with Ariel Sharon for a U.S. publication in 2002, but he refused my request. I would have welcomed the opportunity to ask him about the truth of this story but never got the chance.

197 **"Arafat's children":** "Arafat's children" are well known in Palestinian society: These are orphans that Arafat supported personally. They still live, very many of them, in Ramallah and throughout the West Bank and Gaza. Many have gone on to lead very successful lives.

197 **At times I would sit with Arafat in his headquarters in Ramallah:** I never officially interviewed Yasser Arafat, but I did serve as a kind of unofficial adviser to him from 1990 to the day of his death. This conversation took place one year prior to his death.

202 **We made it to Jerusalem by traveling on settler roads:** It is still possible to travel to Ramallah from Jerusalem, via settler roads, without crossing an Israeli checkpoint. The idea that the construction of the Israeli "security wall" has stopped terrorism is a myth.

203 **A Palestinian friend of mine:** Salah Ta'amri is a renowned figure in Palestinian society. He and his wife, the first wife of King Hussein of Jordan,

worked together in Lebanon after the PLO expulsion from Jordan in September 1970. They befriended the British writer "John Le Carré" (David Cornwell). Ta'amri was apprehended by the Israelis in Lebanon and spent many years in an Israeli jail. He also spent many years in the United States, working as the PLO's unofficial representative, even while the organization was on the U.S. terrorist list.

206 **And then the Haganah came:** "Haganah" is Hebrew for "the Defense." It is the name of a Jewish paramilitary organization that fought the British colonial administration of Palestine prior to creation of Israel. Founded in 1920, it fought until 1948, when it became the core of the Israeli Defense Forces.

207 **Princess Dina:** Sharifa Dina bint "Abdul" Hamid graduated from Cambridge University, taught at Cairo University, and married King Hussein of Jordan in 1955 and separated from him in 1956. She married my friend, Asad Sulayman Abd al-Qadir "Salah Ta'amri"—Abul Hassan—in 1970. She remains in Jordan, a much-beloved figure.

207 **In Tunis I met Sachar Habash:** Sachar Habash is a former member of the Central Committee of Fatah and a former close associate of PLO chairman Yasser Arafat. He lives in retirement in Ramallah. He was one of the original members of the PLO, is a poet, and has a lifelong dream of establishing a Palestinian national library.

208 **the professor wanted me to talk about what it was like to write books:** I am not at liberty to use this person's name, but he is ubiquitous in this text. He served as a translator for me through half a dozen trips to the West Bank and Gaza. His English is impeccable. He has an advanced degree from a British university.

EPILOGUE

212 **"Violence, though definitive of the jihad today":** Faisal Devji, *Landscapes of the Jihad* (Ithaca, NY: Cornell University Press, 2005), 14.

213 **"We have to come to terms with a disturbing and blunt truth":** Geoffrey Aronson, interview by author, April 2006.

214 **Bin Laden and his takfiri allies:** For a discussion of bin Laden's views of Islamic legal restraints, see Devji, *Landscapes of the Jihad*, 125–127.

216 **"there is no line between good people and the rest":** Maurice Merleau-Ponty, *Humanism and Terror* (Boston: Beacon Press, 1969), 41.

216 **"pity is treason":** Simon Schama, "Maximilian Robespierre Before the Revolutionary Tribunal," in *Citizens* (New York: Knopf, 1989).

216 **"power is virtue":** Ibid.

216 **"We have talked with those political Islamists":** Mark Perry and Alastair Crooke, "The Politics of Indignation," *Asia Times*, June 8, 2006, http://www.atimes.com/atimes/Middle_East/HF08Ak01.html.

217 **"We do not condemn Osama bin Laden":** Ibid.

INDEX